Tiger Papa Three

Tiger Papa Three
Memoir of a Combined Action Marine in Vietnam

Edward F. Palm

McFarland & Company, Inc., Publishers
Jefferson, North Carolina

LIBRARY OF CONGRESS CATALOGUING-IN-PUBLICATION DATA

Names: Palm, Edward Frederick, author.
Title: Tiger Papa Three : memoir of a Combined Action Marine in Vietnam / Edward F. Palm.
Other titles: Memoir of a Combined Action Marine in Vietnam
Description: Jefferson, North Carolina : McFarland & Company, Inc., Publishers, 2020. | Includes index.
Identifiers: LCCN 2020017686 | ISBN 9781476681047 (paperback : acid free paper) ∞
ISBN 9781476639543 (ebook)
Subjects: LCSH: Palm, Edward Frederick. | United States. Marine Corps. Combined Action Group, 3rd. Company P. Platoon, 3rd. | United States. Marine Corps—History—Vietnam War, 1961–1975. | United States. Marine Corps. Combined Action Program—History. | Vietnam War, 1961–1975—Regimental histories—United States. | Combined operations (Military science) | United States. Marine Corps—Biography. | Vietnam War, 1961–1975—Personal narratives, American.
Classification: LCC DS558.4 .P35 2020 | DDC 959.7/0434092 [B]—dc23
LC record available at https://lccn.loc.gov/2020017686

BRITISH LIBRARY CATALOGUING DATA ARE AVAILABLE

**ISBN (print) 978-1-4766-8104-7
ISBN (ebook) 978-1-4766-3954-3**

© 2020 Edward F. Palm. All rights reserved

No part of this book may be reproduced or transmitted in any form or by any means, electronic or mechanical, including photocopying or recording, or by any information storage and retrieval system, without permission in writing from the publisher.

Front cover photographs: Edward Palm on radio watch shortly after arriving at Papa Three; the village chief's house and fortified compound in Papa One's village (author images)

Printed in the United States of America

*McFarland & Company, Inc., Publishers
Box 611, Jefferson, North Carolina 28640
www.mcfarlandpub.com*

Table of Contents

Dedication and Acknowledgments	vii
Preface	1
1. The Identification	3
2. Palm and the Delaware Dream	10
3. My Great Expectations	19
4. Mixed Blessings	27
5. How It All Began	30
6. That Other Parris	34
7. The Sticking Point	39
8. Camp Lejeune	41
9. Delaware Revisited	45
10. An Enlightened Gesture of Dissent	48
11. Palm on the Supply Side	52
12. Deliverance	55
13. CAP School	57
14. Papa One Confidential	59
15. Flashback: The Girl I Left Behind	63
16. Tiger Papa Three	67
17. The Dramatis Personae	72
18. Blissful Ignorance	80
19. Flashback: My Great Expectations Revisited, July 1966	83
20. And the Rains Came!	88

Table of Contents

21. Hard Times	90
22. Deus ex Machina the Second	93
23. The Way We Were	96
24. Puff the Magic Dragon Comes to Call	104
25. Schism	108
26. Close Encounters of the Strange Kind	110
27. On Courage—Physical and Moral	112
28. Winning Hearts and Minds	114
29. Boys Will Be Boys—American and Vietnamese	119
30. The R&R Experience	123
31. The Fire Next Time—December 4, 1967	125
32. Confession Being Good for the Soul…	133
33. Innocents Abroad	135
34. A Way You'll Never Be	139
35. Life Goes On	141
36. The Shape of Things to Come	143
37. Coming Home	145
38. Looking Back on Leaving	150
39. A Siren's Spell	152
40. "All the way with LBJ!"	161
41. Shelter from the Storm	163
42. A Chance Encounter with the Third Kind—of Girl	166
43. Palm at Penn	169
44. Men Without a Country	177
45. Vietnam and Modern Memory	179
Epilogue	183
Index	201

Dedication and Acknowledgments

A disclaimer, a dedication, and acknowledgments are in order. The opinions expressed herein do not reflect those of the U.S. Marine Corps, the Department of the Navy, or the Department of Defense—or, for that matter, most of the Marines I served with in Vietnam or elsewhere. Regardless of how my fellow Papa Three veterans may feel about it, however, I'm dedicating this book to them—to Bill Cooke ("Sarge"), Mack Garrett, Larry Scroggs, Robert Yost, Ron Parks, Mike Fink, and Tom Flynn—and, above all, to the memory of Jim Reaves. I'm dedicating this as well to the Papa Three Marines and corpsmen with whom I have yet to reconnect and whose names have faded from my aged memory. Alzheimer's disease, I'm sorry to say, runs in my family. Should that fog begin to descend upon me, I'm sure that the men I've just named, and our time together at Papa Three, will be among the last memories I'll lose.

I owe a large debt of gratitude to the late Colonel John Greenwood, USMC (Ret.), the former editor of *Marine Corps Gazette*, for his unwavering commitment to truth-telling as the paramount obligation of a military professional. Colonel Greenwood had the courage to publish an early version of my combined-action experiences. The Corps in the '80s was largely in denial about Vietnam, and an article critical of the Combined Action Program had yet to appear in any military journal. I have since learned that the best approach to getting veterans past PTSD is to encourage them to share their experiences with one another. Colonel Greenwood greatly facilitated that process for me by publishing "Tiger Papa Three." Portions of that original article appear here with the permission of the *Gazette*.

A short account of my Papa Three experiences, titled "3rd CAG 1967," appeared in Al Hemingway's oral history collection *Our War Was Different*, published by the Naval Institute Press in 1994. The Naval Institute Press has granted permission to expand and expound upon what I had written for Al Hemingway's book.

I am also indebted to former Marine and fellow Vietnam veteran Dennis Pregent. In helping to edit his collection of interviews of Vietnam veterans from his hometown, I discouraged him from seeking a commercial publisher, believing that the time for marketable Vietnam memoirs had passed. Dennis proved me wrong. McFarland's acceptance of his book emboldened me to submit this one.

And I would be remiss in not acknowledging the help of another Vietnam veteran, the renowned writer, poet, and commentator W.D. ("Bill") Ehrhart. Bill has been an inspiration, a sounding board, a confidant, and a good friend ever since we first met in 1991, when I was serving in the English Department of the U.S. Naval Academy and Bill was a visiting writer. He was kind enough to read that first version of "Tiger Papa Three" and to praise it. And he went above and beyond the call of friendship in recommending me to Gary Mitchem, the senior acquisitions editor at McFarland.

Finally, I owe more than I could ever repay to Andrea—the light and love of my life, without whom I might have remained mired in the rice paddies of the mind. Her unrelenting faith in me helped me get on with my life and to achieve more than I ever thought I could.

Preface

I am 73 years old and retired now. But more than half a lifetime ago I was an enlisted Marine serving in a Vietnamese village with the Combined Action Program (CAP). I have moved on since then. I went to college and got married. I went on to graduate school and earned a PhD. Midway through graduate school, I even returned to the Marine Corps as an officer and eventually finished out a 20-year career, retiring as a major. But to paraphrase the leading Vietnam author, Tim O'Brien, it is always back to my CAP experience, back to that village and to the rice paddies of the mind, that I return in trying to figure out how I got from there to here.

In a very real sense, as another of my favorite writers, Paul Fussell, has pointed out, everything processed by memory is fiction. This is true of even the most straightforward attempt at memoir. None of us can completely resist, especially in recounting traumatic experiences and troubled times, the temptation to reorder, to enliven, and to reshape personal experiences in the telling, particularly in those areas in which we may not have lived up to our own expectations. And I would submit that, even if we think we have resisted the conscious temptation to revise our memories to ease our consciences or improve our images, our subconscious minds will take over and do it for us to a certain extent. Still, in what follows, I have tried to be as honest as I can be—with myself as well as the reader.

The problem, however, is that I didn't keep a diary or journal while I was "in country," and nearly 20 years had elapsed between the end of my Vietnam tour and my decision to write the first account of my Vietnam experiences, "Tiger Papa Three: A Memoir of the Combined Action Program," which was published in the January and February 1988 issues of *Marine Corps Gazette*. At the time, I had not been able to locate any Papa Three veterans against whom I could check my memories. I did visit the Marine Corps Historical Center in Washington, D.C., where I consulted the III MAF operations logs before beginning to write. But, while the logs held nothing to contradict my unaided, aging memory, they also contained little to supplement or revive it. The one exception was the after-action report of December 4, 1967. As the reader will learn, that was the most significant date during my time with the third platoon, "Papa Three," of Papa Company, 3rd Combined Action Group.

Then, in the early '90s, through the miracle of the Internet—an invention and an innovation we could not have conceived of back at Papa Three in 1967—I reconnected with six of my fellow Papa Three Marines—Bill Cooke, the "Sarge" of my original account; Larry Scroggs, the former Air Force "brat" I mention in passing; Mack Garrett, the radio operator whom I mention as twice saving the day at Papa Three; Robert Yost; Mike Fink; and Ronald Parks. I have also met and have stayed in touch with Tom Flynn, who was in the original Papa Three start-up group and who, after being seriously wounded in the first attack on Papa Three, was serving back at the Papa Company headquarters while I was out in the "ville," as we termed it.

Together, these Papa Three Marines have helped me fill in many of the gaps regarding things I didn't know at the time, especially about our unit's history and about what was going on behind the scenes. More importantly, they have helped me recover some of the things I had forgotten or repressed, especially about my own role (or lack thereof) in the events of December 4, 1967. There are also things I have never forgotten, and which were still raw in my memory when I first wrote this story in 1987, almost 20 years after the events I recount. Some of these things, I was too embarrassed to relate; others, I realized, would never have made it past the editor and into the pages of a professional military journal. Bill, Mack, Larry, Yost, Ron, Mike, and Tom have inspired and emboldened me to give a fuller, more honest accounting of Papa Three and of myself when I was in it. I thank them for their help and their friendship over the years.

To this day, I do feel somewhat guilty about the way it all played out. But it also makes me wonder sometimes if there is not indeed "a divinity that shapes our ends, / Rough-hew them how we will."

1

The Identification

It was the least I could do. Compared to everyone else, I'd been either incredibly lucky or incredibly unlucky that day. Today, more than 50 years later, I'm still trying to decide which. I only know I felt I had to do something to redeem myself. So when the company gunny came up on the radio and said that someone had to go identify the body, I volunteered.

A half hour later the gunny and I were in his jeep out on Highway 9 (just a dirt road at the time) heading toward Dong Ha and Delta Med.

His name was Jim Reaves, "like the country and western singer," he liked to point out, "only spelled with an 'a.'" I first noticed him some six months earlier, atop a hill in Phu Bai, where we would soon practice artillery spotting. Undaunted by an exhausting climb, he was standing atop a sandbag wall, arms outstretched over the valley below, loudly proclaiming to all who would listen, *"Look at me. I'm God!"* At that moment, he didn't look much like *the* God; but he was tall, blond, square-jawed, and generally imposing, and in another time and place, he probably could have passed for *a* god.

The rest of us were still trying to recover. Wearing helmets and flak jackets in Phu Bai's wet heat, we had just climbed up and along a ridge that seemed to keep rising in steep intervals of at least a hundred yards from one plateau to another, until at last we got to the top. We were a polyglot group of about 20 young enlisted Marines, all of us from different units and backgrounds and all thrown together just days before as "volunteers" for the Combined Action Program, or "CAP" for short. At that point, I doubt that any of us knew exactly what the program was all about, only that we would be sent out to a village to win those fabled "hearts and minds." For some of us, I'm sure, the program seemed to represent a good way to get out of the bush; for others, including me, it represented one last chance to get into it. But before we would get out to our respective "villes," as we called them then, we first had to go through a two-week school at Phu Bai, the main purpose of which seemed to be to ensure that we were tactically and technically, if not culturally, proficient. That's how Reaves and I and the others found ourselves on this hill about to call in real artillery fire from a battery stationed just below us.

Cpl. James L. Reaves calling our attention to the beautiful vista from atop the hill we had just climbed to practice spotting artillery fire as part of the CAP-school curriculum in Phu Bai.

The low sandbag wall that Reaves had jumped up on rimmed the western side of the summit, from which we could we see nearly straight down into a lush green valley, itself made up of gently rolling hills, which themselves soon rose into a series of equally lush but formidable looking mountains extending all the way to the horizon.

The view was spectacular, a point Reaves was not going to let the rest of us fail to appreciate. He soon started reaching down and tugging at the guys within his reach, commanding them to take a good look. "God, that's BEAUTIFUL!" Reaves added, speaking to himself, I suppose. It was a stirring sight, or should have been. As Hamlet says of Polonius, however, most of us were "for a jig or a tale of bawdry or [we slept]." I know I was still trying to recover from the climb and wasn't up for any sightseeing. But Reaves wasn't like the rest of us. As I came to know him, he was sensitive and intelligent and not afraid to show those qualities. Nothing ever seemed to get him down; he was irrepressible, always cheerful and gregarious. He could also be boisterous, arrogant, and even overbearing. At times I didn't like him. But, truth be told, it was a dislike born of envy and resentment at both his background and his ability to relate to people.

I can still picture our company gunnery sergeant. He was a tall, stocky, and dark-skinned Hawaiian man. As the gunny and I were driving along, I

1. The Identification

thought back to how Reaves and I had managed to get thrown together. I suppose that one trait we did have in common was foolhardiness or just reckless bravado. Toward the end of CAP school, one of our instructors asked if any of us would be willing to volunteer for "Papa Company, up north." The program up there, he explained, was new. Papa Company was still "getting established." "A couple of the units had been 'hit,'" he warned. In a cavalier mood, I raised my hand. So, too, did Reaves. I noticed him again on this occasion because he was elbowing the man next to him, commanding him to raise his hand. He dutifully obeyed. I would later come to know this other man—whom I'll call "Scotty"—as a quiet and unassuming Canadian who had enlisted in the Marine Corps to see something of our war.

All the way to Dong Ha, I kept marveling at what a beautiful day it was, sunny and cool, with hardly a cloud in the sky. That's probably what had gotten us all in trouble in the first place. According to the calendar, it was early December, but spring had come to Quang Tri Province up in northern I Corps.

A preview of the monsoon rains had hit hard in September and continued into October in our area. Early that fall, we had even suffered a serious flood caused by a typhoon-driven storm surge. Maybe it's just me. Maybe it's because I never got any farther south than Da Nang. But when I think back on the discomforts of my days in country, Vietnam's fabled heat doesn't even come in as a close second to the monsoon cold.

I realize now, as I think I realized then, that the actual temperature may not have dropped below the 50s, maybe even the 60s. But when the humidity was 100 percent and it was raining, the wind was blowing, and I was soaked with no dry clothes left to change into, and I could see my breath and was shivering—I was cold. I can remember being out on patrol, for example, and getting so wet that my skin would wrinkle up just the way it did when, as a kid, I would stay in a swimming pool too long. Add to this the fact that the Marine Corps didn't think we needed field jackets—we were in a "tropical country," after all—and that's why, to this day, rainy days and cold water get me down.

But what a difference in one's mood and morale a little sun can make. This was long before I'd heard of the pathetic fallacy or the idea of nature moralized. (I confess it: After Vietnam, I spent a lot of time going around in academic circles, pun intended.) At the time, I didn't fully appreciate the irony of our having been ambushed on such a beautiful day, although I think I certainly intuited it.

As we drove along, a part of me wanted to blame the weather. It was as if it had conspired with the other side to throw us off guard. But, as I had to admit to myself, the truth of the matter was that it had been a long time since any of us had really been on our guard. All throughout that fall, we had suffered from friendly folly but not enemy fire. As a result, we had grown complacent and even lackadaisical.

Amazingly, no one seemed to blame our PFs, the Vietnamese Popular Force soldiers we were supposedly there to train and inspire. The patrol team had crossed the river alone, only five Marines and no PFs. The irony was that Papa Three Marines had pretty much been patrolling alone for the past month, ever since the PFs had first refused to patrol the hamlets on the northern side of the Cam Lo River, the Song Cam Lo. "Beaucoup VC," they had given as their reason. I suppose we all realized that the PFs could have said, "We tried to tell you so!"

No, we couldn't blame the PFs. It was not their fault. If my fellow Marines had ignored our CO's directive that day, this trip to Delta Med might not have been necessary. But, then, who was I to criticize? Only a day or two before, I had been the leader of this patrol team, and I don't know how many patrols I had led along that very same route, violating the most basic rule in the book on my own initiative.

The truth is, I was a lousy leader, barely competent, painfully insecure, and Reaves knew it. I still remember the first patrol I ever led. A group of us had gone out earlier in the day to a shallow part of the river to get rid of some old ordnance, mostly grenades. When someone, I forget whom, told our compound leader that a couple grenades had not gone off, he sent us out to retrieve them lest they fall into the enemy's hands. Fortunately, we had thrown them into a shallow bend in the river, and we found the first dud right away. After nearly an hour of wading around on our hands and knees looking for the second one, the guys were starting to suggest that we just "bag it" when suddenly I felt something hard and smooth under my knee. There was our second grenade. On the way back, Reaves slapped me on the back and said I was a "good leader" not to let us give up. I knew it wasn't true. Reaves knew it wasn't true. But it was a thoughtful and generous gesture, and I was grateful to him for making it.

And now Reaves was dead—he was really *dead*!—an idea I was still trying to wrap my mind around as we pulled up in front of Delta Med.

Neither of us knew exactly where to go. We stumbled into triage first, only to have an irritable corpsman abruptly chase us away from a couple of doctors working intently over an unconscious figure. Demanding to know our business, the corpsman directed us to Graves Registration, which was in a small unmarked shack out back. Here we were again challenged, this time by a lugubrious-looking sergeant who opened the door only wide enough to peek out at us speakeasy-style. The gunny explained why we were there, and our Charon for that day grudgingly opened the door, admitting us to the most macabre scene I had ever witnessed.

My dominant impression remains that of a cottage industry of death

1. The Identification

conducted in a matter-of-fact manner that only served to heighten the horror. The building itself wasn't much larger than today's average suburban two-car garage, and except for lacking a garage door, the effect was very much the same. The front door opened immediately into one large room. The floor was concrete and appeared to have been hosed down recently. Set up throughout the room were at least six rustic preparation tables constructed from two-by-fours and sheets of corrugated roofing tin. (As they used to say, "Nothing is too good for our boys.") Three bodies lay out in plain view. They had been stripped naked and apparently hosed off.

Asking us to "wait one," the sergeant went over to a desk at the far side of the room and began assembling some paperwork. He was tall and thin, and his face remained expressionless throughout our visit. It was years later when I finally placed who he reminded me of—the character Raymond Massey plays in *Arsenic and Old Lace*. Completely ignorant of the procedure, I assumed one of the three bodies must be Reaves and that I should be proceeding with the identification.

None of the bodies looked at all familiar at first glance, so I forced myself to walk up to one of the tables for a closer look. Bending over the face, I suddenly realized with a start that I was looking into a flattened, bullet-punctured eyeball.

I had just about convinced myself that this unfamiliar visage must be Reaves transformed by the shock of death when I was startled by a strange, thundering command: "I thought I told you to pick that up!" I just froze, wondering what I was to pick up, when a shy little lance corporal darted in front of me and, with a sheepish grin, bent down at my feet, coming up bare-handed with a fist-sized chuck of brain tissue. I had almost stepped on it.

This distraction, however, had come just in time. Before I could foolishly try to identify the wrong body, this same lance corporal was leading me into a back room saying, "Reaves is this way."

I soon found myself in a narrow room facing a bank of stainless-steel drawers, such as I had seen in any number of television and movie morgue scenes. Checking the numbers on the drawers against a sheet of paper, my guide went to one of the lower drawers and pulled it out between us. I remember that it extended the entire width of the room, touching the opposite wall, and that the room was dimly lit, the only light coming from a high window at the far end.

The body was in a translucent, zippered plastic bag, which the lance corporal unzipped and pulled away along the entire length of the body. This time I was sure. I recognized Reaves at a glance and said so. But before he would let me go, my ghoulish guide insisted upon tilting the head first one way and then the other, in the process revealing a small, neat puncture wound on one side, not even as large as a dime, and a gaping exit wound, large enough to put my fist in, on the other. Much of the brain tissue had been blasted out. What remained looked sort of like pink cauliflower. The eyes were half-open but turned back into the head. The mouth was open and fixed in a strange, half-grin. The teeth were yellow; I had remembered Reaves as having good, white teeth.

I especially remembered those teeth because Reaves, who was irrepressibly outspoken, had a peculiar self-effacing way of defusing the situation whenever he sensed that he had gone a bit too far in his kidding or his candor. With an index finger in each corner of his mouth, he would pull his mouth wide open to reveal clenched teeth and would then shake his head and whinny like a horse. The effect would be to leave you wondering if he were making fun of himself or of you. Either way, he was big enough, and imposing enough, that he always got away with it. "Where be his quiddities now…?" Invariably, I picture Reaves doing his horse laugh whenever I read or hear that line from the grave-digger's scene in Shakespeare's *Hamlet*.

After I don't know how long, my guide looked up at me with a strange half-smile. I suppose he liked his work, especially the esoteric nature of it. He was privy to things that even combat Marines only occasionally glimpsed, and even then didn't allow themselves to dwell on. This guy had perhaps made a study of all the ways a high-powered bullet could damage a body, and he seemed to take a perverse delight in showing them off. Satisfied at last that I had made positive identification, he zipped the body up, slid the drawer back in, and led me out.

A couple of formalities remained. I had to sign a form attesting to the positive identification, and the sergeant asked me to verify and witness a considerable sum of money Reaves had had on him. He handed me a wad of bills, asking me to count them. Ordinarily, it would not have been a difficult task. It was only about $300—remarkably, in U.S. currency rather than in the small bills of government-style Monopoly money, Military Payment Certificates, "MPCs," we were supposed to use in Vietnam. I remember wondering why Reaves had been hoarding and carrying around so much American money. He hadn't been up for R&R. I didn't know until later that he was due to rotate home in days.

I tried to start the count, but I found myself just too shaken to concentrate. I kept thinking in particular of his former girl back home; they had planned to get married. She had sent him a Dear John letter only a month or so before. The worst part of it, from what Reaves had confided, was that she had somehow felt entitled to the entire joint bank account that they had both paid into, over $500, a large sum to enlisted Marines in those days. When would she hear? Would she feel guilty? Would she feel responsible? I had my

1. The Identification

own reasons for taking a special interest in how she would react, even though I had never met this girl and never would.

I was on my third false start when the sergeant and gunny stepped in and counted the money for me. Somehow, I managed to sign a receipt for the money and the rest of Reaves's personal effects—a watch, a wallet, a Marine Corps ring, and a few other odds and ends. The sergeant put them in a green cloth bag and gave them to me to take back to be included in the inventory with the rest of Reaves's things. We were done at last.

Once we were back out on Highway 9, the gunny said, "Hell of a way to make a living, isn't it, Palm?" I agreed it was, and neither of us said another word all the way back to Papa Three.

2

Palm and the Delaware Dream

Here is a variation on the opening of what some consider to be *the* great American novel: Whenever I'm inclined to reflect back on my regrets, my missed opportunities, and my failures, I remind myself that not everyone has had my disadvantages.

Above all, I suppose, it was my misfortune to serve in the original "wrong war in the wrong place at the wrong time." That was quite an awakening for me and my generation, the World War II Baby Boom generation. Raised in relative prosperity and nurtured by the great American myths, we grew up believing that God was on our side and that "truth, justice, and the American way" was a redundancy. We were destined to wake up from that American dream to the American nightmare of Vietnam. But maybe we took it all too personally. Other generations have had it much worse.

Too much has been made of Vietnam as a class war. America's underclass black kids from the ghetto and impoverished white kids from just about everywhere else were indeed drafted, and even killed and wounded, all out of proportion to their percentage of our population. That is a fact. But, in my experience, it falls far short of the essential and existential truth of that war. The poor kids I served with didn't complain much. They had never put their faith and trust in the American dream to begin with; hence, they weren't very surprised or disappointed when that dream turned into a nightmare. I have to wonder if the real character and tone of that war couldn't be attributed to kids like me instead—those of us who had grown up neither rich nor poor and just smart enough to realize, to paraphrase Philip Caputo, that the land of suburbs and shopping centers somehow didn't seem to be the America we had been promised.

Such, at least, was the reality where I grew up, in northern Delaware—a prosaic land of suburbs, shopping centers, factories, and chemical plants in those years. As I look back on it now, like so many of the guys I found myself serving with, I joined the Marine Corps in search of adventure and to escape

2. Palm and the Delaware Dream

the industrial-strength boredom that would be my legacy should I stay. The problem is that most of my family members and friends back then counted that boredom as one of our principal blessings. "Better things for better living through chemistry" was the DuPont Company slogan and the Delaware dream in those years, with the emphasis on *things*. It was a prosperous place and a prosperous era. We were living in the chemical capital of the world, and most Delawareans took either an innocent or a perverse pride in that distinction. Hercules, Atlas, and DuPont were all headquartered, and all had plants, in the greater Wilmington area. That made us a prime target should the Cold War ever turn hot, my Uncle Al liked to remind people. But we were fatalists all, and in any event, we were working class and couldn't see that there might be alternatives to letting a corporation or a company take care of us.

Like so many giant and formerly paternalistic corporations, DuPont in the '80s began to renege on its promise of secure, lifelong employment, and credit card companies began to displace chemicals as the mainstay of the economy. But back when I was growing up DuPont was still king, and the entire Wilmington/New Castle area was very much a company town.

The Delaware dream when I was young was to "get in with DuPont." "DuPont pays really good," I can still remember Mother saying when she was in one of her expansive, dreamy moods. "Unions have tried to get in DuPont," she'd continue, "but they can't. DuPont's employees don't need a union. They treat their people right."

"Look at *so and so*," she would say. "He's been with DuPont now for over 20 years, and he gets six weeks of vacation. Every time you turn around, he's off."

I don't know how many of these little sermonettes I endured during my high-school years. Before then, when I was about 12, my grandfather died, and the funeral obviously had a profound effect on my mother. There for a while she was encouraging me to become an undertaker and even talked about helping to pay my way through the Philadelphia College of Embalming. But, later, during my sophomore year of high school, my mother and stepfather divorced and, suddenly, we scaled way back, both in our standard of living and in our expectations.

There is a reason, of course, why a sense of place looms so large as one of the great themes in American literature. For better or worse, I believe, our mental horizons are conditioned by issues of geography and topology. Too many of the Appalachian kids I came to know, both the transplants I grew up around in Delaware and those I would later teach in West Virginia, spent too much time hemmed into the narrow valleys they call "hollers." They had lost the capacity to dream their way out of poverty. As for me, I spent my formative years in "one of those places," as a New Yorker once described it, "you have to go through to get there."

I grew up virtually in the shadow of the Delaware Memorial Bridge in a tract neighborhood called Collins Park. One of the first of many bedroom communities to spring up in our area after World War II, it was located south of Wilmington and only a few miles from old New Castle. Collins Park was also a neighborhood in transition when we moved in. There was a ranch house section, which I suppose had started out as working class. But the two-story colonial section, where we would buy, had clearly started out middle class. By the late '50s, however, most of the original buyers already had, or soon would, move on, drawn to newer and more desirable developments west and north of Wilmington. The "two-story" section of Collins Park, as we called it, was filling up with prosperous working-class people, and the "ranch" section had devolved, and devalued, to the lower end of the working-class scale. That's how "two-story" houses in Collins Park came within reach of working-class people like my mother and my stepfather, an auto mechanic.

Our house was on the last street back, Riverview Drive, which did indeed afford a view of the "Twin-Span" Delaware Memorial Bridge and the Delaware River, less than a mile away from my backyard. About a third of the way back, there was a railroad track, still an active freight line back then. Beyond the track, a few hundred yards of land, covered mostly by low scrub, belonged to a rod and gun club, which employed a full-time caretaker and security guard to keep us kids out. They did so for good reason. It was an active club, stocked with small game and featuring hunting and skeet shooting. Sporadic shooting, and even sustained volleys of gunfire, echoed up to our house with great regularity. Even if I could have managed to sneak past the club's caretaker—and on a couple of occasions I did—between the club land and the river lay another couple hundred yards of impenetrable marshes, complete with wide streams and sucking mud. I never got all the way to the river.

From my backyard, I can remember watching trains go by and cars and trucks passing to and from New Jersey as well as freighters, tankers, and even warships sailing up and down the river on the way to Philadelphia and back down toward the Atlantic Ocean. But I always knew that most of the people in Collins Park weren't going anywhere.

Most of the people who lived in Collins Park, however, probably felt they had arrived. These were the years when one wage earner, particularly if he were in a good union or one of the paternalistic companies, could swing a home in the suburbs and a good car—maybe even two. In my experience, there were actually two working classes in those years—the aspiring working class and the acquiring working class. The former, believing in the American promise of upward mobility, worked to get their children into college so they could enjoy the kinder, gentler life of the middle class. The latter—lulled into complacency by the unprecedented material prosperity of the times and un-

2. Palm and the Delaware Dream

able to imagine better lives for themselves or their kids—worked to acquire things. To borrow a phrase from F. Scott Fitzgerald, the objects "commensurate with the capacity for wonder," in my neighborhood, at least, seemed to be cars, boats, color TVs, and finished basements. It was to this group, the acquiring working class, that I was born. My mother, Margaret Elaine Masarik Palm Whitlock, was a charter member.

In the words of the poet, "getting and spending, [my mother laid] waste [her] powers." To this day, she ranks as the vainest, the most self-centered, and the most acquisitive person I've ever known. I can still remember my stepfather, her third husband, complaining that "Marge is never satisfied." And that was early on, when they were still otherwise happy. It's not that she was greedy or even selfish. She was capable of great generosity when things were going well for her. It's just that she really did think that the world revolved around her and that happiness could indeed be bought, one object or status symbol at a time.

In all fairness, I should concede that she had come of age during the last years of the depression, graduating from high school in 1939. The widespread unemployment, poverty, and privations of those years seemed to mark everyone who lived through them, my uncles and aunts included, with an almost pathological need to own things. But my mother's restless, relentless materialism seemed to be driven by something even deeper. She wasn't simply overcompensating for not having had "a pot to piss in or a window to throw it out of," an expression she was especially fond of and routinely applied to people she felt economically superior to. Truth be told, she had never had it that bad. She was the youngest in her family, the baby sister that everyone doted on. She grew up in a warm, loving extended family that managed to get by, despite the depression, by sticking together and pooling their resources. Despite, or maybe even because of, that experience, she wound up terribly insecure and in need of constant reaffirmation.

Not that I understood that until recently. Growing up, I certainly didn't appreciate where she had been or even think about her needs. Throughout my teenage years, I hated her. Truth be told, one of my major motivations in joining the Marine Corps was to spite her and to run away from home. I spent much of my early adult years blaming her for just about everything that had gone wrong in my life—only to discover in a final bitter confrontation the Christmas before she died that she had been blaming me for much that had gone wrong in hers. Now, over 40 years after her death, I realize that what she was in search of all along was what we all need, only her need was more pronounced than most.

"No man needs only a little salary," Uncle Charlie remarks at Willy Loman's funeral in Arthur Miller's *Death of a Salesman*. My mother's need too was finally for self-affirmation. Each new object—whether a jewel, a fur, a piece of bric-a-brac, a husband, a boyfriend (and they were all objects to Marge)—represented an attempt to recapture a golden past when she was the center of attention and all the world seemed kindly disposed toward her. To borrow what Arthur Miller once wrote in defense of his own play, Mother was merely trying to secure her dignity on her own terms, and she remained faithful to a platonic conception of herself and her own worth long after most people would have sought a comfortable accommodation. And in the end, that stubborn persistence destroyed her. I can see now what I couldn't see then. Her life was the stuff that tragedies are made of.

Still, Mother was ahead of her time; I have to give her that much. Divorce, single-parent homes, live-in boyfriends—all these things are common today. But they weren't when and where I was growing up. At least all through grade school I always seemed to be the only one whose mother had a different last name than my own. The only one whose father didn't live with him. The only one who was called by his middle name instead of his first name. The only one whose grandparents didn't speak English. The only one who wore glasses, a trait I inherited from my mother. Far-sightedness ran on my mother's side of the family. My father, a pilot, had always had 20–20 vision. The rest of her family, while they sided with her against my father, disapproved of the way she lived, particularly after my stepfather left, and often told her so. Her two older sisters in particular were scandalized by her lifestyle. But she never let their concerns deter her.

I always knew when one of them would call to complain about the sort of example she was setting for her son, even though they typically spoke Slovak to one another, and I never learned the language. "Your Aunt Jo and Aunt Rose," she would remark, in hanging up the phone, "they act like they just came over on the boat."

My mother, on the other hand, had been born here—on September 13, 1922, in Newark, New Jersey. She was the youngest of six children born to Joseph and Katherine Masarik, a Slovak couple who had been living in and emigrated from Hungary around 1910. (The records no longer exist, and their own papers seem to have been lost.) My grandfather, who had learned leather tanning in what is now Slovakia, was lured over to take a job at a tannery in Newark—in those years, as a couple of Philip Roth's novels attest, the virtual center of the leather industry in America. My mother had been a change-of-life child, a complete surprise to my grandmother who thought she was finished with all that and who, when she began to feel bad, imagined that she was seriously ill.

According to family legend and lore, my grandmother went to an old-school doctor, himself a Slovak émigré, who diagnosed heart disease and told her she would not live much longer. My grandmother was ever the stoic, and her immediate response was to herd the entire family to a photographer

2. Palm and the Delaware Dream

for a formal portrait; she thought that the children would need something by which to remember her.

Shortly after the portrait was taken, of course, my grandmother realized that her Slovak doctor had been wrong. She wasn't dying, but being pregnant again didn't exactly give her a new lease on life either.

I had often wondered how my mother, a second-generation Slovak-American, got such a WASPish name when her siblings all got names that could have stood them in good stead in the Old Country—"Joseph," "Josephine," "Rosa," "Albert," and "Julius." According to my Aunt Rose, back when my mother was born poor immigrant women still gave birth at home. But hospital interns, as part of their training, rode along in ambulances and would come out to help women give birth. Such were the circumstances of my mother's birth. A young intern came out to their apartment house to help, and as chance would have it, my aunt said, my mother's birth was the first at which he alone assisted. He was obviously more impressed by the experience

The formal family portrait my grandmother had taken in 1922. She thought she was dying of heart disease. The "disease" turned out to be my mother, who was born on September 13, 1922. Back row, left, standing: Rosa Masarik (later Rose Masarik West); back row, middle: Josephine Masarik (first born, later Josephine Sickinger). Front row, from left: Albert Masarik; Katherine Omelka Masarik (matriarch, of course); Julius Masarik; Joseph Masarik (patriarch, of course); Joseph Masarik, Jr.

than my grandmother, who admitted that she had not yet given a thought to a name for the new arrival. The intern suggested his wife's name—Margaret Elaine. My grandmother, having no alternatives in mind, went for it.

Her lukewarm welcome to the world notwithstanding, Margaret Elaine Masarik grew up petted, pampered, and spoiled. By all accounts, her big brothers and sisters in particular doted on her. She was precocious and pretty and smart. She was the only one in the family to graduate from high school. She took the commercial course rather than the academic one; education for education's sake simply was not understood in her family. But still, relatively few people finished high school in those years. It was an accomplishment she remained proud of throughout her life.

The family did struggle during the Great Depression—my grandparents lost a rooming house they had bought as an investment—but they never went homeless or hungry. They lived together and pooled their resources. Even when they married, my uncles and aunts typically started out by bringing their brides or husbands home to live. As extended families often did in those years, they stuck together, physically as well as emotionally. And eventually they got back on their feet. The lessons of the depression, however, were not lost on my mother. For the rest of her life, she would remain close to her family and at regular intervals would fall back on them for moral and financial support. As I've already mentioned, she would also become obsessed with *having* things. When she would urge me to "get in with DuPont," for instance, it was always so that "we can have something"—her unspoken expectation that I would stick around and repay my raising just as she and her siblings had done with their parents.

I had nothing of the sort in mind, especially since I was experiencing my first serious romance at the time. (More about that anon.) When it looked as if my girlfriend and I were definitely headed toward marriage, she suggested that we could live with her "if we were good kids."

My mother was hardly one to give marital advice—a point I would finally make in that bitter confrontation the Christmas before she died. (We never really reconciled, not even in the course of her final illness the following spring.) She had been married the first time right out of high school to a man I still know almost nothing about. His mother, I was told, didn't approve, and the marriage was annulled. She would meet my father in 1945 at a dance held at the New Castle Air Force Base Officers Club. He was an Army Air Corps lieutenant and a B-17 pilot just back from the European Theater at the time. They were married within a few months of that fateful meeting, and true to form, lived at first with my grandparents.

They separated when I was two years old, mostly over my father's decision to go back in the service. Although she and my father lived apart from that point forward, my mother seems to have stalled on making their divorce final until he finally forced the issue in 1953. He had met the woman who would become his second and final wife.

Shortly thereafter, my mother, perhaps on the rebound, met the man who would become her third husband and my stepfather, an auto mechanic named Reese Whitlock. That marriage would last until my sophomore year of high school, 1963, at which time Reese left my mother for another woman. A succession of boyfriends followed. By my senior year of high school, however, Mother had settled on one, an artful dodger I'll identify only as Joe. He would live with her continuously, aside from periodic fights, until her death in 1978.

My mother and father on their wedding day, July 21, 1945.

Joe was at the center of what undoubtedly turned out to be the saddest period of my mother's life. When they first met, soon after I began my senior year of high school, Joe passed himself off as a retired New York City cop and a widower who was then working at a Ford plant in New Jersey. They met at the Kent Manor Inn, a restaurant, nightclub, and motel that catered to jaded middle-aged singles and cheaters on the prowl. I still remember my mother coming home that night, excited as a schoolgirl and eager to tell someone about the great guy she had met. He had turned her head with his gold-colored Lincoln Continental and with a wallet that, as she described it, was "full of $20 bills."

It couldn't have been more than two or three weeks later that Joe moved in—although, as I look back on it now, Joe always seemed poised for a quick getaway. He kept most of his clothes in the trunk of his car. A little later that fall, a friend of a friend tipped my mother off; the reports of the death of Joe's wife were somewhat exaggerated. She was alive and living in their house in northern Wilmington. That explained one of Joe's unusual habits. He would get up and leave every morning at 0-dark-thirty; his explanation was that he and some of his co-workers liked to meet at a particular diner for breakfast before beginning work at Ford. Joe was leading a double life, jumping from my mother's bed back into bed with his wife.

Once he was found out, Joe's initial cover story was that his wife was dying of cancer and that he just didn't have the heart to divorce her. Before my senior year was out, however, Joe's wife would show up at our door, hale and hearty and very vocal about how my mother was robbing her of the sexual attention to which she was entitled. (It seems Joe was telling her he was impotent.) I thought that that would be the end of the affair. But I underestimated Joe. He confessed that he and his wife owned property together and that he was afraid he would lose his interest in their property should he be the one to file for divorce. That was a consideration my mother could understand and respect. Somehow, my mother thought she and Joe could wait out his wife and not have to share any of Joe's assets.

It wasn't that my mother was stupid or gullible. Far from it. She was afraid of being alone. That's certainly one reason why she settled for Joe. But, more importantly, like Arthur Miller's Willy Loman, America had sold her "all the wrong dreams." Her childhood somehow left her with the conviction that she was destined for a happy ending. And, like Willy Loman, she somehow thought she could make it all fall in place by force of her personal attractiveness. She remained trim throughout her life, had green eyes and, for the last 13 years of her life, sported bleached blond hair that suited her and her values. But she couldn't seem to conceive of her happy ending in other than material terms.

As short on money as she claimed to be after my stepfather left, Mother periodically found enough to spend on fortune tellers. One of them told her she could see me leading men in Vietnam and that I would do well. (Go figure.) Another one told her she could see her wearing furs and jewels and riding to Florida in a Cadillac.

I suspect she took that first prediction with a grain of salt. She always considered me clumsy and lacking in common sense. But I'm sure she believed that latter prediction would come to pass. "Someday, our ship will come in!" was her favorite cliché. Somehow, she never understood that she was responsible for launching that ship.

As I look back on it now, ours was always a clash of values. The problem was that, like a character out of Dickens, I was growing up with "great expectations" that she disapproved of and did all in her power to suppress.

3

My Great Expectations

The best thing my father ever did for me, I realize now, was to disappear from my life when I was only two. One of my earliest memories is of the beginning of the end, when he left to go back in the service.

I must have been less than two years old, so most of the details are hazy. What I remember is like a movie scene—as if I'm outside of myself and watching a little boy and two other people on a gray day.

I see a woman, a man, and a little boy out on a sidewalk in front of a car. It must have been a taxi.

A man kneels down and hugs the little boy. The man gets in the taxi, and it drives off. I didn't understand what was going on, but I could sense that this was an unhappy scene.

The final break up came not long after this scene, after my mother and I had joined my father at his new duty station in Japan. There had been a drunken dalliance with a Japanese maid, and that was that. My mother and I returned to the bosom of her family—the safe place she had never really wanted to leave.

From then until I turned 18, as part of the divorce settlement, he sent us $100 a month, without fail. But in all that time, while he would write occasionally and usually send a gift for my birthday, I remember his visiting me only twice. In fact, it wasn't until I was 19 and a Marine lance corporal that he sought me out and we established a tentative father-son relationship. But, from the time I was able to understand who and what he was, my father would loom large in my imagination.

To me, a child of the working class, growing up in the midst of the Cold War, to be a pilot and an Air Force officer seemed a wondrous accomplishment. Even better, he won hands-down in the "What-did-you-do-in-the-war, Daddy?" contests of my youth. My father had been a B-17 pilot and, to my mind, had really fought in the war that was being mythologized in the films and television programs of the '50s. My stepfather, by comparison, had been a mere sailor and was hidden below decks as an electrician on a prosaic LST. Further—unlike my stepfather, my uncles, and the fathers of all my friends—

my father had gone to war twice. He flew a light artillery spotter plane in the Korean War, an assignment just as dangerous and heroic to my mind as bombing Nazi Germany, and for which he won the Distinguished Flying Cross. And he was continuing to serve, helping to keep our skies free from the Russian bombers that threatened our peace of mind in the early years of the Cold War.

I understood very little about the military's caste system when I was growing up. But, from what I learned watching war movies, I understood early on that my father inhabited a station of life above the one I was living in. Not that my mother ever openly acknowledged that there was anything to admire in what my father had achieved. For as long as I can remember, she had always disparaged my father as lazy. At my mother's insistence, he had gotten out of the service briefly, but the job market was saturated with returning veterans after the war. My father worked, in turn, as a short order cook, a taxi driver, a mailman, and an operator in a chemical plant—all of which proved to be quite a come-down for a man who had lately been an officer and a gentleman. My mother, however, couldn't or wouldn't see that. "Your father didn't want to work," she would tell me, "so he decided to stay in the service." I never believed that. Moreover, from what my uncles would say about my father, usually when my mother was out of earshot, I could tell that they had liked and admired him. "Remember that there are always two sides to every story," my Uncle Al confided long before I would hear my father's version of why he and my mother had divorced.

But I didn't much care which party was primarily responsible for the failure of my mother and father's marriage. Just hearing the family legend and lore associated with my father imbued me with a special sense of destiny. It wasn't anything as crass as expecting my father to show up someday and to raise me to my rightful place above the working class. The legend that resonated the most with me was how, by a combination of luck and pluck, he had pulled himself up and out of an impoverished single-parent home. He grew up fascinated with airplanes and with a single-minded determination to learn to fly. Working after school and throughout his summer vacations, he managed to pay for flying lessons and earned his private pilot's license while still in high school. On the strength of only a high-school education, he later qualified for the Army Air Corps' Aviation Cadet Program. The story of my father's early success was a lesson and an example that was not lost on me. I grew up believing that I had to be heir to whatever innate potential my father had had and that I too would somehow rise above the place of my birth and become something special.

The innate quality we really shared, I eventually came to realize, was a degree of vanity that my mother feared and despised. Whenever she became especially angry with me, which happened more and more as I grew older, I

3. My Great Expectations 21

would hear a variation on the same bitter lament: "You're getting more and more like your father Ed Palm every day!" I, of course, couldn't see that as a bad thing. But to her the analogy seemed to sum up everything she couldn't understand about either of us and therefore disapproved of. Both of us, to her mind, thought we were too good to work for a living. And having failed to humble my father, she seemed to make it her mission in life to cut me down to size.

One of the things we especially fell out over was my education. While I may have lacked my father's early focus and drive, I did have two distinct advantages my father had not had. I had a doting grandmother and a doting aunt, my mother's oldest sister, my Aunt Jo. By their Old-Country standards, my mother was a scarlet woman and a bad influence on me. She had been a bobbysoxer as a teenager and a night-clubber as a young woman, and just as they feared, she had grown up to become a divorced woman and a single parent. All the time I was growing up, even when I had a stepfather, both Aunt Jo and my grandmother remained outspoken advocates on my behalf and constant critics of my mother's modern American mores and lifestyle. For her part, my mother always bitterly resented their meddling, but she never severed her ties with the extended family she remained emotionally and, at times, financially dependent upon. And probably the best thing my mother ever did for me was to acquiesce in my grandmother and my Aunt Jo's wish that I get a good high-school education.

As often happens in life, too late I realized how much I really owe to my Aunt Jo in particular. She volunteered to pay my tuition to the best Catholic high school available to the likes of our family in those years, the Salesianum School for Boys. Run by the Oblates of St. Francis de Sales, the "gentleman saint," "Sallies," as it was widely known, had been a respected Wilmington institution since its founding in 1903. The curriculum is strictly college-prep, and the school's no-nonsense approach to discipline, dress, and grooming is legendary. The students are expected to comport themselves as "Sallies gentlemen." They are required to wear coats and ties at all times when on the school grounds, even for athletic and social activities. Prospective students and their parents are told to expect three hours of homework a night (a promise that, in my experience, held up through the sophomore year). Judging from the photos Sallies now has online, the grooming standards have been relaxed, but in my day, "Sallies gentlemen" had to be clean-shaven and were allowed no more than two inches of hair.

Rule breakers were—and I believe still are—subject to a distinctive form of detention known as "jug." The unfortunates "placed in jug" reported to a designated classroom after school, and under the watchful eye of the duty priest or seminarian, spent an hour sitting up straight, with their feet flat on the floor and their hands folded and resting on their desks, staring at the crucifix affixed to the wall in front of them. I was a frequent visitor. I once had occasion to do two back-to-back 10-day stints—an ordeal that made me a minor folk hero among my downtrodden classmates. I was caught smoking, the penalty for which was 10 days in jug. Then, before serving out my first sentence, I was caught again. Suffice it to say that I had a lot of time for reflection.

All things considered, though, I was fairly happy to be what passed for a Sallies gentleman—at least at first. The public high school in my district was a disaster zone. It was notorious for low standards and discipline problems. More to the point, the public high school was very much our neighborhood school, and had I gone there, I would have continued to keep some of the bad company I had fallen in with around Collins Park. Salesianum took me away from all that. It seemed the gateway to an altogether better life. Suddenly, I found myself thrown in with kids from solidly middle-class and aspiring working-class families, kids with caring parents who wanted to give them every advantage they could conceive of and afford. As I look back on it now, Sallies seemed to be the first real sign that, like my father before me, I too was among the elect. And I did well there—for my first two years.

Initially, my mother was fairly supportive. Sallies grads had a reputation for networking and for sticking together. "If a Sallies grad is going to hire somebody, and he sees you're wearing a Sallies ring," she told me, "you'll get the job over someone who didn't go to Sallies." Her attitude would change dramatically, however, after my stepfather left. She began a campaign to get me to transfer to "Brown"—not the university but the vocational high school in Wilmington, where I could have "taken up" something practical like plumbing, electrical work, or auto repair. The great advantage to going to Brown, as she reminded me repeatedly throughout my junior year at Sallies, was that Brown had a cooperative program whereby students learning some trades went to school two weeks and worked for two weeks—and got paid!—throughout their senior year.

"You could be bringing some money into this house, and then we could *have* something!" she would lament. Ahead of my time, I dug in my heels and said, "Hell no, I won't go!" She never understood my intransigence. "There's no money for college, if that's what you're thinking," she once reminded me, making such an ambition sound as unrealistic and extravagant as harboring an expectation to be sent on the Grand Tour of Europe after graduation.

I knew full well there was no money for college. (Years later, my father, who faithfully sent $100 a month toward my support, was shocked to learn that she had put away none of that money for my education, not even when she and my stepfather had been doing well. Having lived with her, I wasn't surprised. She saw that money not as support for me but rather as reparations due to her.) When I was a junior in high school, I wasn't sure what I wanted

3. My Great Expectations

to do. I just knew I wanted a good high-school education at least. But, as soon as I was able, I would have to meet her halfway.

From the time I was 15, I had a series of summer and after-school jobs. I caddied at the Wilmington Country Club; I made French fries at Gino's, a McDonald's precursor; I was a bellhop at the Gateway Motor Inn, a motel with pretensions; and I worked in the housewares department of Wilmington Dry Goods, a bargain department store. Often on school nights, especially throughout my senior year, I wouldn't get home until nearly midnight. Still, Mother bitched about how I wasn't bringing enough money into the house. She would even hound me—a hungry teenager—at meal times: "I see there's nothing wrong with your appetite for someone not bringing any money into this house." She would complain about how I was only making enough to pay for my lunches and my bus fare.

One of the money-making schemes she hit on soon after my stepfather left was to rent out my room. Again, I suppose I was ahead of my time. Before he left home, Harry Potter had to live in a closet beneath the stairs. I was moved into the smallest room in the house, a five-by-eight-foot room at the end of the hall. There was barely enough room for a narrow daybed/couch combination and a small desk. Most prison cells are bigger. My only enduring complaint, however, is about the daybed. My mother had not invested in a regular mattress for it; she expected me to spread a sheet over the couch cushions, every square foot of which was adorned with a quarter-inch raised, hard button. I eventually got used to it, but it's a wonder that I don't still have a series of small regular indentations up and down my sides and back.

I got Mother her first roomer, a desk clerk I worked with at the Gateway Motor Inn. I'll call him Bill. He was tall and heavy set, with curly black hair. Also, his demeanor and speech bordered on the effeminate. His backstory was that he had been in the Navy for 10 years. When I asked Bill why he hadn't stayed for 20 and gotten a pension, his answer was cryptic: "Regulations are one thing, but I can't go along with chicken shit." The Navy, I would later come to learn, had always been more tolerant of gays than the other services—so long as they were discreet. Bill must not have been. He had obviously been put out for being gay, an orientation that would eventually become apparent. On more than one occasion, late in the evening, when we weren't busy, he would grab me from behind, lift me off the ground, and challenge me to break free.

One thing I can say for Bill: He was always friendly and helpful with the guests. Women especially loved him. I remember one night in particular. An attractive forty-something woman checked in alone. Another desk clerk and I were on duty, and as it was my turn, I showed the woman to her room. She hadn't been there a half hour when she called the desk.

Just by listening to Bill's side of the conversation, it became apparent that the lady was lonely and was inviting Bill to come to the room to talk and to keep her company for a while. The other bellhop and I were trying to cheer him on. He politely declined, claiming he wasn't allowed to leave the desk. We told him to call her back and go, that we were fully capable of manning the desk until his return. But he held firm. He was proof against temptation—from that gender, at least.

Mother too loved him. He was clean and polite and paid his rent on time. On only one occasion, when Mother was working the nightshift as a hospital admitting clerk, did he try to hit on me. Hollering from his room (my former room) to mine, he tried to invite me to join him, to "keep him company." When I declined, he became more explicit about what he had in mind, asking me if I had ever been with a man and didn't I want to try it. I said "no" in no uncertain terms, and he gave up. It wasn't long after that that he decided to leave—both our house and the Gateway Motor Inn. I don't remember exactly what he said about why he was leaving, only that it was as vague as his explanation for leaving the Navy.

From my standpoint, at least, the best roomer my mother ever took in was one "wild and crazy guy" I'll just call Steve. Steve came on the scene during my senior year of high school. He had just taken a job driving a car carrier delivering new cars for a major motor freight company headquartered in our area, and my mother thought it was great that he would be away, on the road, for two to four days at a time.

Newly divorced and a former Marine, Steve was always on the make. Initially, he even tried to hit on Mother; unfortunately, he didn't have the sort of assets that would have interested her. But Steve always thought of women as buses; if you didn't catch one, another would be along in 15 minutes.

Watching Steve hit on waitresses was one of the great entertainments and educational experiences of my misspent youth. He had a devil-may-care attitude, an inspired and quick wit, and a boyish charm that allowed him to get away with off-color jokes and double-entendres that would have gotten other men slapped by waitresses and ejected from restaurants. It also didn't hurt that he had a hot car, a Pontiac Grand Prix—which he always referred to as his "Grand Prick." I don't recall that he ever got any phone numbers, but the objects of his attentions always seemed to find his overtures amusing and not threatening, even when he would tell them about his "Grand Prick" and offer to take them for a ride.

Steve also had his sensitive side. He could see how badly my mother treated me. I suppose that's why he befriended me. He treated me as a peer. He took me, at the advanced age of 17, drinking. He regaled me with colorful stories of his times in the Marine Corps and even confided in me about his marital problems. I knew I was destined to enlist in some branch of the service, but it was Steve who inspired me to become a Marine.

3. My Great Expectations

I don't mean to imply that my life was all bleak in those years. There were moments of real grace, and there were people who were better to me than I had a right to expect.

My cousin Doris, 10 years my senior, agreed to teach me to drive when my mother wouldn't. Rather than disappoint me, she took me out for my first lesson at night in a serious snow storm. I drove us around the empty Acme parking lot until the snow got to be about six inches deep.

There was my next-door neighbor, Bob Burns, who was personable, friendly, and blessed with the gift of gab. Photography had been my passion ever since my father sent me an adjustable 35 mm Edixa camera when I was 12. Bob encouraged my interest in photography and once gave up an evening to drive me to the *News Journal* office. I couldn't have been more than 12 or 13 at the time. I had photographed an accident scene near our neighborhood and was hoping the paper would run one of my photos. It did. I told Bob that he could just drop me off, that I could take the bus back home. But he went in with me and seemed just as interested as I was in watching one of the paper's professional photographers develop my film and print one of the photos.

Also, Bob had served in the Air Force on Guam, and his stories helped ignite my interest in joining the military. If working for DuPont was the Delaware dream back when I was growing up, getting stuck on the soul-deadening assembly line at General Motors or Chrysler was the Delaware nightmare. Bob had been stuck for a time on the GM line but had managed to escape. I still remember his telling me about one of his co-workers, who during his lunch break would bite into his sandwich as if attacking it, saying, "I'm gettin' the hell outta here!" over and over again. I don't recall what Bob, who had a wife and three kids, was doing for a living at that time, but it was evident that he looked back on his military service as the best time of his life. He was a good man. I wish I had somehow repaid his kindness or told him how much his interest and help had meant to me while I was growing up.

And there was Warren Yap. It was Bob Burns who put me onto him. Bob told me that Warren too was into photography and that I should meet him. Warren lived about three doors down from Bob on our street. He was Indonesian and a chemical engineer at DuPont (which made him one of the last of the solidly middle-class homeowners in Collins Park at the time, a real holdout). One evening, I brashly knocked on his door, introduced myself, and told him what Bob had said about our mutual interest in photography. He handed me a stack of photo magazines and told me to come back on Saturday and we could talk. Despite having a beautiful blonde Dutch wife and infant daughter, Warren found time to befriend me. He had an Omega D2 enlarger he was "keeping for a friend." We went to Wilmington's major camera store, Lincoln Camera, bought the necessary chemicals and paper, and printed some photos in his basement.

Warren also had two good 35 mm cameras, a Nikon S2 and a Voightlander Vitessa. He was nice enough to loan me the Voightlander to use on a weekend Boy Scout camping trip. (That summer, I had lost the Edixa camera my father had sent when my stepfather accidentally swamped an 18-foot runabout boat he had just bought.) Somehow, I got some dirt in the viewfinder of the Vitessa. Warren was angry. I was embarrassed, and that was the end of our friendship.

The last time I saw Warren was after I had become a Marine officer. I was back visiting the old neighborhood and ran into him. He made it clear that he was disappointed in me for becoming a Marine. And that was that.

There were also my Aunt Rose and Uncle Bill, who lived just two streets down from us in Collins Park. (We lived on 134 Riverview Drive; they lived on 134 Rodney Drive.) And there was my Aunt Jo. They all stepped in and took up the slack when I was growing up.

4

Mixed Blessings

Now that I've gotten to a certain age, I often find myself wondering at the ways in which the world has changed since I was young and thinking of some of the modern advances we couldn't have conceived of when I was in Vietnam. Dick Tracy's wrist radios, I suppose, foreshadowed cell phone technology, but we never expected to enjoy such a reliable and miniaturized means of communication in our lifetime, especially those of us who occasionally humped the Marine Corps' bulky 25-pound tactical radios. Today, people have cell phones in Vietnam. Likewise, a computer was something that Captain Kirk regularly consulted on *Star Trek*, but we never imagined that we'd all be needing and using personal computers by the time we reached middle-age. Back in 1967, mail usually took at least five days to get from the States to Vietnam, and your loved ones could count on another five- or seven-day delay before they heard back from you. Today's soldiers—the ones we sent to Iraq and those still in Afghanistan (as of this writing)—can stay in touch through cell phones, e-mail, and Skype. And when I was in Vietnam, I couldn't have imagined what an "Internet" would be used for or why we would someday want to make regular use of it.

(Personally, I'm glad we were not able to phone, e-mail, or Skype home when I was in Vietnam. It's bad enough to be in a combat zone without feeling obligated to check in with loved ones daily lest they assume the worst. Many of today's deployed troops must consider our modern means of instant communication to present as much of a burden as a blessing.)

It was through the miracle of the Internet that, starting in the mid-'90s, the guys I served in Vietnam with and I began to find one another. Or, more accurately, they began to find me through Vietnam photos I had begun to post to a couple web sites. The first was Larry Scroggs, who lived in El Paso. (He died in 2019.) The next was my old platoon sergeant, Bill Cooke, who grew up in and returned to Grand Rapids, Michigan. Then there was Mack Garrett, of Orange County, California. Later, I would reconnect with Ron Parks and Mike Fink. I'll have much to say about each of these characters and our past lives together as I go along. The one I should dwell on at this point was the last to find any of us, Robert Yost. (He died in 2018. I have corresponded with his daughters, who approve of my using his real name.)

Yost, who grew up in a small Midwestern town, struggled with post-traumatic stress disorder throughout his postwar life. When we were still in touch, he confided that he found himself unwelcome when he first returned home. His family and friends, put off by his moodiness and erratic behavior, soon found themselves afraid of him. So he went out to L.A., where he drifted from job to job and joined the counter culture. He claimed to have lived for a time with Lynette "Squeaky" Fromme, the former Manson family member who would later attempt to assassinate President Ford. And he drank—more and more as time went on.

At some point, he pulled himself together enough to get married and to father two daughters. But it proved to be a troubled marriage. His wife did her best to stick by Robert and to try to help him get the treatment he needed for his alcoholism and his PTSD. But shortly before Yost came back into my life, after he had some sort of brush with the law, she had left him for good. They remained in close contact, however, and she continued to care about him.

Shortly after Yost first got in touch with me, in early 2004, I was surprised to receive an e-mail message from his wife. I'm still trying to decide if the tone of that message was bitter or just anguished. She let me know, in no uncertain terms, that she just didn't understand why people like me had managed to put Vietnam behind them and go on to make something of themselves when her husband was still haunted and troubled, and ultimately disabled, by his Vietnam experiences.

I wrote back, but I admitted that I didn't have a good answer for her. I suppose that this book, in part, is an attempt to answer her question.

Frankly, I've done much better than I ever deserved to do. I'm what the people who believe in standardized testing would call an overachiever. I rose above my raising in a working-class broken home. I'm the second in my family to go to college and the first to earn graduate degrees. I've made it into my 70s with no major health problems. I've been married only once, and my marriage, as of this writing, is going on 50 years and counting. Our son, daughter-in-law, and grandson are all doing well. I managed to conjoin a military career with an academic one, serving as a department chair and tenured professor at a state college. I went on to hold dean appointments at two other colleges, and I now enjoy a comfortable retirement.

As I look back on my life today, I can see a kind of Dickensian pattern to it: Simple working-class lad from New Castle, Delaware, a child of a broken and at least a verbally abusive home, goes bad for a while, but ultimately rises above it and finds safe harbor. One word of warning before I go much further:

4. Mixed Blessings

My writing tends to be allusive—not "illusive," I hope—maybe even a little showy. I know it. But, as I've had occasion to tell people before, I didn't study English literature for 10 years only to have to think for myself, thank you very much! If Milton, Shakespeare, or some other literary lion said it best, why not let them speak for me in places?

5

How It All Began

Here's a variation on a line from Tennyson: "In the spring, a young man's fancy lightly turns to [escape and to dreams of glory]."

"I'm gonna go talk to the Air Force recruiter today after school," Roger said. "Wanna come?"

It was our lunch period in April 1965, the spring of our senior year. Roger Frantz, my best friend at the time, had just come up to my table in the cafeteria.

"Actually, Rog, I'm going to try to join the Marine Corps," I replied. "But they're both in the same building. I'll go down with you, and I'll talk to the Marine recruiter while you talk to the Air Force recruiter."

So after school on that fateful day we set out together—to the Old Customs House on King Street in Wilmington, Delaware. I remember that it was a beautiful spring day, the sort of day people don't get too many of in that part of the Middle Atlantic region. We always seemed to go from winter to summer without much of a spring in between.

When we got to the Customs House, the directory in the foyer indicated that all the military recruiters were on the second floor. When we got up there, we found that the Marine recruiter's door was the first one on the right, and the Air Force recruiting office was at the end of the hall.

"Okay, Rog," I said, with my hand on the door knob. "If I get done first, I'll wait downstairs for you, and you do the same."

"Ah, I'll come in to hear what he has to say," Roger replied.

We entered what at first seemed to be an empty office. But at the sound of the door closing behind us, a tall Marine came out from around a partition, demanding, "What do you guys want?" To say that he seemed less than welcoming would be an understatement. In fact, he seemed irritated, as if we had interrupted something. He was tall and dressed in the uniform I would come to know as "Blue Dress C"—dress-blue trousers with a red stripe down the seams and a short-sleeved tropical wool khaki shirt with the three-stripe chevron of a sergeant on the sleeves. Having come straight from school, we were both dressed in the coats and ties

5. How It All Began

that Sallies required. I suspect he wasn't used to having applicants walk in so-attired.

"We're interested in joining the Marine Corps," I said.

"What makes you guys think you're good enough to be Marines?" he demanded, staring down at us. I didn't know what to say, so I said nothing. Roger too stood on his right to remain silent. Fortunately, the sergeant broke what was becoming an uncomfortable silence. "Where do you guys go to school?"

"Salesianum," I replied. Suddenly, his demeanor changed. If not friendlier, he at least didn't seem to feel so put-upon by our presumptuous presence. Later, much later, it occurred to me that he and his fellow recruiters had never managed to recruit from Sallies, Sallies being college prep, and that netting two of us would be a real coup for him.

"Well, I have a test here that will tell me if you two are smart enough to be Marines. It takes less than an hour. Do you have time to take it now?"

We were certainly smart enough to be Marines, but not smart enough to see through the sergeant's reverse-psychology tactics. We soon found ourselves sitting at separate desks taking a two- or three-page multiple choice test. As I recall, it was a test of reading and of basic math. There may also have been some verbal analogies comparable to the ones I encountered in the Scholastic Aptitude Test I would take a few years later. Roger and I finished within a half hour, and the sergeant scored the tests right then and there. We each scored a 99 percent. I don't remember which question or questions I may have missed.

"Well, you guys are certainly smart enough to be Marines," he conceded. "But I need to know if you're physically capable of being Marines. I can get you out of a day of school to go to the Induction Center in Philadelphia to take the physical. Do you want to go next week? No obligation. If you pass the physical, then we'll talk." Before we knew it, we had train tickets and a physical appointment for the following Wednesday.

Roger never did talk to the Air Force recruiter. Within a couple weeks, we had both enlisted under the buddy program—meaning we would be in the same platoon at Parris Island—with a 120-day delay. We were to report to Parris Island on August 10, 1965.

I had mixed feelings about our going in together under the buddy program. "Roger, please, I'd rather do it myself!" I remember thinking. But there was no graceful way to decline the recruiter's offer without offending Roger. And truth be told, I suspected he would show me up. And he did! I had a difficult time in boot camp; Roger sailed through it. He was one of the top performers promoted to PFC on graduation day at Parris Island. He went on to serve as a helicopter door gunner in Vietnam, extending his tour of duty twice, and finishing his enlistment as a drill instructor at Parris Island. He even made staff sergeant in under four years—quite an accomplishment back then. After our enlistments, we would both go on to college under the G.I. Bill, except that Roger had the good sense to major in business rather than English. He became a DuPont executive.

But why did we enlist in the first place? We had both grown up in single-parent homes. I'm sure that, like me, Roger had no prospects for college. Growing up in that time and place, we would both have been drafted anyway. But, ultimately, I can speak only to my own motivation. It certainly wasn't out of patriotism. All the working-class people I knew were cynical and distrustful of business and government institutions—all of which, in their view, were only out to exploit you. All my uncles had served in World War II, but they had waited to be drafted. Only my father had volunteered, but as I recounted earlier, even he waited until he could qualify for what had always been his heart's desire—flight training. Still, my generation had grown up steeped in the films and television programs that had glorified World War II service. They made the camaraderie and challenges of military life look appealing.

But I didn't enlist to go to war. I was a typically self-absorbed teenager at the time. I hadn't paid much attention to news reports. I did know that Marines had landed to guard the airfield in a place called Vietnam. No one I knew, however, foresaw that within only a few months Vietnam would become a major American war.

The truth of the matter is that I needed to earn that uniform to shore up my flagging self-esteem. To say it the way Sylvester Stallone's Rocky character might say it, if I could "go the distance" as a U.S. Marine, then I'd know "I wasn't just another bum from the neighborhood." And there really didn't seem to be any other avenues to distinction open to me at the time.

Mark Twain was right: "History doesn't repeat itself, but it does rhyme." I had signed up under the 120-day delay program, so there was plenty of time to break the news to my mother that I had enlisted in the Marine Corps. But I kept putting it off. Then, one bright day, the Marine Corps did it for me. Mother received a nice letter from the commandant of the Marine Corps—a form letter, of course—congratulating her on having a fine son who had qualified for enlistment in the United States Marine Corps.

In 1978, after my mother had died, I found a letter to my mother from a Major John J. Hunter, USAF, who at the time was assigned to Headquarters United States Air Force. Hunter was responding to a letter from my mother, and he was explaining that "officers of the civilian components are recalled to active duty only upon their own request." Hunter went on to explain that "First Lieutenant Edward G. Palm" had submitted his request and that "it is regretted that your husband's action in applying for extended active duty did not meet with your approval." The letter is dated May 19, 1948.

5. How It All Began

Clearly, my father had not been honest with my mother. He must have led her to believe that he had been involuntarily recalled to active duty when, in fact, he had volunteered. I suppose Mother was right: I was becoming more like my father "Ed Palm" every day.

Given how strained our relationship had been throughout my teenage years, I was genuinely surprised when she burst into tears on the morning I was leaving to go to boot camp.

6

That Other Parris

Every year around August 10, I find myself reminiscing about Parris—not the one in France, but the one spelled with two Rs. After traveling all day on August 10, 1965, and most of the night, I found myself standing on those fabled yellow footprints in front of the receiving barracks at the Marine Corps Recruit Depot, Parris Island, South Carolina. To borrow a phrase from the Leon Uris novel *Battle Cry*, "the gates of mercy" had closed behind me.

Our senior drill instructor happened to be African American, and his welcoming words, after all these years, still ring in my head: *"My name is Sergeant *****. If you have any motherfucking prejudices, you better forget 'em right now!"* And we did—immediately—even the recruits from the Deep South. After that warm welcome, it was no more Mr. Nice Guy.

Marine boot camp has long been legendary for physical and psychological abuse. The opening scenes of the film *Full Metal Jacket* convey some sense of what it was like. But worse than the physical abuse, in my experience, was the psychological torment—not the least of which was a strictly enforced code of silence. For the entire eight weeks (shortened from 12 due to the Vietnam build-up), we never got to talk to one another, or to anyone except our drill instructor, and then only when spoken to.

Between tumbling out of the bus and onto those yellow footprints and graduation day eight weeks later, for instance, Roger managed to say only one thing to me. It was after Taps, the only time we were allowed to make head calls (to go to the bathroom) without asking permission from our drill instructor. Roger was coming out of the head; I was on my way in. "You and your big ideas!" he whispered. I never got to say anything to Roger.

It was, therefore, a supreme relief when, halfway through the program, our platoon went on mess duty. Because an abscess, caused by an ingrown hair, had come up under my chin, the mess sergeant insisted I be kept out of sight. Hence, I found myself alone with one other recruit in the pot shack behind the mess hall. Our mission—and our only choice was to accept it—was to scrub spotlessly clean a seemingly endless supply of dirty pots large

6. That Other Parris

enough for boiling missionaries. But at least we could relax and talk to one another like normal, free human beings.

My fellow pot-scrubber, I learned, was from a broken family in Arkansas and had dropped out of high school to join the Marine Corps. But what really floored me was when he said he would be "out of here by this time next week." We still had four weeks to go on "the island."

He was only 16, he explained. He had gotten in so much trouble in high school that his mother, at her wit's end, agreed to lie about his age and to sign the papers so he could enlist. After four weeks at Parris Island, however, he was seeing things from a different point of view, and he was especially looking forward to rejoining his high-school class.

"You know," he said, his voice reverberating from the bottom of a huge pot, "I used to think school was the worst thing that ever happened to me. But, when I get back in that classroom, they're going to have to beat me out with a stick!"

I wish I had written down that recruit's name and had kept track of him. I would bet that his change of heart was permanent and that he went on to become a doctor, lawyer, or successful businessman. At the very least, he was able to write one hell of an essay on the perennial topic of "how I spent my summer vacation."

I, too, have come a long way since then. I'm a retired Marine officer, a retired professor, and a former college dean now. To stay busy, I write a regular opinion column for a daily newspaper, and I dabble in freelance photography. A lot of people along the way have helped me get here, but whatever success I've had I owe mostly to those guys wearing those Smokey-the-Bear hats back there at Parris Island. From them, in no uncertain terms, I learned to accept responsibility, to persist in the face of adversity, and to respect authority. But, most of all, what they taught me was that self-esteem can't be bestowed; it has to be earned. Our public schools don't seem to be doing a very good job teaching these life lessons anymore.

Today's all-volunteer force, in many respects, is better than the military of my day. The Department of Defense now requires that at least 90 percent of enlistees be high-school graduates, and the latest demographics indicate that the majority are doing quite well on the Armed Forces Qualification Test, a nationally normed test of math and reading ability.

But one thing I can say for the Marine Corps of old: It was the best reform school we had. While military readiness might suffer, our country would certainly realize a "peace dividend" if Marine D.I.s could have a crack at the Jerry Springer set and the Court TV crowd.

But to return to those thrilling days of yesteryear, of course my pot-shack companion and I got caught. We soon found ourselves in front of the mess hall doing squat thrusts until our D.I. "got tired" (of watching us, that is). By the time he was "tired" enough to let us stop, we had both dug ruts about a foot and a half deep in Parris Island's sandy soil.

As I mentioned in the previous chapter, Roger returned to Parris Island as a D.I. a few years later. When, in 1969, we met again, he swore that those ruts were still visible outside the 1st Battalion Mess Hall.

It is indeed good to have made one's mark on the world.

But it was only later, much later, that I was able to see the humor in much of what I went through at Parris Island. There was a dark side to Marine Corps boot camp in those years.

The abscess under my chin that put me in the pot shack kept getting bigger, and our junior drill instructor—a white sergeant with a distinctly Scottish name and a gravelly voice well suited for the drill field—was intent on curing it himself. (I later realized that abscesses and boils were probably viewed as an indication our D.I.s weren't paying enough attention to our hygiene.)

"Private Palm, report to the junior drill instructor with a clean handkerchief!" he commanded one evening.

I did as ordered. He wrapped the handkerchief around the offending bump and proceeded to squeeze as hard as he could. But, try as he might, he couldn't get it to pop open and drain on that occasion. If I say so myself, I managed to remain stoic throughout the procedure. Finally, he said, "It must not be ready yet" and let me go.

He tried on at least two more occasions, but the abscess refused to comply. Along the way, I remember his holding up his two index fingers about 10 inches apart and saying, "I once took a hair this long out of one turd's face."

A day or two later, a captain, our series commander, was paying an informal visit to our squad bay, and he happened to notice me. "Sergeant *****," he said, "has that man been to sickbay about that thing on his face?"

"He is going today, sir," our junior D.I. replied.

And so it was that I found myself at sickbay getting my abscess professionally lanced by a doctor who was kind enough to give me an anesthetic first. Closing the wound required a couple stitches, and much to my surprise, I found myself admitted for the next 24 hours.

But before that kindly doctor treated me, he asked a pointed question: "Have your drill instructors ever hit or otherwise abused you?"

It was a question our senior drill instructor had prepared all of us to answer. In the very first week of the program, he warned, "We drill instructors are a tight group." He went on to tell us that there would be two unpleasant consequences to informing on a drill instructor. "You'll be taken out of training while an investigation goes on, and you'll be set back. You'll have to start all over again," he warned. "And your next drill instructor will know what you did!" In those days, most recruits decided it was better to keep their mouths shut and get off the island on time.

6. That Other Parris

The fact of the matter is that we had all been hit—usually in the solar plexus. Our D.I.s knew better than to leave visible marks. And we had been harassed and abused. Watching us try to do the manual of arms with footlockers was a favorite D.I. pastime, as was having us do bends and thrusts in our hot, un-airconditioned squad bay until the floor was wet with sweat.

In my own case, once, while our junior D.I. was marching us around, I kept getting out step—I never did learn to march well—our senior D.I. called me into the barracks, smacked me up alongside the head, and said, "Wake the fuck up!" As much as I hate to admit it, that wake-up call was just what I needed at that point. The anger carried me through, and I marched much better from then on.

Still, there were lighter moments—usually enjoyed at the expense of some hapless recruit. Woe unto the private who received a stick of chewing gum in a letter. He was allowed to chew it, but without removing the foil. Woe likewise to the private whose girlfriend wrote "SWAK" or some other form of endearment on the envelope of her letter. The D.I.s took that as license to read the letter out loud to the platoon. One private had a Polish name that began with a "Y" and was difficult to pronounce. Hence, he went by the shortened version "Yancy." His girlfriend had written "SWAK" on the flap of the envelope, and her salutation read, "Dear Yancy Baby." Our drill instructor, I must say, shared some morale-boosting details regarding the sexual favors Yancy Baby's girlfriend was promising to deliver when he got home. Her boyfriend was known as "Yancy Baby" throughout the rest of the program.

Then there was the day when the D.I. was required to ask if any of us had ever been arrested. One recruit made the mistake of admitting that he had once been arrested for "surfing too close to the pier" at some beach. The D.I. had him get up on the table in the middle of our squad bay and ordered four privates, two on each end of the table, to act as waves. He then ordered the private on the table to demonstrate his surfing prowess as the other privates rocked the table back and forth. Of course, the D.I. ordered the "waves" to get rougher and rougher until the surfer fell off his table/surfboard. A good time was had by all but the surfer.

In point of fact, hazing, physical abuse, and unauthorized training have always been against regulations, and D.I.s have been reduced in rank and even sent to the brig for flouting the regulations. But there was—and maybe still is—a subculture committed to keeping recruit training as tough as possible—presumably as tough as the D.I.s had it when they were going through the program. And I know from talking to former D.I.s that peer pressure used to play a major role in motivating the abuses. There were D.I.s who valued the respect of their fellow D.I.s more than they feared the repercussions of being caught abusing recruits. And, again, maybe there still are such D.I.s.

Be that as it may, the following story should give the uninitiated some idea of what it used to be like on Parris Island, for D.I.s as well as recruits. I heard it from a former junior drill instructor who daily lived in fear that the senior drill instructor would get them both court-martialed.

It seems that one day—in the barracks, behind closed doors—the senior D.I. was amusing himself with the pastime I already mentioned—having the platoon practice the manual of arms with foot lockers. Picture it: *"Right shoulder—footlocker! Left shoulder—footlocker! Present—footlocker!"*

One hapless recruit lost control of his footlocker and ended up with a serious cut on his forehead.

Unperturbed, the senior D.I. bellowed, "Give me a private brain surgeon up here on the double!"

A demented recruit ran up and sounded off: "Sir, Private Brain Surgeon reporting as ordered, sir!"

"Go get your sewing kit, maggot," the D.I. commanded.

Private Brain Surgeon did as ordered. He took the injured recruit into the head and sewed up his cut.

The former D.I. who told me this was sure that that was the end. He and the senior D.I. would be going to jail. But no one outside the platoon noticed, and the cut healed up just fine.

Not all the former D.I.s I met throughout the course of my career confessed to perpetrating or witnessing such abuses, but they all agreed on this much: They were relieved to get off the drill field with their stripes intact and their careers unblemished.

The standard defense of recruit training in the "Old Corps" held that it instilled the discipline and presence of mind to survive in combat. There is much to be said for that. But, to my mind, it was essentially an intense fraternity initiation aimed at making us proud to be Marines.

Throughout my four enlisted years, I met a lot of Marines who hated the Corps and couldn't wait to get out. But I never met a Marine who didn't take pride in telling you how tough his D.I.s were or who harbored any ill will for the hazing and abuse he claimed to have withstood.

It's a Marine Corps thing. If you were never a part of it, you wouldn't understand.

7

The Sticking Point

The patrol that morning was one we had run over and over again. We were crossing the river and doing a round robin through the large ville on the other side. The only hairy part was crossing the river. We used the village ferry service—two small boats. We never paid them. It seemed to be a free municipal service of sorts. Their presence, I realize now, was probably what kept the enemy from opening up on us in midstream. But, at the time, we were all 19 or 20—armed with M16s and grenades and armored with the reckless bravado of youth. And, besides, we'd crossed so many times before, and nothing had ever happened.

There were 10 of us in all—four Marines, one Navy corpsman, and five Vietnamese Popular Force soldiers, "PFs" for short. The PFs were a motley crew. They wore uniforms cobbled together from various types of American war-surplus fatigues. No two looked exactly alike. Some wore the blackened high-top tennis shoes favored by the Army of the Republic of Vietnam. The better heeled wore the same jungle boots we wore. Most wore flip-flops or plastic sandals, even when we were on patrol. Their weapons were generally war surplus M1 carbines, although a few carried full-size M1 rifles that looked almost as tall as they were.

We had briefed them and had even shown them the patrol overlay before setting out that morning. They knew where we were headed, and none voiced any objection or betrayed the least concern during the briefing. Normally, they were the ones who hailed our water taxis. They spoke the language. We didn't. But when we got to our familiar crossing point, a set of stone steps that led down to the river, they promptly sat down, refusing to budge or even to hail the boats.

One PF in particular—a young, arrogant-looking man who had never mixed much with us and who had always managed to frown and look resentful in our presence—emerged as the ringleader and spokesman. He spoke to the others in Vietnamese, and it seemed to be at his direction that they all sat down and remained seated despite our puzzled attempts to wave them toward the river. After several minutes, the sullen-looking PF finally spoke up. "*Beaucoup* VC" was his common-sense excuse.

We tried to get him and his cohorts to see that as more of an opportunity than an obstacle, an opportunity we were mutually obligated to exploit. Truth be told, we didn't speak Vietnamese, or even French beyond the few words that had long ago passed into the pidgin by which we tried to communicate. "*Beaucoup* VC NUMBER ONE," we insisted, pantomiming shooting them down with our M16s. A Marine I'll introduce later, "Heinie," especially hammed it up, doing his rendition of sneaking up on and slaughtering an unsuspecting VC. But they remained unmoved—in both senses of the word. "Number 10! *Beaucoup* VC Number 10!" they kept repeating.

At an impasse, we radioed back for instructions and were told to "wait out." After an extremely awkward 10 or more minutes of staring at one another, word finally came back to let our allies "*didi*" (to run off) and to patrol the other side of the river without them. The captain was going to take care of the problem back at Cam Lo. That's what we were told. In the meanwhile, we were to show the PFs that we weren't afraid to patrol across the river, *beaucoup* VC or no VC.

In my mind's eye, I can still see our PFs that day, cheerfully diddy-bopping back down the trail toward the compound and laughing it up along the way.

"So much for *combined* action," I remember thinking as we crossed the river that day.

8

Camp Lejeune

As with most who enlisted in the days before the military began to bribe people with "'choose-before-you-enlist' technical training and educational benefits," I harbored vague dreams of glory. But they were hardly inspired by Vietnam, a war I knew almost nothing about and which I couldn't imagine lasting long enough for me to get into. As I mentioned earlier, no one I knew back in Delaware in 1965 imagined that Vietnam would become a major war. Mostly, I was running away from home, fleeing northern Delaware and the blue-collar life of "quiet desperation" I seemed destined for.

As for the Marine Corps, despite their shortening boot camp to eight weeks, the war must not have quite taken hold by the fall of 1965. One indication of that was the MOS (Military Occupational Specialty) I drew out of boot camp. I still remember, toward the end of the program, our senior D.I. holding a list and calling off our MOS assignments. Only one recruit in our platoon, Platoon 163, got an infantry MOS. "Don't ever give it up!" our senior D.I. counseled. My "buddy program" friend Roger got water supply—as I've already related, an MOS he was able to surmount as a helicopter door gunner. I got "0400, logistics." Our D.I. appeared to be puzzled by it. I certainly was. Back then, I didn't have an inkling of what logistics was all about.

Because every Marine, regardless of MOS, was supposed to be a rifleman, the next stop after boot camp was "ITR," the Infantry Training Regiment. For East Coast Marines, that was at Camp Geiger—a Quonset hut village adjacent to Camp Lejeune. Infantry types went through a six-week program, the rest of us a four-week one. We learned the basics of scouting and patrolling. We got to throw grenades and to fire just about every weapon the Corps had, including the bazooka and the flame thrower. It was a relaxed, low-stress program with no harassment or abuse whatsoever.

I can remember one day in particular. It was a cool, crisp, sunny autumn morning. We had hiked out to a cleared area on the perimeter of the base adjacent to a civilian highway. There had been a scheduling mix-up, and we found ourselves lounging in the grass waiting for an instructor who never showed up and some sort of lecture or demonstration that never happened.

As I watched civilians driving by, presumably on their way to work, I felt worry-free and perfectly at peace with myself and my situation—one of the few times in my adult life I've felt that way.

I also remember getting base liberty on Sunday afternoons there at Camp Geiger. In my mind's eye, I can still see what we euphemistically called "dark-green Marines" (African Americans) dressed in impeccably starched and ironed khaki uniforms and gracefully dancing to soul music at the humble base club—the "slop chute," in Marine Corps parlance. They would jump up, twirl around, and sway back and forth in time to the music—usually with a 3.2 beer in one hand and without spilling any. It was a homophobic time and place, and I heard more than one Marine, out of earshot from the dancers, grumble that they must be "faggots." But, as I saw it, they weren't men dancing together. Each Marine was dancing alone—no doubt forgetting where he was and imagining himself back in a better time and place. I don't remember how, but I knew they were going through the longer infantry program and were headed to Vietnam. I've often reflected back on that scene, wondering how many made it home.

From Camp Geiger, it was on to Camp Lejeune, where, after a 20-day boot-camp leave, I was assigned to a force-service support regiment. It was soon apparent that they didn't quite know what to do with a logistics private. As I recall, I could spell "logistics," but I couldn't define it, much less know how a private could contribute to it.

Another thing I remember: While I was waiting for a colonel and another officer to decide my fate, I was approached by a staff sergeant who obviously assumed I was an admin clerk assigned to that office. "I need a favor," he said.

He explained that he had just gotten back from Vietnam, where he had been assigned to a headquarters unit in Saigon. "I had it made there," he boasted. He showed me a photo of a young, attractive Vietnamese woman and said, "I was living with her. I was working 0800 to 1600, Monday through Friday, as if I had a civilian job back in 'the world.'"

"What I need for you to do," he explained, "is to type a letter for me, as if it had come from my unit in Saigon, saying they really need me back there."

Clearly, he wanted cover for his wife back in the States. I gave it a shot, but I wasn't familiar with naval-letter format, much less the kind of language a high-ranking officer might employ in such a letter. The result hardly looked and sounded official. "That's okay," he said. "I'll find somebody else."

Soon thereafter, I was summoned into the office to meet a stocky gunnery sergeant with a friendly demeanor and a Hispanic name. I'll call him Gunny Flores. The colonel explained that the gunny was in charge of the "Mount-Out Project for the Second Marine Division" and that he was assigning me to help with that project.

8. Camp Lejeune

Once again, I was at a loss for what I was going to be doing. The gunny drove me to a little building in the industrial area of the base and gave me a bunch of orders on the inception and mission of the program to read. They might as well have been written in Greek or Serbo-Croatian. Eventually, Gunny Flores explained that what we would be doing was building a computer database of all the equipment, repair parts, and supplies each unit in the division would need to support them for 120 days were they to "mount out"—to deploy to a war zone and engage in combat.

What it amounted to was having senior representatives in from each of the units—especially warrant officers and senior staff NCOs—to review stock lists and to tell us what and how much of the various listed items they would need. Their needs were computerized, and they would then be invited back to review the printouts for accuracy and adequacy. My role in it largely consisted of cleaning up, making coffee and tearing the printouts apart for the various units to review. It wasn't hard work. It was boring work that took me no closer to understanding logistics than when I was first assigned the MOS.

Early on, the gunny asked me what my "GCT"—my General Classification Test score—was. At the time, I thought it was 131. (I later learned it was higher than average, but not 131.) From that time forward, I was "131," which was how the gunny would address me, except when he was being sincere.

One such instance was when I asked him once why I had never seen a black officer. "Because we're prejudiced, Palm. You got any other stupid questions?" Then he went on to explain that most of our generals at that time were from the South and that they would have to pass on before we saw an integrated officer corps.

Such chiding aside, Gunnery Flores was nothing if not paternalistic. He once got me out of trouble when a snowstorm kept me from getting back in time from a weekend trip to Delaware. He convinced the CO to charge the lost time as leave rather than give me an "Article 15," an administrative punishment that would have been on my record. He also saved me from myself when a quota for the air delivery field came down, and I wanted to volunteer for it. Had I gotten it, the first stop would have been Jump School at Fort Benning, Georgia. "You don't have to go to Fort Benning, Palm," he said. "I'll break both your legs right here." He went on to explain that when something worthwhile came along, he would let me volunteer but that air-delivery was a career-limited field.

One field that did have career potential was the one the gunny himself—after an infantry tour in Korea—had reenlisted for: supply. "You don't want to keep that 0400 MOS," he said. Without giving me a choice in the matter, gunny went to the colonel and got my MOS changed to supply. I know the gunny was just trying to look out for me. His heart was in the right place. But that act of kindness ultimately did me no good.

I had been working with Gunny Flores on that mount-out project for a little over a year when my number came up. I had orders to Vietnam. By that point, I wanted go, but Gunny Flores was intent on keeping me. He tried to get me out of it, but the answer was "No, we're all going, and it's Palm's turn."

Shortly before I left the gunny's clutches, he was selected for the temporary officers program and commissioned a second lieutenant. I asked him what it was like to suddenly become an officer. "I'll tell you, Palm," he said. "It's like being black all your life and one day waking up white."

Gunny Flores was also nothing if not honest.

9

Delaware Revisited

More than one person, upon first meeting me, has remarked that I'm the first person from Delaware he or she has ever met. That stands to reason. Delaware is the second smallest state, in terms of population as well as size. Only about half a million people live there. Rhode Island, of course, has the distinction of being the smallest state. Rhode Island can also claim the cultural distinction, and the cachet, of being in New England. Delaware is a Mid-Atlantic state. It is neither North nor South. The Mason-Dixon Line actually runs down Delaware's western boundary. But most Delawareans couldn't tell you where the line is.

The Great Delaware Divide is not the Mason-Dixon Line, however. It is the Chesapeake and Delaware Canal, connecting the Delaware River to the Chesapeake Bay, thus forming a convenient shipping route from the Delaware Bay to Baltimore. "The Canal," as Delawareans generally refer to it, completely bisects Delaware, dividing what used to be the heavily industrialized northern third from the still predominantly agricultural southern two-thirds of the state. It is typical of Delaware's fortunes that its physical integrity was expendable compared to the economy of Baltimore and of the Mid-Atlantic region. Just ask the people of St. Georges, a small eighteenth-century town that the canal's planners decided to cut through rather than go around.

Delawareans typically refer to the two regions as "North of the Canal" and "South of the Canal," signifying a cultural divide more than a geographical one. Northern Delaware lives under the hegemony of Philadelphia, southern Delaware under the hegemony of Baltimore. Hence, there is no distinctive Delaware accent. People from "above the Canal" typically sound as if they come from Philadelphia, those from "below the Canal" as if they come from Baltimore. As for me, I'm proud to have come from "North of the Canal"—the New Castle area, to be exact. Again, in trying to place my accent, more than one person has imitated Sylvester Stallone's Rocky in the delivery of one of his most memorable lines, "Yo, Adrian!" (Close enough. My wife's name is Andrea.)

Delaware's greatest claim to fame, as proudly proclaimed on its license plates, is that it was the "first state." Delaware was indeed the first of the colonies to ratify the Constitution. But, as historians will tell you, especially historians from larger states, it's not that we were any more forward thinking than people in the other colonies. We had only three delegates to the Constitutional Convention, and we were right next door to Philadelphia.

In all fairness, millions of people from all across America pay monthly tribute to Delaware—via their credit card companies. Several banks and credit card companies are incorporated in Delaware. Numerous other corporations are as well, although the bulk of their operations are not there. In an effort to promote economic growth, Delaware has always kept its corporate taxes low, and as a consequence of that strategy, Delaware has no sales tax. Never has. But while corporations have flocked to Delaware, jobs have not necessarily followed. The largest employer in Delaware today, I read recently, is the state itself.

This is in marked contrast to the Delaware I grew up in during the '50s and '60s. Back then, the giant DuPont Company was the largest employer in the state. As I mentioned before, Delaware used to promote itself as the "chemical capital of the world," and in a very real sense it was. We had both Atlas Chemical and Hercules Chemical, but the undisputed leader was the DuPont Company, whose world headquarters is still located in Wilmington. Again, DuPont's slogan—before the '60s counterculture would give it an ironic resonance—was "Better things for better living through chemistry."

I realize that I touched on this theme before, but it bears repeating: The Delaware dream when I was young was to "get in with DuPont." The Delaware nightmare—often held up as a cautionary tale to keep kids in school—was to wind up on the assembly line at General Motors or Chrysler, both of which had assembly plants in northern Delaware when I was growing up. The car plants, even then, offered high wages and good benefits, but the tradeoff was having to endure stultifying boredom performing the same repetitive task for eight hours a day.

DuPont, on the other hand, was still one of the great paternalistic companies. DuPont offered high wages and good benefits and seemed to promise secure, lifelong employment—even for high-school graduates who could qualify for one of their technical or support jobs. But even presumptive promises, I suppose, are made to be broken, and DuPont certainly reneged on theirs. Many of the people of my generation who threw their lot in with DuPont have long since been laid off or forced into early retirement as the company in the '80s began to cut back and to sell off several of its divisions.

There but for the grace of God I would have gone, another early DuPont retiree with no skills or experience marketable outside the DuPont Company.

9. Delaware Revisited

The Marine Corps became my escape route. It seemed to offer a reasonably secure, irrevocable escape from a dead-end life in Delaware. And who would have thought back then and there—Delaware in the early spring of 1965—that Vietnam would become a major American war? Not me. I was just a kid suffering from romantic yearnings undefined.

10

An Enlightened Gesture of Dissent

A long time ago, back when my generation too thought "freedom was on the march," I got caught up in something extraordinary. Through a combination of chance and circumstance, I became a Combined Action Marine in Vietnam.

Like most of the pacification and nation-building programs we tried in Vietnam, the Combined Action Program was grounded in the neo-imperial presupposition that, deep down inside, the Vietnamese were just like us and that by merely associating with us they would adopt our cultural values and ideals. It was also grounded in a neo-imperial article of faith—that young American boys were irrepressible and eminently likeable. But on the plus side, the Marine Corps at least deserves high marks for recognizing the importance of the insurgency that supported the North Vietnamese maneuver units the Army was obsessed with defeating. The Marine Corps further recognized that the only way to wage a successful counterinsurgency was to seduce the people away from the other side.

The Marines and PFs of a combined action unit were to form a cohesive team, pursuing a twofold mission. First and foremost, the unit was to root out the Viet Cong infrastructure and protect its village from further enemy incursion. The Marine role in this ambitious undertaking was principally to train and inspire the PFs, raising their morale through our presence and example. Together, then, the Marine-PF team could go on to tackle the secondary but vitally important mission of winning the loyalty and support of the people. This was to be done by providing both effective security and assistance with practical self-help projects aimed at raising the standard of living in the village.

Military historians and veterans alike have joined in touting combined action as one of the few things we did right in a war gone wrong. Large-scale search and destroy operations occasionally produced high body counts from among North Vietnamese Army (NVA) and main-force Viet

10. An Enlightened Gesture of Dissent

Cong units, but they usually left the communist infrastructure intact, and they often alienated the people through their indiscriminate and disproportionate use of our awesome firepower. Inherent drawbacks aside, however, search and destroy was always meant to be only the leading element in a larger three-pronged strategy; the other two elements were clearing and pacifying. General William C. Westmoreland relegated the last two largely to the South Vietnamese, insisting that American forces bear the brunt of searching and destroying. Recognizing that precious little clearing and pacifying was taking place, and that a low-level insurgency could smolder almost indefinitely despite the apparent gains of search-and-destroy operations, the Marine Corps began to experiment with combined action as early as August 1965.

The Corps began by sending out small groups of Marines to train and patrol alongside Vietnamese "Popular Force" (PF) soldiers in their home villages. In fairly short order, the Corps' leadership recognized the potential intelligence advantages and the certain public relations value of combined action and decided to regularize the program. Throughout their area of operation, Northern I-Corps, the Marines formed permanent combined action companies, each of which established garrisons in a number of villages. Thus was the Combined Action Program—"CAP" for short—born.

The Corps received little help and no encouragement from Westmoreland's Military Assistance Command Vietnam, but Lieutenant Generals Victor H. Krulak and Lewis W. Walt, among other high-ranking officers, had faith in the concept and would not let the program die. It was consolidated and expanded in February 1967, under the leadership of Lieutenant Colonel William R. Corson, and the units were actually moved into villages on a full-time basis. It was a daring move on the Marine Corps' part, tantamount to

The distinctive pocket-flap badge combined-action Marines were authorized to wear when I first joined the program. The inscription above the eagle translates to power or strength. We were soon ordered to stop wearing the badges when the command learned that "CAC" was Vietnamese slang for the male sex organ.

breaking ranks in the eyes of some. But much to its credit, the Corps felt it had to dissent from a strategy that clearly was not working and which was proving to be self-defeating. As I've long maintained, the Combined Action Program was an enlightened gesture of dissent.

What made CAP unique was not just the opportunity to get up close and personal with the Vietnamese and their culture but also the extraordinary degree of trust and confidence the program reposed in young enlisted Marines. There were no officers out in the "villes."

On the Marine side, the typical combined action platoon, or "CAP," consisted of 13 enlisted Marines and a Navy corpsman. The ranking member and compound leader was usually a sergeant, and given the way Vietnam had accelerated the promotion process, most of the compound leaders were still on their first enlistment and were not career Marines.

On the Vietnamese side was a platoon of Popular Force soldiers. Popular Forces were roughly analogous to our National Guard, except that they were not nearly as well trained, equipped, or disciplined as our National Guardsmen. An irregular component of the Army of South Vietnam that the French, under our tutelage, had formed in order to put a Vietnamese face on their imperialism, Popular Forces were part-time soldiers who served in their home villages under the direction of the village chief.

Popular Forces were part of the fiction we all subscribed to back then, which was that the enemy was alien to the people of South Vietnam and won their support mainly through fear and intimidation. Most of us didn't know that South Vietnam had been our creation and that we had encouraged the man we had put in place, President Ngo Dinh Diem, to renege on the plebiscite that would have reunited North and South Vietnam in 1956 under whichever form of

A young PF armed with an M1.

10. An Enlightened Gesture of Dissent

government the people chose, democracy or communism. We didn't know that the term "Viet Cong" was our coinage and that, insofar as the people were concerned, we were fighting the same nationalist forces who had forced the withdraw of our French predecessors in 1954. We didn't know that the same clandestine network that had waged guerrilla war against the French, and which had helped hide and supply the People's Army of Vietnam—the Viet Minh, as they were then called—was still latent in the villages and the back alleys of the cities. We didn't know that America had bankrolled that First Indochina War and had even convinced France to stay the course when they were ready to throw in the towel after a disastrous ambush in 1950.

But the Vietnamese knew. They knew they had struggled against Chinese domination for a thousand years and eventually prevailed. They knew they had struggled against French domination for a hundred years and that the French had eventually tired of the struggle and gone home. They knew that we had seized on the French departure as an opportunity to remake South Vietnam over in our image, thereby demonstrating the superiority of our way of life over communism. They knew, or they would come to know, that we believed the end to justify the means and that the right of self-determination didn't apply to them. We knew what was best for them—or we thought we did. They knew they could count on the spirit of Vietnamese nationalism, and on the longstanding xenophobia of their culture, to outlast our half-hearted and half-baked commitment to "nation building."

11

Palm on the Supply Side

I realize that Gunny Flores meant well in getting my MOS changed to supply. But because I had worked in that special program, I learned virtually nothing about the Marine Corps supply system. More to the point, I hated the thought of working in it. And it was just my luck to find myself working for a supply master sergeant who hated me.

That was in the 3rd Engineer Battalion, my first stop in Vietnam. If I thought long and hard, I could probably recall that master sergeant's name, but I'd rather not. We got off on the wrong foot because he seemed to feel cheated. Thanks to Gunny Flores's patronage and the accelerated promotion system at the time, I was a corporal when I reported to 3rd Engineers. This master sergeant was expecting an experienced supply NCO. Instead, he got me. I was more than willing to learn. I'd seen enough to know that the Marine Corps Supply system was not nuclear physics. But this master sergeant seemed to have no interest in teaching me. Instead, he relegated me to the humiliating task of merely filing supply documents.

Just to relieve the boredom, I kept volunteering for the perimeter patrols that went out every few days, always with a different officer in charge. (It must have been a rotational duty, like officer of the day.) While we called them perimeter patrols, we often went out several hundred yards and didn't circle our base camp. The actual purpose seemed to be to familiarize ourselves with the area. I remember two patrols in particular.

It was an especially hot and humid morning, and the lieutenant in charge seemed to be setting a forced-march pace. (Maybe he didn't want to miss chow in the officers mess.) Finally, he called for a break, and I sat down in a clump of brush apart from the main group. Suddenly, both my legs cramped up. The pain was excruciating, and I began to worry that I would be left behind. We were an ad hoc group. We didn't know one another, and the lieutenant didn't know us. I wouldn't have been missed. Fortunately, the cramps eased up just before the lieutenant called an end to the break. I later learned that dehydration can cause severe cramps. That's what did it.

On another occasion—when our battalion rear was in the Phu Bai

11. Palm on the Supply Side 53

area—we set out at dawn. We had been out "humping" (as we called it) for a half hour or so when we came to and climbed up a significant hill. Looking down to the east, we could see a section of Hue with exotic-looking buildings rendered golden in the warm light of the early morning sun. I remember thinking I'd never seen such a beautiful sight. Later, much later, when I read James Hilton's *Lost Horizon*, that view of Hue is what I pictured in my mind's eye when Hilton described the utopia of Shangri-La.

Contrary to popular belief, there was nothing remotely utopian about being "in the rear with the beer" in Vietnam—at least, not so far as the Marine Corps was concerned. I realize we had it better than the grunts who were out humping the bush, subsisting on two C-rations a day, and sleeping on the ground for weeks at a time. In the six months I was with 3rd Engineers we moved three times. We started out in Da Nang, moved to Dong Ha, and finally settled in the Phu Bai area. In Da Nang and Dong Ha, we lived in strong-back "hooches," as we called them. They were plywood buildings with galvanized tin roofs set up a couple feet on pilings. In Phu Bai, we lived in large general-purpose tents with wooden-pallet floors. At each location, we got to sleep on standard G.I. cots. Not long after I got to 3rd Engineers in Da Nang, one of the old salts advised me to buy a poncho liner—a kind of nylon quilt—at the "gook store" just outside our gate. He said I'd need it when "the hawk," the monsoon cold, was out. He was right. I did. How that store acquired those U.S.-government-property liners, I don't know.

I got to Vietnam in late November 1966. By that time, there was no liberty. It was deemed to be unsafe. We worked seven days a week. The food was terrible, and there was never enough of it. I remember going away from every meal still hungry. There were discipline problems. We all took turns standing perimeter guard, but not all of us took that responsibility seriously. The prevailing assumption was that we were in a safe area and that guarding the perimeter was just part of the general harassment package.

But then one Marine I knew got caught sleeping while on guard. I remember him well. He was a Hispanic Marine from Los Angeles, and he might as well have been a member of the L.A. Chamber of Commerce. He used to boast by the hour about the beauty of the area and how he could go swimming in the morning and snow skiing in the mountains in the afternoon. He got a special court martial and six months in the Long Binh jail. I saw him as he was being led away in handcuffs. He had clearly been crying. I told him I was very sorry this had happened to him—although I was well aware that he had done it to himself. I never saw him again. I don't think there was much sleeping on guard after that.

On one occasion, I helped hold down a Marine who was intent on fragging our company commander for holding a personnel inspection. This Marine had been a court-martial prisoner in the infamous Portsmouth Naval

Prison in Maine. I don't recall what he was there for, but because he had been a model prisoner, he was allowed to return to active duty. He probably shouldn't have been.

There was racial tension, and there were drugs. I still remember one Marine late at night waking everyone in our tent and asking if anyone had any pot. Another Marine, a friend of his, was trying to tell him to forget it. "That stuff will get you in trouble."

As I look back on it now, while we weren't doing hard labor, my six months in the 3rd Engineers rear must have been what life on a Georgia chain gang was like.

Toward the end of that stint, my nemesis, the supply master sergeant, found a way to get rid of me. He got me reassigned to be the Headquarters and Service Company supply NCO. All I had to do then was watch over the company's treasure trove of mostly unnecessary supplies and occasionally issue something to someone. Still, it was boring, unfulfilling work. But even worse than the boredom was the thought of coming home after 13 months in country only to have to admit that I had sat out my tour in safety, filing supply documents and issuing out equipment in a base camp.

12

Deliverance

I had probably established my reputation as the worst supply clerk in the history of the 3rd Engineer Battalion when I first heard of the Combined Action Program. One day at chow a sympathetic company clerk happened to mention that we had been assigned quotas for the program and that a team would be coming through the very next week to interview prospective "volunteers." (I seem to recall the quotas were mandatory, but I could be mistaken.) He went on to tell me what he knew about CAP, which wasn't much, only that it entailed living and working with the Vietnamese and that anyone with at least four months in country and a clean disciplinary record was eligible.

I had heard enough. Combined action seemed a ticket out of supply and an opportunity to see some of the war I had come halfway around the world to see. I was the first or second to sign up for the interview. I am not sure, but the battalion postal clerk, a fellow sufferer and friend, may have beaten me to it.

Up to this point, my contact with the Vietnamese had been limited to supervising laborers on two or three occasions and to a weekly haircut from the barber who set up shop under a tarp just outside our wire. I really had no strong feelings about the people, or about the war, one way or another. I had gone on those patrols around the perimeter and through the neighboring villages, but they were uneventful. The only thing I had going for me was the enthusiastic recommendation of my commanding officer, who was probably only too glad to get a disaffected and unmotivated supply clerk off his roles so he could get a better one.

The interview, as I recall, was perfunctory at best. It was conducted by a gunnery sergeant and lasted less than five minutes. He asked how long I had been in Vietnam, how much contact I had had with the Vietnamese people, and how I felt about them. I, of course, built my occasional supervision of Vietnamese laborers into a warm and richly rewarding experience. In truth, I hadn't even known their names and wasn't able to communicate with them beyond simple gestures and a few words in Vietnamese-English pidgin.

But the clincher was a hypothetical situation. The gunny asked me to imagine I had been assigned to the program and that a PF had stolen my camera. What would I do? The right answer was self-evident, and I laid it on with a trowel. Drawing on the liberal sentiments I had heard just seven or eight months before in a one-week jungle warfare course at Camp Lejeune (I was in the first group fortunate enough to bypass staging at Camp Pendleton), I answered that I realized we seem extraordinarily rich to the average Vietnamese and that the temptation to take what they think we can afford to lose must often prove overwhelming.

I claimed I would never take matters into my own hands, but would report the theft to my squad leader, expecting that he would take up the matter with the senior Vietnamese. Pretending to Christian sufferance and forgiveness, I concluded that if my camera were never returned, I would humbly chalk it up to experience, being careful never again to put temptation in the way of some poor PF. Whether he believed me or not, the gunny had obviously heard what he wanted to hear. He told me on the spot that I was accepted for the program, provided I didn't mind working out of my occupational specialty. I would be assigned as a rifleman. I couldn't believe my good fortune, having just talked the Marine Corps into throwing me into the briar patch of my choice.

Leaving the interview tent, I caught up with my mail clerk friend who had also been looking to escape the humiliating trials of life in the rear with the beer. He, too, had made it through the interview. The gunny had told us both we could expect orders in about two weeks, and true to his word, it was just about two weeks later that the mail clerk (unlike me, a Marine who would be missed) and I, along with a third man we didn't know, found ourselves leaving 3rd Engineers forever.

13

CAP School

The first stop was the program's headquarters and school in Phu Bai. The school, which was non-graded, lasted only two weeks. The curriculum, as I recall, was more tactical than cultural. We were issued and fired the M16, which was new at the time to those of us in combat-support and combat-service-support units. As I related earlier, we spent a solid day learning to call in and spot artillery, hiking to the top of the highest hill in the area for live-fire practice. We reviewed the rudiments of squad tactics, patrolling, and map reading. We brushed up on communications.

We did hear at some point from a sergeant who ran one of the Phu Bai area units. The theme of his talk was Vietnamese sexual mores, and he seemed somewhat obsessed, implying that we could all expect to suffer what might seem to us homosexual advances. Such practices, he explained, were considered the only acceptable sexual outlet before marriage in the Vietnamese culture, and it would at least be a sure sign of acceptance should a PF come on to you. For the sake of the program, he counseled us, it might be better to acquiesce than create an incident. Most of us, I suspect, resolved not to get too close to PFs if we could help it.

We also received a few hours of language instruction from a young Vietnamese lieutenant who treated us, a group of lower-ranking enlisted Marines, with all the deference one might accord a gathering of major generals. Nevertheless, we went off to our respective villes armed with the Vietnamese equivalent of *la plume de ma tante* and other useless phrases.

I remember little else of the curriculum. But the school does stand out in my mind as a time of eager anticipation and as probably the most pleasant couple of weeks I spent in Vietnam.

I suppose I have never been one to half-step. As I related before, toward the end of the school, one of the instructors asked if any of us were willing to volunteer for Papa Company up north. Papa Company, he explained, was new and the program was not yet well established up there. Units had been hit, and the villagers were still aloof and largely indifferent to our civic action overtures. It sounded dangerous and exciting, and after what that sergeant had told us, I thought I might prefer my Vietnamese a little distant and not too friendly. In a cavalier mood, I raised my hand.

So too did Reaves and his Canadian friend.

14

Papa One Confidential

Our joint odyssey began with a C-130 flight to the Papa Company rear in Dong Ha, where we were assigned first not to Papa Three but to Papa One in Cam Lo. Papa One was very much the company showplace. It was located less than a mile from the district headquarters that housed both our commanding officer and his Vietnamese counterpart. This meant that Marines and PFs alike were on their best behavior and that even the villagers were fairly friendly.

I remember one occasion in particular. We were in the middle of a day patrol, walking through the center of the village, when a middle-aged man

The village chief's house and fortified compound in Papa One's village.

stepped out of his house to greet us. He waved us into an open-air patio section of the house where there were a table and chairs. He said something to his wife, and she brought out a platter of fresh pineapple slices. Smiling and motioning for us to eat, the man said, "I have beaucoup." It was a hot day, and the pineapple was cool. I'd never had fresh pineapple before, and I remember thinking that I had never tasted anything so wonderful.

Two Papa One Marines in particular stand out in my memory.

There was Tony, a gregarious New Yorker who had worked a deal with our compound leader. Rather than go out on patrol, he ran our little mess hall and looked after our supplies.

His meals weren't memorable, but they were okay by Vietnam standards. He had adopted a dog, and I remember his deflecting any and all criticism of his cooking with the comment "My dog is the one suffering!"

There was also a gaunt 27-year-old—an old man by our standards—whose name I can't recall, but whose story has stayed with me all these years. He was the first Marine draftee I met.

"I had a good job with the railroad," he told me soon after I met him. "But my wife was running around on me. When I found out, she called the draft board and reminded them that they'd forgotten me."

His bad luck hadn't ended there. "I was at the induction center. I'd passed the physical and had my orders for the Army, when this Army PFC walked up and picked four of us at random. He took our orders and said, 'Come with me. You're going in the Marine Corps!'"

This hapless Marine was clearly an alcoholic. He seemed to drink Vietnamese beer, brand name "33," non-stop. He was also afraid to go out on patrol and not ashamed to admit it. He too had worked a deal with the compound leader. He cleaned up and did odd jobs around the compound.

Apparently, Papa One had never been hit, and there were those who arrogantly assumed it never would be. With one exception, the day patrols were pleasant walks in the sun. And with one exception, the night ambushes were uneventful. (More about that anon.) In the three or so weeks Reaves, Scotty, and I spent there, we took one sniper round.

The patrol leader swore he felt the round crack by within inches of his head. On the other side of the tree line from which we thought the round had been fired, we found a young woman. There was no sign of a weapon, and the young woman didn't seem at all nervous or apprehensive. Nevertheless, we took her into custody and delivered her to the village chief for interrogation.

As for that night ambush patrol exception, it was understood that the local VC owned the night. Knowing the area, they could roam about, reassemble, and collect taxes under cover of darkness, and we couldn't be everywhere. Someone from way up high had decided that the way to disabuse our enemy nightcrawlers of their relative sense of safety was to fire an artillery

14. Papa One Confidential

shell or two or three at random intervals at trail junctions and other suspected rendezvous sites. The practice was called "harassment and interdiction Fire," or "H&I Fire," as we generally referred to it.

It was during my very first night on ambush patrol with Papa One that an H&I shell landed close to us. We immediately hit the dirt, and another one came—this time close enough that we were showered with dirt clumps. Fortunately, that was it. But, when we got back to the compound, I discovered that it had been my bad luck to have plopped down on a fresh pile of water buffalo shit. I suppose that was the enemy's form of H&I.

On another occasion, one of our claymore mines exploded spontaneously, injuring no one.

Then there was the time that another Marine and I had been engaging in horseplay, chasing one another, when I ran right smack into the corner of a tin roof. Blood began streaming down onto my face. I found that I had sustained a significant cut just under the hairline on the upper left side of my forehead.

Our corpsman diagnosed the cut as definitely needing stitches, and he gave me two alternatives: (1) He could send me to Delta Med to be stitched up, or (2) he could do it himself right there at Papa One. But there was a catch. He had a suture kit, but he had no xylocaine to numb the wound. "You'd be surprised," he added. "There aren't many nerves up there, and it really won't hurt very much if I do it."

It was a Hobson's choice. On the one hand, I would have felt terrible taking time and attention away from seriously wounded Marines to suture a minor cut I sustained through my own carelessness. On the other hand, the thought of getting stitches without an anesthetic was off-putting. In the end, I "screwed my courage to the sticking point"—literally, I suppose—and opted to let "Doc," our corpsman, do it. And he was right. I felt a little jab each time he pushed the needle through my skin, and some pressure, but it really wasn't bad at all. Doc gave me five stitches. The cut healed up fine and with a scar that was barely visible.

Earlier, I mentioned my love of photography. I had been developing and printing black-and-white photos since I was 13. What little money I could scrape up went to Lincoln Camera—the major camera store in Wilmington, Delaware, and my Mecca throughout my teenage years. My dream was to become a photojournalist. Thus it was that when a Papa One Marine about to rotate home offered to sell me his Yashica single-lens reflex camera with two lenses and a leather gadget bag for the low price of only $75, I took him up on the offer. As events would unfold, it might have been better had I declined the offer. Then again, maybe not.

Our time at Papa One might have been idyllic had it not been for the leadership. No matter where I go, it seems ever my fate to arrive just after or at least in the waning days of the golden age. Papa One's charter members were all short by the time I got there, and the original platoon sergeant—a young, laissez-faire sort—rotated within a week of our arrival. He was replaced by an archetypal lifer, a third- or fourth-term staff sergeant named Garcia (not his real name). Garcia had a mania for neatness and order and a talent for squaring things away. Under his direction, we pulled weeds, restrung and tidied up our barbed wire, raked the dirt under the hooches, and did all manner of disagreeable things we expected to do in garrison but not in a combat zone. Garcia was relentless and generally led by example, pitching in and getting dirty along with us. But we remained unimpressed and uninspired, engaging in frequent petty mutinies and nearly constant satire.

Deliverance came in the middle of August. We awoke one morning to learn that Papa Three had been hit in force overnight. They had held, but barely. One Papa Three Marine was dead; two had been seriously wounded. Papa One was ordered to make up the losses, and I was neither surprised nor unhappy when Garia chose me, Reaves, and Scotty for transfer to Papa Three. In fact, I welcomed it. In volunteering for Papa Company, I had imagined I would be struggling for the program's very survival. But Papa One had seemed more sinecure than struggle.

But the important thing is what CAP had seemed to represent to me at the time. Those first six months in country had left me with too much time to think. I had decided I wanted to start my life anew—that there was a better future waiting for me than the one I had seemed destined for when I left for Vietnam—including the life I had seemed destined for with the girl I had left behind. I had the feeling that destiny was calling and that I must be on my way.

15

Flashback: The Girl I Left Behind

Say what you will about war. It has always been good for at least one thing: seducing girls. Generations of shameless young men about to ship out have evoked the specter of everlasting regret should their girlfriends not give them a beautiful memory to sustain them in the face of death. At least, that's the way it used to be before the age of sexting and casual sex.

To say it the way that Sergeant Joe Friday of *Dragnet* fame would have said it, I was working the evening shift out of housewares at Wilmington Dry Goods, a longstanding Delaware institution and department store that sold irregular and overstock merchandise at bargain prices. It was my senior year of high school, and I had already signed on the dotted line to join the Marine Corps that August.

I'd started working at Dry Goods after school and on weekends in November. I'd been hired to help out with the Christmas rush in the toy department. They kept me on after Christmas but transferred me to housewares. My mother being the way she was, I needed some kind of job just to keep the peace at home, but I'd already made up my mind that a future in retail sales would have been even worse than the industrial-strength boredom I mentioned earlier. And stocking and tidying up shelves in housewares was proving to be even more boring than working in the toy department.

Of course, the pay was low—one dollar an hour, the minimum wage at the time. The worst part, however, was a practice I'm sure was illegal, but which they got away with nevertheless. At closing time, the department managers would send us up to clock out but would order us to come back. We were expected to spend 20 to 30 minutes off the clock straightening up the stock and cleaning up.

On this one night, as I was heading upstairs to clock out, another teenage employee, a guy I barely knew, approached me and said, "There's someone who wants to meet you—a girl from my department."

"Really?" I said, not quite sure what to make of this overture. "Why?"

"I don't know, man. She thinks you're cute or something."

We agreed that he and the girl would wait by the front door and that he would make the introductions.

"Erin, this is Ed Palm," he said, and promptly walked off without another word.

I found myself face to face with an attractive girl of 5'6" or 5'7" with a fair complexion, green eyes, and short hair of a somewhat indeterminate reddish color. As I would later learn, she was in the cosmetology and hair-styling program at Brown Vocational High School. Her class projects must have involved experimenting with various color rinses. Her hair was a slightly different color every time I saw her, ranging from brunette to auburn and various shades in between. On one occasion it even had a slight purplish tint.

I remember saying hello. I think we exchanged information about where we lived and went to school. I know I told her I would be going in the Marine Corps in August, and she said she loved the Marine Corps—"they're the best!" She gave me her phone number. I said I would call her, and I did, a couple days later.

For our first date, I took her to the Ellis Drive-in Theater. The Ellis would later become our local passion pit, but not that night. We mostly just talked.

I should perhaps explain that the sexual revolution was slow in coming to Delaware. That, and I was shy, insecure, and naïve. I had engaged in some heavy necking—"making out," we called it back then—but I had never even tried to get to second or third base, much less to steal home, so to speak. Looking back on it now, I realize that with at least one girl in particular I should have pressed my case and probably could have gotten to second base at least. But our world was still divided between the "good girls" who wouldn't and the "bad girls" who would, and those fabled "bad girls" always seemed to be in short supply. At least, I hadn't managed to connect with one.

I am enough of a child of the '60s to believe that the sexual revolution, by and large, was a good thing. It got us past the arbitrary and repressive division of women into the "good girls" who would not and the "bad girls" who would. It ended that inequitable double standard by which a man was forgiven for sowing his wild oats and the woman who failed to keep him in check was left holding the bag, morally as well as literally. The pill was not widely available while I was in high school. A pregnant high-school girl used to be forced to drop out of school while the boy who did the deed not only got to continue his education but was actually admired and envied by his sexually repressed male classmates.

Still, I don't envy today's young people who are growing up too fast and too soon where sex is concerned. We were repressed, but they must be growing up jaded. Today, if the media is to be believed, sex comes too easily. Girls signal their interest in a boy by sexting—by sending smart-phone selfies of

15. Flashback: The Girl I Left Behind

themselves in provocative poses and even in the nude. I've read that most young people today consider oral sex to be less intimate than intercourse and that nearly 50 percent of high-school students today have had intercourse before graduation. For most of us in my generation, seduction was a matter of siege warfare. You had to wear the girl down gradually, over a protracted period of time, with each new intimacy representing a victory. But that made it all the more special and exciting.

It must have been May of 1965, at least three months before I left for Parris Island, that I took my first liberties. We were at New Castle's Battery Park, overlooking the Delaware River.

The cool guys referred to taking a girl there as taking her to the "submarine races"—the main objective was to induce the girl to help raise a periscope.

It's ungentlemanly to kiss and tell, I realize. Suffice it to say that over the next year, before I left for Vietnam, I got home on the average of once a month. A pattern of intermittent gradual escalation ensued before she finally surrendered completely to me. But it was not an unconditional surrender. She attached one condition to her surrender—that we would get married.

We soon found ourselves having sex on a regular basis—whenever I was home. But, still, it was evident that a part of Erin—the good Catholic girl part—remained guilt-ridden. She seemed to submit as a form of tribute or even martyrdom. Erin never really seemed to enjoy sex. She had been indoctrinated to view her virginity as her "pearl of great price." And the only way in which she could rationalize losing it was to view it in sacrificial terms—something precious that she gave up for me.

Part of my strategy, I'm ashamed to say, had been to assure Erin that we were headed toward marriage and that I was onboard with her goal of eventually bringing five or six good Catholic children into the world. For a time, I even believed I was sincere.

Erin graduated from Brown Vocational a year after I graduated from Salesianum. She became a licensed hairdresser. And, by all accounts, a good one. While she was still in school, she was chosen to style the actress Barbara Bel Geddes' hair when she was playing at the Wilmington Playhouse. After graduation, Erin was hired at one of the best salons in Wilmington, one that catered to the upper crust. She was bringing home upwards of $120 a week back when that was good money. Ours would have been a financially secure life, at least.

But there were signs it never would have worked out. For one thing, fornication notwithstanding, Erin was determined to keep the faith. Whenever I was home on a Sunday, I had to appease her by going to mass. She just couldn't stop being a Catholic.

She was also a hopeless romantic. She believed there was one marital partner ordained by God for each of us, and that, in some measure, would mitigate our sin—provided that I redeemed and sanctified her sacrifice through the sacrament of marriage. I made the mistake of trying to tell her what my senior religion teacher, Father McGovern, had told our class—that there are any number of people a person could be happily married to. Erin wouldn't hear of it. She insisted that Father McGovern was wrong. She was understandably insecure about our relationship, sensitive to any and all signs that I may not be the one God had chosen for her and that my intentions may not be honorable.

On one occasion, we were watching an old movie on TV—the Cary Grant and Deborah Kerr film *An Affair to Remember*. I was less than worldly wise in those days, and I innocently asked Erin what they meant by "an affair." She immediately got in my face, and her tone became challenging, if not outright hostile.

"People having an affair have sex with no intention of getting married. Is that what we're having, Eddie? Are we having an affair?"

"Yeesh! Of course not. I was just asking," I said, while trying to hug her back into a peaceful and pleasant frame of mind. Touchy, touchy!

(Also, it was later during that fateful summer when Erin capitulated that something happened that would paint our relationship in a different light. But that's the subject for another chapter.)

And that was the way the world was when I first met Erin on that night in April 1965 at Wilmington Dry Goods. I sometimes wonder what it must be like for today's young people, for whom intimacy and sex come so easily and are not considered the ties that bind.

I know that I started this account crediting war with being good for that one thing—seducing girls. But it occurs to me that I have to give it credit for something else. Vietnam made me realize that I was too young to be terminally tied down. "The world was all before me," to borrow a line from Milton, and I wanted to be free to restart my life. I sent Erin a "Dear Erin" letter soon after I was transferred to Papa Three.

I suppose there is something to be said for the old saw about the good dying young. Erin—a "sadder but wiser," good Catholic girl—died in 1996, at age 49. She had married, while I was still in Vietnam. My mother sent me a clipping of her wedding announcement. I don't know if it was a happy marriage. But according to her obituary, it produced a son and a daughter and three grandchildren, and she was still married when she died. The cause of death was listed as "respiratory failure"—whatever that means.

Looking back on it all, I feel bad about the way I behaved. To say it the way that President Clinton once did, I took advantage of Erin "because I could." I was duplicitous, selfish and insincere. I racked up a lot of bad karma that came back to bite me later and which probably is not done with me yet. As I would eventually learn, all's not fair in love and war.

16

Tiger Papa Three

"Tiger Papa Three," back before we realized the enemy may be listening, was the constant radio call sign of the 3rd Platoon of Papa Company, 3rd Combined Action Group, operating between Dong Ha and Cam Lo in Vietnam's northern Quang Tri Province. As a Papa Three rifleman and patrol leader, I took special pride in the "fearful symmetry" of that call sign—even though, as the ensuing pages may suggest, we never burned very bright in Vietnam's jungle of the night. We at least belonged to a romantic and select group, the Combined Action Program (CAP) in Vietnam. Ours was not simply to search and destroy. Ours was to win hearts and minds at the grass-roots level.

The author on radio watch shortly after arriving at Papa Three. (I'm wearing a South Vietnamese Army chevron for corporal on my "cover"—the Marine Corps term for a hat.)

Papa Three was located along South Vietnam's Highway 9 in the hamlet of Cam Hieu, part of a large village complex called Thon Vinh Dai. That, at least, is the name appearing on the map I now have, and it must have been on the tactical maps we used then. But none of us paid any attention to Vietnamese place names. I don't recall anyone referring to Cam Hieu as anything other than the "ville." And truth be told, I never heard that name until 1994, when I reviewed a book by a Marine who had been in Papa Three's start-up group. (More about that anon.) Highway 9, of course, was a "highway" by Vietnamese standards only. It was a dirt and gravel road, barely two lanes wide. But it was an important route linking Dong Ha and Cam Lo with points west.

We were a "platoon" of 13 Marines, a Navy corpsman, and approximately 40 PFs. That, at least, was what our Table of Organization called for. In reality, we were never up to T/O strength. As I've already related, PFs were not regular soldiers but were roughly analogous to our National Guard. They served only part-time, living in the village when they were not soldiering with us. They were a mixed lot made up largely of men hoping to avoid the draft through PF service, as well as a few supposedly not qualified for full-fledged service, and an occasional veteran who had managed to survive five years in the regular army. We were led by a Marine sergeant, who had no direct authority over the PFs and by a PF sergeant, who had no authority over the Marines, nor any obligation to take direction or advice from them. The relationship between the two sergeants was collegial at best, nonexistent at worst. Papa Three answered to parallel Marine and Vietnamese commands. These commands were head-

Trung-si (sergeant) Nguyen, our PF leader.

16. Tiger Papa Three

quartered together at Cam Lo. But, as events would prove, they, too, were a house divided.

What the program lacked in effective joint command and control, however, it should have made up for through its freedom and autonomy. Papa Three certainly could not complain of over-supervision or micromanagement. We saw the company gunnery sergeant, who usually made the rounds with the supply truck, for at best a few minutes each day. The company commander would perhaps drop by once a week. For the most part, the day-to-day operation of the unit was left to our young buck sergeant (whom I'll identify anon). He was responsible for everything, including the planning and execution of patrols. The patrol overlays, of course, had to be encoded and radioed to the company commander for approval. But I don't recall any of Sarge's proposals ever being rejected. As long as Papa Three met the program mandate of two patrols a day—one a daylight excursion, the other a night ambush—he was pretty much left to run things as he saw fit. Sarge was easygoing, friendly, and unflappable, his leadership style tending toward laissez-faire. Consequently, all of us liked him, and most were well aware that life in Vietnam could be much worse than what we enjoyed at Papa Three.

I know I was happy to be there. Early in the program, CAP Marines were all combat-tested veterans, but not by the time I got there. As I've already confessed, CAP had been my Deus ex Machina, lifting me out of a boring job as a supply clerk in the 3rd Engineer Battalion rear.

As I've already related, the Marines and PFs of a combined action unit were to form a cohesive team, pursuing a twofold mission. First and foremost, the unit was to root out the Viet Cong infrastructure and protect its village from further enemy incursion. The Marine role in this ambitious undertaking was principally to train and inspire the PFs, raising their morale through our presence and example. Together, then, the Marine-PF team could go on to tackle the secondary but vitally important mission of winning the loyalty and support of the people. This was to be done by providing both effective security and assistance with practical self-help projects aimed at raising the standard of living in the village.

Papa Three's two patrol teams served in succession, setting out with five to 10 PFs on a daylight patrol one day and a night ambush the next. For the team that wasn't patrolling at any given time, there was guard to stand and work to do around the compound. The PFs must have been assigned to patrols on an ad hoc basis, as we never seemed to get the same group twice despite our best efforts at suggesting, and even demanding, some semblance of stability and team cohesion. For my part, I found myself promoted from rifleman to patrol leader within a couple of weeks of my arrival at Papa Three. I rose, I must admit, more through default than merit. Next to Sarge's assistant, I was the only corporal, and there were no volunteers for the job.

Papa Three was responsible for patrolling an unrealistically large area, one encompassing nearly nine grid squares and two major village complexes. Making matters worse, a deep and fairly wide river, the Song Cam Lo, cut diagonally through the area from northwest to southeast, dividing it nearly in half. Our only means of patrolling the northeastern half, containing two large hamlets, was to cross the river by boat. As we had no boats of our own, we would proceed to a particular point along the southern bank, a place marked by a set of stone steps, where our PFs would hail a couple of elderly Vietnamese, a man and a woman, and occasionally a child, who would row over to get us in flimsy canoes with single fishtail-type oars. Just who these rowers were, or who paid them, I never learned. But they seemed always on call and ever ready to row us across the river, usually by twos and threes.

It was a time-consuming and inescapably dangerous practice. It made a mockery of patrol security, virtually broadcasting our imminent arrival and practically inviting an ambush. Why the enemy never took advantage of the invitation, trapping half of us on the northern side and shooting the rest of us like fish in a barrel, I'll never know. Perhaps they thought it too easy and were suspicious. More likely, they had bigger things in mind and didn't want to attract attention. Whatever the reason, we never took so much as a sniper round in crossing the Song Cam Lo. That river, nevertheless, would be at the

One of the boats we would use to cross the Song Cam Lo. An unidentified Papa Three Marine is sitting in the bow. Three PFs are in the middle. The rower is pushing off from the stern.

16. Tiger Papa Three

center of our problems, aptly symbolizing in the end a cultural gulf we never could get across.

As I've already recounted, it was on the banks of the Song Cam Lo, on a beautiful day in late September, that we first fell out with our PFs. I cannot claim Marines and PFs had ever been especially close at Papa Three. But up to this point, the bolder and more curious PFs would mingle with Marines in the evenings, joking and cadging C-rations and cigarettes. And since my arrival, at least, all the PFs had seemed willing to follow along passively on patrol, wherever we would lead. Papa Three had not made contact with the enemy since the August attack, and we had seemingly settled into a comfortable routine, and had even grown somewhat complacent, when for no apparent reason our PFs mutinied, refusing to cross the river because there were "beaucoup VC" over there.

We were to play out this same frustrating scene several more times, always with the same result: a sit-down strike on our side of the river. Eventually, we were ordered to patrol on the other side without PFs, an order we initially carried out with great trepidation and which eventually would have tragic consequences. There were indeed "beaucoup VC" over there.

17

The Dramatis Personae

Papa Three seemed to renew the promise, holding out the lure of danger and excitement to young men as green as Reaves, Scotty, and I were at the time. The attack that had brought us there, to my mind, was an important validation. Some VC bodies had actually been left in the wire. Moreover, the village was rumored to be unfriendly, with the VC still pretty much in control. We didn't know about the unit's early history and were led to believe that Papa Three had never made any significant civic action inroads there.

My early experience with Papa Three certainly seemed to bear out that assessment and all the rumors. Shortly after my arrival, we awoke one morning to the sounds of general consternation in the village. Investigating, we discovered the VC had slipped in and assassinated a government official.

Not long after that, in broad daylight and within sight of our compound, a truck hit a command-detonated mine. After medevacing the driver, who seemed to have suffered serious internal injuries, we found the wires and the place in a stand of tall grass less than 50 feet from the road where the VC had lurked, waiting and watching the highway. Clearly, we were tested and even taunted periodically at Papa Three. But the day-to-day life was hardly as dramatic as these two incidents might suggest. On balance, it is now clear that the most pressing problem we faced that fall was forming a cohesive team.

(The Marines I'm about to name and/or describe are by no means the only ones I served with at Papa Three. They're just the ones I remember best, and, with a couple of exceptions, they're the guys I've reconnected with over the years. Unless otherwise noted, with their permission, I'm using their real names.)

Once again, I had arrived to find a unit in transition. Within a week or two, most of the old guard had rotated and only three remained: a quiet and unassuming corpsman; Al Hein (since deceased), a gregarious Illinois farm boy who answered to the nickname "Heinie"; and an embittered loner of a lance corporal who held himself aloof and viewed all the new arrivals with contempt. I still remember how this guy would brag about his first kill to anyone who would listen.

17. The Dramatis Personae

"I came up on him before he even knew I was there," he said, with a sadistic smile on his face, "and I shot him right through the heart. I was so proud; I hoisted this gook up onto my shoulder, as if he was a dead deer, and I carried him all the way back to the compound. He bled all over my shirt, but I didn't care." Fortunately, this Marine left within a week of my arrival. Aside from these three, the unit was literally reconstituted with people drawn from other Papa Company platoons, along with a few from a newly graduated CAP school class. We were an odd assortment. Here, to paraphrase Vietnam novelist Tim O'Brien, is who we were or pretended to be.

"Heinie," Al Hein, was a German-American and a self-styled fascist who had been encouraged in his affectation by another member of the old guard, a superannuated lance corporal also of German extraction and with a reputation for erratic behavior. "We Krauts have to stick together," this individual had supposedly told Heinie, and Heinie never tired of singing his praises. Heinie credited this Marine with jumping into the wire with a K-bar in his teeth during that mid–August attack. He had been seriously wounded—in the groin, according to Heinie.

As I reported earlier, I have since been in contact with Tom Flynn, another member of Papa Three's old guard, who had been part of the reaction force during the August attack. Flynn seriously doubts that anyone did anything so foolish as jumping into the wire during that attack. Apocryphal or not, however, the legend spread throughout Papa Company. I later heard the tale from a former Papa Two Marine, but I have to wonder if it originated with Heinie. He was a gifted storyteller and a compulsive talker. He was never one to let the literal truth get in the way of a good story, and believed, along with Emerson, that "a foolish consistency is the hobgoblin of little minds." He seemed to hold contradictory opinions on everything ranging from PFs to war protesters back home. Depending on his mood at the moment, for instance, Heinie either planned to beat up the first protester he encountered or to let his hair grow and join the movement himself.

There was a black machine gunner from a line battalion via another CAP unit I'll call Rodney. A gentle soul who had either found religion during his time with the grunts or brought it with him (I never knew which), Rodney, upon joining us, quite publicly confessed his fear of the field, volunteering to do the cooking and cleaning. All of us respected his candor and humility, and Sarge honored his request. Rodney became our cook and seldom went out on patrols.

As Rodney spent most of his spare time reading the Bible, behind his back we called him "the Reverend Mr. Black," after a popular song of the day. But he was obviously sincere, and no one ever worked harder to honor his share of a bargain—although he did lack both talent and inspiration in the cooking department. I remember suggesting to him on one occasion that a little salt and pepper, not to mention some hot sauce or Worcestershire, could go a long way toward making our meals a bit more interesting. Rodney, however, just didn't feel he had the "right to season another man's food."

Of course, there was only so much Rodney could do to make our meals interesting. We had B-rations (large cans, mostly beef stew) and we had C-rations. Occasionally, we were able to buy fresh French rolls from a kid who would come out from Dong Ha. (They were good but full of insects that we would just pick out as well as we could.) What we didn't have was something most young men imagine they wouldn't miss—vegetables. But miss them we did. "If I don't get something green soon," Reaves was heard to complain, "I'm going to start grazing in the grass."Later that fall, Rodney, who had been seriously overweight, contracted amoebic dysentery. None of us realized how serious it was at the time. When Rodney couldn't extricate himself from our little outhouse, which featured half-screen construction and commanded an excellent view of the wire in one sector, we thought we saw a way to make the best of a bad situation. Passing his rifle and cartridge belt in to him, we asked if he wouldn't mind standing guard, seeing as how he was stuck there anyway. Never one to complain, Rodney meekly agreed. We medevaced him the next morning. He came back about three weeks later and 30 pounds lighter.

There was Mike Fink from Denver, Colorado. I remember him as quiet but also as clearly not a man to be trifled with. His MOS was 2532, radio relay operator. Another Papa Three Marine with whom I've reconnected, Ron Parks, knew Fink better than I did and has even visited him in recent years. Parks describes Fink as "a rigid hard ass and a pure Marine" as befits the son of a World War II Marine.

Robert Yost, the Marine I described in Chapter 4, was also there. He had gone to another Papa Company unit after CAP school and had also been transferred in the wake of the August attack. I remember him as a loner who seemed to have no end of trouble adjusting to the program and getting along with the rest of us at first. It all came to a head one afternoon, precipitating a minor crisis and an especially painful memory.

He had adopted a puppy that cried incessantly—it was obviously too young to be taken from its mother. When Sarge insisted he do something about the problem, he stormed out with a shot gun and blew the puppy to bits. A fight with Mike Fink ensued, and none of us were sorry to see Yost lose. The incident troubled all of us, raising serious questions about his stability and reliability. But whatever was bothering him seemed to have been purged on that terrible afternoon. He settled down after that, going on to do just fine when it really counted.

Ron Parks from Houston, Texas. He was transferred to us from Papa Five. By primary MOS, Ron was an auto mechanic and had served with a motor

17. The Dramatis Personae

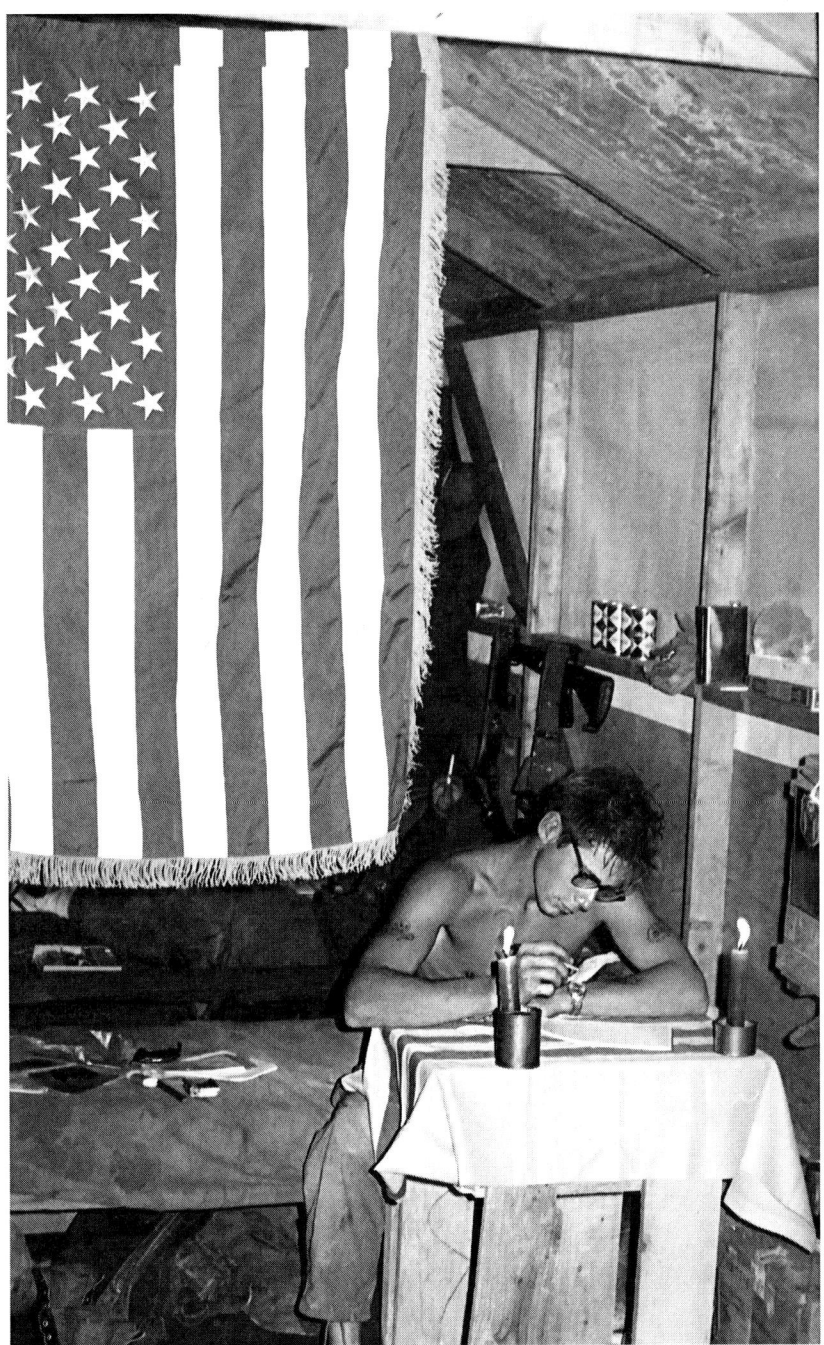

Yost writing home from the reconstructed Papa Three.

transport battalion before becoming a rifleman with the Combined Action Program.

At least three Navy corpsmen served with us during my time with Papa Three. I can't remember any of their names. I remember a heavy-set, blond-haired corpsman best. He was intelligent and possessed of a good sense of humor. He's the one pictured below during his first crossing of the Song Cam Lo.

No squad is complete without one. We were blessed with our own Gomer Pyle, a well-meaning but feckless young PFC who seemed never quite tuned into what the rest of us were doing. I think he infuriated all of us at one time or another with his inability to get up on time for guard duty. But he was unpretentious and humble about his shortcomings, and none of us could stay mad at him. I'll call him Nordberg. He, too, came out all right in the end—which, as the reader will discover, may be a cruel pun.

By far, the Marine who would emerge as the most competent among us was McClain "Mack" Garrett. He was a motor transport driver by primary MOS, and he had come to us from 3rd Medical Battalion. Because he was so quiet and self-effacing, I suppose, I don't have a single photo of him. That was a serious lapse on my part. As the reader will discover, we would all owe our lives to Mack on one occasion, and he more than proved his mettle in an even more desperate situation.

But if Nordberg was our Gomer Pyle, his opposite number had to be Reaves, easily the most self-assured and self-possessed of the Papa Three's cast of characters. He was a radio operator and had come to us via a radio battalion. That experience, coupled with reading Leon Uris' *Battle Cry*, had confirmed him in the belief that communicators are uniformly smarter than other Marines, a position he would good-naturedly defend by the hour. Always outspoken and opinionated, he could occasionally be overbearing. He was physically imposing as well, solidly built and well over six feet tall. But his judgment was usually sound, and he seemed to be one of those people who always know just what to do or say—a born leader, to use a much-abused phrase.

I watched him defuse a fight once, disarming both parties with gentle humor and irony. On another occasion, I watched him resolutely help retrieve a badly decomposed body from a river, a nauseating task requiring more intestinal fortitude than most of us could muster. Even when his fiancée sent him a "Dear John," appropriating their entire "joint" savings account, he managed to laugh it off. I think we all admired and respected Reaves. But I remember him most for his wry sense of humor and his obvious intelligence. He was simply smarter than most of the people around him, and he knew it. His plan, he once confided to me, was to get out of the Marine Corps to go to college under the G.I. Bill. He had seen enough of the mud and blood. If he came back in service at all, it would be as a Navy officer on a submarine. I can still see him crouched down, hanging by the elbows from an imaginary periscope, mimicking the languid pose Hollywood submarine officers all strike. I think he was serious about college at least, and I count it a great loss he never got to go.

Reaves and one other Marine, the son of a career Air Force NCO, Larry Scroggs (since deceased), seemed to be the only Papa Three Marines to have had the benefit of a solid middle-class upbringing. I understood Reaves to have been the son of some sort of consulting engineer and that he had lived in several parts of the country. The "Air Force brat" had spent his teen years in France. I still remember his complaining about how French women didn't

On patrol in Cam Hieu. Reaves is in front. Scotty is behind him.

shave their legs or armpits and that body odor was oppressive in French buses and in the Paris subway. He clearly had mixed feelings about having lived in France. He also told us that the best way to insult a Frenchman was to refuse to shake his hand.

I've already mentioned Scotty, the Canadian who had enlisted to see something of our war. I don't recall his real name. I'm sorry to say that I never got to know him very well, but I do remember him as uncomplaining and as exuding an air of quiet competence. The rest of us were provincial by comparison, distinctly working class and largely nondescript.

Al Hein had come to Papa Three from an infantry battalion, and to my knowledge, he and Sarge

Larry Scroggs taking a break from helping to build a sandbag bunker.

Sergeant Bill Cooke about to cross the Song Cam Lo.

were the only ones who had had extensive combat experience. "Sarge" was Sgt. William "Bill" Cooke. He had been a squad leader in the 3rd Battalion of the 3rd Marines. But he never spoke about those days. He had extended his tour for six months, joining the program and Papa Three immediately following his 30-day extension leave back in Grand Rapids, Michigan, his hometown.

By a remarkable coincidence, our senior corporal, James Anikowski (deceased), Sarge's assistant, was also from Grand Rapids. They had never met before reporting to Papa Three. But they apparently had friends and favorite haunts in common, and they soon became inseparable. Together, they formed our command element while the rest of us formed two five-man patrol teams.

18

Blissful Ignorance

It was a good thing that I didn't know then what I would later learn about Papa Three's history.

Papa Three had been attacked not once but twice before I got there. This I didn't know until 1994, when the editor of the *Marine Corps Gazette*, the professional magazine of Marine officers, sent me a self-published book to review. The title was *A Voice of Hope*, and the book was the memoir of former Marine Thomas Flynn, who had been in Papa Three's original start-up group. In being assigned to CAP, Flynn was told that he and his fellow Marines would be "the people's voice of hope." Hence, the title of Flynn's book.

Flynn doesn't pin down the date, but Papa Three had been started at some point in the early spring of 1967. Flynn describes the PFs as lackadaisical and difficult to deal with from the beginning. The villagers, on the other hand, initially seemed to be receptive. They routinely took advantage of the rudimentary medical care Papa Three's corpsman could give. At one point, they even treated the Marines to a feast, much of which they were hard-pressed to eat. In addition to rice, it featured rare chicken and pork along with intestines, brains, and clotted chicken blood. But Flynn describes how they all did their best to eat a little of everything so as not to offend. He also mentions thinking of how much food we waste in the States. Still, passing through some of the hamlets, especially at night, Flynn had the feeling that the people were as afraid of the Marines as they were of the Viet Cong.

The original Papa Three group, moreover, was certainly more conscientious than we were. In addition to meeting their mandate of a day patrol and a night ambush patrol each day, they routinely went out on four-man "EKT," or enemy kill team, patrols without the PFs. It was on one of these EKT patrols, in a hamlet on the north side of the Song Cam Lo, that they stumbled upon three Viet Cong. Flynn describes how they saw the VC before the VC saw them and opened fire, killing one and wounding the other two, who managed to escape. This incident, and the apparent inroads Papa Three was making with the people, must have convinced the local VC that Papa Three had to go.

As Flynn recounts, on the last day of April, the village chief had passed

18. Blissful Ignorance

on an intelligence report that Papa Three was going to be hit. A few tense days passed with the compound on 100 percent alert before they resumed business as usual. Then, on May 15, 1967, at about 4:45 a.m., just after Flynn had been awakened for guard duty, all hell broke loose. A satchel charge brought the roof of his strong-back hooch down upon him. In grappling for his M16, Flynn found only the barrel. It had been blown apart.

Flynn crawled out from under the debris, only to find several VC within the compound. He tried to make a break for one of the bunkers, where he knew he could get a weapon, but ran smack into a VC who drew a large knife. Flynn managed to wrest the knife away from him and to stab him in the chest. All the while explosions were going off and rounds were whizzing past him. He then noticed a dazed VC whose arms were limp, holding his rifle down in front of him. Flynn tried to grab his rifle, but as he did, he felt a hard blow to his neck and face. He'd been shot in the upper neck and fell to the ground semi-conscious. The bullet had traveled up through and broke his jaw, lacerating his tongue and exiting through his cheek, taking a few teeth with it. A VC proceeded to try to drag Flynn by the hair, but he managed to break free and to get up, only to be bayoneted in the hand. He fell back down, and several VC ran over top of him before one threw a grenade that hit him in the thigh and went off. Flynn finally managed to crawl to a bunker from which the surviving Papa Three Marines were returning fire, and one of the Marines pulled him inside. Help in the form of helicopter gunships had arrived by then, and Flynn and another wounded man were loaded onto a medevac chopper while the battle was still raging. Two bullets ripped through the chopper as it was lifting off. Flynn describes looking down and seeing that all the hooches were "burning bonfires." He remembers feeling relieved and joyful but also guilty about leaving while others were still caught up in the battle. He also remembers praying, "Thank you, Father, for allowing us to live!"

Flynn was stabilized at the medical facility in Dong Ha and quickly flown to the hospital in Da Nang, where he stayed for several weeks before being transferred to the U.S.S. *Sanctuary*, a hospital ship. Everyone thought, Flynn most of all, that he would be medevaced back to the States, but in the end, he was sent back to Papa Three. He soon found himself suffering from flashbacks and nightmares and unable to sleep. The company commander, sympathetic to all he had been through, reassigned Flynn to the company headquarters at Cam Lo.

According to a history Flynn found online, the second attack took place on August 14, 1967. Flynn joined an impromptu reactionary force assembled at the Papa Company headquarters in Cam Lo, and it joined up with a company-sized reactionary force accompanied by two tanks. They quickly repelled the attackers, and Flynn helped with the mop-up. There were 11 dead VC in the compound and in the wire. They found another body close to the compound and killed a wounded one who wouldn't surrender and kept trying to crawl away despite repeated invitations from an interpreter.

One Marine had been killed. Flynn calls him "Banes" in his book, but he was actually Lance Corporal Mark Black. Another Marine, whom Flynn calls "Wells," had been seriously wounded. A round had passed through his leg and into his groin, piercing his intestines before exiting from his buttocks. Al Hein, who had survived the attack and who stayed on at Papa Three, identified this Marine as the fellow German-American who had gone berserk during the attack, jumping down from the top of a bunker into the fray.

I don't remember the exact date, but it was within days of the August 14 attack that Reaves, Scotty, and I reported to Papa Three. And within a week or two, Hein was the only member of the original start-up group still with us at Papa Three.

19

Flashback: My Great Expectations Revisited, July 1966

The duty NCO had just handed me a note. It was another typically hot and humid July day at Camp Lejeune. The note read, "Call Betty Palm," and included a phone number in the Upper Peninsula of Michigan. My father, who was stationed at the K.I. Sawyer Air Force Base at the time, was inviting me up to renew our relationship and to meet his wife and my half-brother and two half-sisters. I requested and was granted a week's leave, and Betty made the flight arrangements.

It was anything but easy to travel from Camp Lejeune to the U.P. in those days, and I imagine that it still isn't. I had to catch an early morning bus to New Bern—a two-hour trip—and from there, I had to fly to D.C. From D.C., I flew to Green Bay, Wisconsin, where I had a two- or three-hour layover.

That part of the trip stands out in my memory. It was a bright sunny day with the temperature only in the 70s and the humidity delightfully low compared to what I was used to in eastern North Carolina. From Green Bay, I flew to Marquette, arriving just after sundown. I had been traveling at least 14 hours in a wilted summer uniform. Servicemen and women in uniform used to be able to fly for half-price on military standby, and the flights were seldom full back in the days of airline regulation. It was understood that I would save my father money by flying military standby. I didn't mind.

My father and his family could not have been nicer. Betty in particular went out of her way to make me feel like part of the family, even going so far as to voice an expectation that I would henceforth be a regular visitor. She told me to be sure to wear my uniform overcoat and gloves when I come up in the winter.

On the second or third afternoon, everyone contrived to leave me alone with my father, who proceeded to give me his side of the story regarding the

Lt. Col. Edward G. Palm, USAF, and L. Cpl. Edward F. Palm, USMC, at K.I. Sawyer Air Force Base in the Upper Peninsula of Michigan, June 1966.

break-up with my mother. He painted a picture of a spoiled, petulant young woman who was not above suicidal gestures to get her way. Her favorite tactic, according to my father, was to stick her head in the oven and threaten to turn on the gas. Their main irreconcilable difference, however, was my mother's inability to understand that, having been an officer and a gentleman, my father would never be content as a blue-collar worker. Also, my mother just couldn't conceive of leaving her family and Delaware in search of opportunity. By 1949, my father was back in the service and stationed in Japan. It was some time before my mother, who was punishing my father with letters hinting at playing around, grudgingly agreed to join him in Japan—taking two-year-old me along.

We were not in Japan very long before a shameful episode between my father and a Japanese house girl occasioned their final break-up. According to family legend and lore—as kept alive by my aunts—there was no backstory to this incident. My father had been drunk and oversexed, and my mother had been the soul of offended innocence. The truth was that their relationship had long been strained and that my mother too had taken her marital vows lightly. That much was confirmed by letters I would find after my mother's death in 1978.

The high point of the week—literally as well as figuratively—came when

19. Flashback: My Great Expectations Revisited, July 1966

my father got permission to take me up on a training flight, and not just for the ride.

In my mind's eye, I can still see how the slant of the setting sun made Lake Superior look like a giant golden pond as we were flying over it that evening. I can still hear the whir of the servos as the pilot trimmed the plane for level flight. We had taken off at 1715 from K.I. Sawyer Air Force Base in a KC135A jet tanker—a modified Boeing 707. I still have a copy of the log from that flight. It lists my father, Lt. Col. Edward G. Palm; a captain; two first lieutenants; a master sergeant; and me, Lance Corporal Edward F. Palm, USMC. The mission was to practice 60-degree banks and touch-and-go landings.

There I was, behind the pilot, marveling at the view from the cockpit, when the copilot suddenly got out of his seat and motioned for me to sit down and to put on the headphones. The pilot told me to take the yoke, and he proceeded to talk me through putting the plane into a few 15-degree banks. He had me apply back pressure to maintain altitude in going into a bank and forward pressure in coming out of the bank. Talk about power steering! Moving that huge plane around the sky seemed almost effortless.

When it was over, he told me I had done a better job of maintaining altitude than many a new copilot. I'm sure it wasn't true. But it made me feel good.

After that, my father and the master sergeant took me to the rear of the plane and let me fly the refueling boom. They even had me jettison 500 pounds of fuel. The environment and the price of jet fuel were not major concerns in those days.

Two other things about that flight stand out in my memory. I wondered why the flight yokes were inscribed with the Boeing Company logo and the designation "Boeing 707." Was that to try to sell an Air Force pilot on buying one of his own? Also, no one told me we would be pulling two-and-a-half Gs when doing 60-degree banks. Suddenly, it felt as if a giant hand was pressing down on me.

That flight stands out in my memory as the nicest thing my father would ever do for me and the high point in our relationship. As I look back on it now, however, I realize that the real turning point in my life came when Betty, innocently enough, asked me if I had a girlfriend.

I did indeed have a girlfriend, Erin, the subject of a previous chapter. I must admit that, when she had taken the initiative to meet me back there at Wilmington Dry Goods, it seemed like an act of grace in my otherwise blighted life. The fact that I had already committed myself to joining the Marine Corps made our meeting seem all the more poignant. By that summer, as I already admitted, ours had become an exclusive, serious relationship. Throughout my first year in the Corps, I managed to "swoop" home to see Erin at least one weekend a month.

I was proud of Erin and of our relationship and fully expected Betty and my father to approve. Our relationship had already progressed to the physical tie that binds. But during that week in the U.P. my head had been turned by a vision of a middle-class life that I suddenly found myself heir to—or so it seemed at the time.

"A hairdresser?" Betty asked, her tone clearly expressing disapproval. My father's silence and his half smile seemed to express assent.

"Oh, Ed, you don't want to get tied down to a hairdresser," Betty added. "You need to find a good college girl."

Think of Dickens' *Great Expectations* and how Pip's vanity and ambition lead him to turn his back on his one friend, the good and kindly blacksmith Joe. That is exactly what I did—long before I first read Dickens' novel. I found myself suddenly feeling ashamed of Erin and thinking that she would hold me back and keep me from realizing my own new-found great expectations.

Before the week was out, Betty even introduced me to the kind of girl she felt would befit my new station in life—a colonel's daughter who was home from college. We went out on one date, during which we locked lips alongside a small pond on base. We even corresponded for a while. But she was far away and, as a college student, lived in a different world. Before the summer was over, that fizzled out, and I found myself drifting back to what had been a sure thing—Erin. But the seed had been planted. I never again felt the same about Erin as I had before that week in the U.P.

Truth be told, the way that week ended did give me pause. Betty and my father explained that they would be happy to pay for my return airfare but that it should also be possible for me to fly back for free using space-available military flights—commonly referred to as "military hops." It just so happened that there was a daily flight from K.I. Sawyer to Wright Patterson Air Force Base in Dayton, Ohio, and from there, my father explained, there were flights going all over. I was frankly apprehensive and more than a little disappointed. But I was also eager to please, so I agreed to give it a try.

If taking a bus and commercial flights up to the U.P. had been a trial, my return trip was an absolute ordeal. I got to Wright Patterson easily enough—only to learn that there were no scheduled flights heading south. I remember sitting there in the terminal, with visions of getting in trouble for overstaying my leave, when the Palm luck intervened. A small two-engine Navy prop plane, en route from the Great Lakes Naval Air Station to the Patuxent River Naval Air Station in Maryland, had unexpectedly landed for refueling. The pilot agreed to give me and another passenger, a soldier, a hop.

All well and good—except that we ran into a thunderstorm. After all these years, I can still see the lightning flashing all around us and feel the plane being buffeted from side to side and suddenly dropping a hundred feet

19. Flashback: My Great Expectations Revisited, July 1966

or so at a time. I found myself seriously frightened and more than a little airsick before it was over.

It was late in the afternoon when we finally landed, and the problem was that Patuxent, Maryland, is still pretty far from Camp Lejeune, North Carolina. I had to catch a bus to D.C., and from there, it was a long overnight Continental Trailways bus ride to Camp Lejeune. I got in at about 5 a.m. with only a few hours to spare before I would have been marked "U.A."—short for "unauthorized absence."

20

And the Rains Came!

Someone was shaking me and saying something that made no sense: "Better get up; the water will be over your rack soon." I turned over at that point, dropping one arm over the side of the cot and into the wading pool that had been our strong-back hooch. I had awoken to the wonder of "water, water, everywhere."

On balance, I would have to admit that much of what we suffered at Papa Three was more tragicomic than tragic. Like Shakespeare's unfortunate Ophelia, "too much of water" had we in the fall of 1967.

It started raining heavily one morning, continuing steadily into the night. We had gone out on patrol that afternoon and had noted that the streams and the Song Cam Lo were running high, prompting us to cancel a planned cross-

The Marine I've called Nordberg about to step down from our strongback hooch (left) into our flooded compound. The hooch was set up on two-foot pilings.

20. And the Rains Came!

ing. But no one seemed unduly alarmed, and I remember hitting the rack that night at about 2130, expecting to be awakened for guard at 0400.

Looking at the waterproof Seiko I had bought at the Phu Bai Post Exchange while going through the Combined Action school, I noted it was not yet midnight.

As the water was almost over my cot already, and as our hooches were built on two-foot stilts, there must have been at least four feet of water covering our compound. The cheap Vietnamese footlocker containing my clothing was submerged. Somehow, I managed to find my boots. Fortunately, as we usually did, I had slept in my clothes, and my rifle and cartridge belt were safely hanging on nails in the wall. We went on 100 percent alert—not because we feared an attack but because no one had a dry place to sleep, and there was nothing else to do.

By the time it stopped raining the next morning, the flood had crested at more than five feet and was over our heads in the lower parts of the compound.

Just the day before, however, Cam Lo had received intelligence we were going to be hit, and we had been reinforced by a squad of grunts. They had taken the flood in stride and were spending the morning merrily wading and splashing around the compound on air mattresses. There was nothing to do at that point but join in the fun. Those of us who lived there, however, realized there would be a bill to pay for this impromptu pool party and that it wouldn't be paid by our grunt guests.

21

Hard Times

The month following the flood ranks as the toughest I spent in Vietnam. The water receded within a day, and the weather turned clear again and even pleasantly cool. But everything was covered with a couple of inches of vile-smelling paddy silt. Out of concern for our health, as well as the likelihood of further floods once the monsoon began in earnest, the company commander ordered us to abandon the original Papa Three and to rebuild on the high ground on the southern side of the highway directly across from the old site. It was much more easily said than done, we soon discovered, as we reluctantly moved out of our now contaminated but still relatively luxurious (by Vietnam standards) strong-back hooches, taking up lodgings in fighting holes and shelter halves on a barren hill. (A "shelter half" was half of a pup

After the flood: (from left) Anikowski, two unidentified PFs, Sarge.

21. Hard Times

tent. The expectation was that two Marines would join their halves and erect a tent they could share.)

Combined action Marines, I now realize, were spoiled compared to their counterparts in infantry battalions. But we in Papa Three can at least claim to have had the crash course in unaccommodated grubby living. We had no clothes other than the ones that had dried on our backs. Our others were full of silt, and we were a long way from any laundry services. One or two of us tried washing clothes in the river, but too much mud remained suspended in the water, leaving the clothes not much improved.

Word of our plight somehow filtered back to Dong Ha, and an enterprising Vietnamese laundress came out to collect our dirty clothes. Giving them to her was an act of faith, but she delivered—for a modest fee, of course. I went to change the socks I'd been wearing for two weeks. They disintegrated as I tried to pull them off.

Meals were now three C-rations a day, whereas we used to feast on two B-ration meals and one C-ration each day. Worse, when we were not patrolling or standing guard, we were now attempting to salvage as much as we could from the old compound to build a new one from scratch. It was hot, back-breaking work, made all the more difficult by our inexperience and ignorance of combat engineering. We got so that we actually looked forward to patrols as a welcome break from the tedium of filling countless sandbags (most at the original site were too rotten to recover) and stringing endless strands of barbed wire without gloves.

Filling sandbags: (from left) Rodney, Yost, Sarge (William Cooke).

It was during this period that an ugly rumor began to circulate. Our commanding officer, so the story went, had been warned by the village chief not to locate Papa Three in a low area so close to the river, as the area often flooded during the rainy season. The story had it, however, that based on his engineering experience from Georgia Tech, our commanding officer felt he knew better than any unlettered village chief. Hence, all our trauma may have been avoidable.

I now know that there was no truth to the rumor. The flood had been caused by a typhoon in the South China Sea, not by an early monsoon weather pattern. Also, like most rumors in Vietnam, it had that apocryphal quality so many stories in Vietnam had, that "I-heard-it-from-a-friend-of-a-guy-who-was-there" kind of quality. But we believed it at the time because we were bitter and it seemed somehow easier and more reassuring to see ourselves as the victims of friendly folly than an indifferent universe. The fact is, the original Papa Three site never flooded again while I was there, despite torrential monsoon rains that came later.

Still, it would have been nice had someone warned us that a typhoon was coming and that a storm surge was likely.

22

Deus ex Machina the Second

"What unit is this?" We'd seen a jeep drive past us on Highway 9—only to make a sudden stop, back up, and then drive up toward us. We thought it was our company commander or company gunny. But we suddenly realized that the man asking the question had three stars on his collar and was trailed by a captain we didn't recognize.

Hard times, of course, are supposed to bring out the best or the worst in people. The flood had hardly brought out the best in our PFs, making a bad situation even worse. Resentment had been building ever since the PFs opted out of patrolling the other side of the river, and now it seemed that rebuilding our compound was to be strictly an American responsibility as well. Our compound, after all, wasn't their home, only their appointed place of duty. They could afford to be cavalier about the flood. "Beaucoup nuoc" (a lot of water) they had laughed and joked at first, and we had all joined in at the time, buoyed up with a good feeling of shared adversity. But that feeling of camaraderie was short-lived. The humor paled as day after day passed with Marines filling sandbags and stringing barbed wire almost totally without PF assistance.

We would complain almost daily to Trung-si (sergeant) Nguyen, their platoon sergeant, who agreed in principle that it was our joint compound and that Marines and PFs alike had a vested interest in making it as defensible as possible in the event of attack. That is, in "principle" he agreed. In practice he never managed to scare up more than an occasional PF or two to work along with us on the compound defenses, and the unlucky selectees invariably seemed to find some excuse to leave after only an hour or two of work. The other PFs, of course, made it their practice not to hang around the compound, reporting only for guard or patrol duty. In rebuilding, as in patrolling the far side of the river, Marines were on their own.

Worse, we soon came to feel our own headquarters had abandoned us as well. Barbed wire was dribbled out stingily a spool or two at a time. We had, as I recall, two shovels, but only one sledgehammer for pounding stakes and no barbed-wire gloves. We often resorted to pounding stakes with large rocks rather than idly awaiting a turn with the sledgehammer. Without carpentry tools, much less carpentry skills, there seemed little hope of improving our living conditions. Morale soon ebbed, and our progress became halfhearted and desultory.

Sarge managed to keep us working after a fashion but was never able to buck us up. We needed to be shaken out of our lethargy and self-pity. Sarge, however, seemed capable only of shaming us into working. Without saying a word, he would simply pick up a shovel or a spool of barbed wire and set to work. One by one, we would join in. But our hearts just weren't in it, and after nearly a month on the hill, all we had to show for our labors was one sandbag bunker and an unfinished triple-concertina and apron perimeter. We had pretty much despaired of ever seeing the reconstruction completed when that chance visitor from on high wrought a dramatic change in our fortunes. Looking back on Papa Three today, I can see just how much we owed to dumb luck and to a kind and forgiving fate. This personage, who would contribute so much toward our recovery, had never intended to visit us. He was merely passing by and stopped, probably out of idle curiosity.

We had been filling sandbags on our hill overlooking Highway 9 when

Building a bunker: A Marine whose name I can't recall, Heinie (Al Hein) on top of the bunker, and Larry Scroggs carrying a sandbag.

22. Deus ex Machina the Second

we noticed that lone jeep stop short just past our compound. When it backed up and started up the hill toward us, our first thought was that it must be the company gunny or commander on his way somewhere else, on second thought, stopping off to check on us. But when the jeep finally got up to us, out jumped two men we had never seen before. One was big, burly, and middle-aged. The other was thin and young. Both were wearing helmets and flak jackets, and it wasn't until they were virtually on top of us that we realized we were face-to-face with a lieutenant general. Before anyone could jump to attention, much less salute, he had begun shaking hands and introducing himself all around, saying, "Hi, I'm General Walt. What unit is this?"

I think we were still in shock when General Walt seated himself on a sandbag, inviting us to do the same and to tell him about our unit and our problems. And that's just what we did. Everyone from Sarge on down poured out his heart and soul in an impromptu and animated *general* (pardon the pun) gripe session. We related the story of the flood, repeated the unfounded rumors, complained of shortages, maligned the PFs for not pitching in and for not patrolling the other side of the river, and in general (pardon the pun—again) painted ourselves as orphans of the storm. All the while the younger man, obviously the general's aide, stood off to the side, taking notes. General Lewis W. Walt listened patiently to our lament, never interrupting. When we were through, he promised in a relaxed and folksy manner to do what he could to help us out; and without further ado, he and his aide got back in their jeep and drove off.

For several minutes after the general's departure, we sat in stunned silence as the enormity of what we had done began to sink in. Most of us had never even seen a lieutenant general close up, much less poured out our hearts and souls to one. We were sure nothing good could come of it, and more than one of us expected reprisals for jumping our immediate chain of command.

Much to our surprise, we never did hear from our company headquarters. But we did indeed hear from General Walt. Word came about a week later in the form of a detachment of Seabees who suddenly showed up one morning with heavy equipment, ready to go to work. Within three days, our hilltop was leveled, a defensive trench was dug, and two hardback hooches and an outhouse were built. Papa Three had recovered from the flood, and we no longer had any excuse not to get on with the quest for hearts and minds. Lieutenant General Lewis W. Walt—a veteran of World War II and Korea, the holder of two Navy Crosses, and the future assistant commandant of the Marine Corps—had indeed kept his promise to do what he could to help us out.

23

The Way We Were

The flood stands out in my memory as a clear line of demarcation in Papa Three's progress. As our fundamentalist cook Rodney could have pointed out, our history had taken on a distinctly biblical cast. This time it had been the flood. Would it be the fire next time? But in the interim, we could look back on our own antediluvian period. The formative events of that age had been the attack in August, the rotation of the old guard, and the refusal of the PFs to patrol the other side of the river. The first remarkable event of the post-diluvian period, of course, had been our impromptu audience with (then) Lieutenant General Lewis Walt. In Marine Corps parlance, this would have been called a "request mast," which refers to a Marine's right to speak to any officer in the chain of command.

By intervening in the course of Papa Three's events, General Walt was responsible for rebuilding not only our compound but our morale. The PF problem was far from solved. We were still patrolling the far side of the river alone, and there was lingering resentment over the conspicuous absence of PFs during the dark days of reconstruction. But overall, we were again living a relatively comfortable life by in-country standards, and more importantly, we no longer felt abandoned by those who put us out there in the first place.

There have been too many popular depictions of Vietnam as a place of unmitigated horror and a moral vacuum where men sank to pre-civilized states of barbarism and savagery. (The My Lai massacre, of course, looms large in the modern memory of Vietnam.) Such was not my Vietnam experience.

Likewise, while drug use was prevalent in Vietnam, especially in the base camps, drugs were not a problem at Papa Three. To the best of my knowledge, there was only one occasion when Papa Three Marines indulged. It was in the early evening, before dark, that we began to hear resounding laughter, seemingly apropos of nothing, coming out of a bunker. Sarge went to investigate. There were only two Marines in the bunker, and the odor of marijuana was unmistakable. It was the one and only time I ever saw Sarge angry. He told the two Marines—whom I will refrain from identifying—that they were relieved from guard duty that night and that if he ever caught them smoking marijuana again, he would write them up. The next morning, both Marines apologized to all of us.

When I consider how most of my days in the Combined Action Program (CAP) were spent—when I recall "the way it mostly was," to borrow another phrase from Vietnam novelist Tim O'Brien—I remember a daily routine that was usually neither onerous nor unpleasant, and I recall that the evenings especially, in O'Brien's words, "could sometimes be fine."

Trung-si Nguyen and two or three of the bolder PFs would very often come over in the evenings for coffee. The image of two or three PFs and as many Marines sitting around a table in thoughtful silence, sipping C-ration coffee from improvised grenade canister mugs, haunts me still. Under the circumstances, even C-ration coffee could seem a treat, and the company wasn't half bad either. These occasions were the closest we ever came to a rapprochement. The atmosphere seemed imbued with at least some degree of fellowship, a mute recognition that, on both sides, we do what we must do.

I also have fond memories of bull sessions we had that fall, some of the most interesting of which were inspired by Bobbie Gentry's teasingly ambiguous "Ode to Billy Joe." From the first time we heard it over Armed Forces Radio, we were captivated by the song. Our little open-air seminar met one night after chow, Papa Three's unlettered scholars ranged on sandbags offering various opinions about why Billy Joe jumped from the Tallahatchie

A rare treat, enjoying a weinie roast: (from left) Sarge, Rodney, Ron Parks, Al Hein.

An evening coffee klatch: (from left) Trung-si Nguyen, an unidentified PF, Sarge.

Bridge and on what role the young female narrator had played in bringing him to his private doom.

We got the gist of it: the girl and Billy Joe used to hang out on the Tallahatchie Bridge. They must have broken up for some reason, and he took it hard—hard enough to jump off the bridge, leaving her mourning over what might have been.

All the while, Rodney—aka "the Reverend Mr. Black"—must have been off on a tangent of his own.

"With Billy Joe outta the picture, ya think she'll hook up with that 'nice young preacher'?"

"Not a chance!" Reaves replied. "I got the early watch tonight," he added. With that, class was dismissed.

The "Ode to Billy Joe" struck a sympathetic chord of self-pity in all of us, and we would inevitably get side-tracked to the topic of the girls we left behind and the omnipresent threat of the Jodys of the Vietnam era, draft dodgers and war protesters. Reaves in particular seemed able to relate. His fiancée had apparently been growing restless for some time. She had sent him that "Dear John" letter, adding injury to insult. She felt entitled to all the proceeds of a joint savings account they had opened. But by our self-indulgent standards, at least, he took it stoically. Armed Forces Radio Vietnam, however, was very much a mixed blessing. It kept us up on the latest popular music and news from back home, but it was also the propaganda arm of our military establishment back then. In between songs, and even episodes of the comic series "Chicken Man" ("He's everywhere, he's everywhere!"), we were treated to commercials on the importance of keeping your M16 clean and on other tactical imperatives. The command was obviously trying to put a patina of normalcy on the absurdity of war.

This is why I caution anyone who will listen not to be taken in by the film *Good Morning, Vietnam* and its depiction of AFR DJ Adrian Cronauer as a rebel. The only original, and possibly unauthorized, thing Cronauer ever did was to begin his morning broadcasts with a resounding "Good morning, Vietnam"—and even that was only mildly irreverent. The real Cronauer was nothing like Robin Williams's portrayal. In fact, he was as bland and institutional as the average announcer on Radio Moscow.

Nevertheless, we did appreciate his opening riff. I can still hear Sarge chiming in with Cronauer every morning, hollering, "Good morning, Vietnam!" while facing the ville. But that was followed by the Vietnamese national anthem, and none of us could chime in on that.

Aside from Armed Forces Radio, our main source of music was Sarge's battery operated, 3-inch reel miniature tape recorder. When he was home on his 30-day extension leave, Sarge had recorded some of the latest "sounds," as he called them, straight from his car radio. That, and the limited dynamic range of the recorder, made for a screechy sound I'll never forget. But we all listened nevertheless. To this day, I flash back to that time and place when I hear one of the pop hits from the '60s that Sarge had recorded.

I also remember the evening when, somehow, we got on the topic of which is better English: *"you all"* or *"youse guys."* Reaves led the southern contingent, arguing for *"you all."* I joined the northern *"youse-guys"* group. But, secretly, I had to agree that *"you all"* was preferable. By sheer force of his personality, Reaves carried the day and had the last word.

Our enthusiasm for the strange war we found ourselves in would wax and wane regularly, often within the course of a typical day. Never at a loss for words, Heinie generally articulated what the rest of us felt—although perhaps not so strongly as he did. We could always count on Heinie to feel especially bloodthirsty first thing in the morning with the sun shining brightly.

"I'll tell ya what we should do. Two or three of us should slip out in the middle of the night. We could swim the river with K-bars in our teeth and our rifles in plastic bags. We'd be what they call an 'enemy killing team—an EKT.' And without any PFs, we could sneak into the ville at the northern edge of our TAOR and quietly kill a couple VC. Then we could slip back out before anyone knew what happened."

Thus Heinie would sow the seeds of terror among our enemies. By afternoon, without reference to his first proposal, he would usually scale down, presenting a somewhat less daring plan. The keynote would still be stealth, but the killing team would terrorize our own side of the river. By late afternoon or dusk at the latest, our Rambo precursor could generally be heard declaiming on the ingratitude of "these people" and questioning the wisdom of going out on patrol at all.

There were also days when Heinie would reflect on the antiwar movement back home. "When I get back in 'The World' [as we used to say], I'm gonna punch out the first protester I see!" Only a day or so later, he would turn around and say, "When I get back to 'The World,' I'm gonna let my hair grow, and I'll be right out there protesting with them."

"Why should we risk our asses for people who won't fight their own war?" That was Heinie's bottom line.

Why indeed? But I realize today we were as frustrated by our own ineptitude as by the reluctance of our PFs. Past events and the general indifference of the people had made it abundantly clear we were not operating in a pacified area. The enemy was out there and, as we were to learn in early December, out there in force. Yet between August and December, Papa Three never made any significant enemy contact.

Only one night ambush was ever triggered during my tenure. Our unsuspecting victims that night turned out to be a group of wild VC pigs. They squealed in terror, but even they apparently got away unscathed. The conventional wisdom back then—and the rationale behind many an inflated body count—was that the enemy often managed to carry off their dead and wounded. That must have been what those VC pigs did.

I would like to write that we likewise struck fear in the hearts of our human enemies, or at least inspired a healthy respect, but I think I would be overstating the case.

The inevitable suspicion, of course, was that our PFs were in league with the enemy and were tipping them off about our patrols. Our suspicions were seemingly confirmed one night when a Marine professed to have caught a PF signaling the village with a flashlight just as we were about to set out on patrol. The PF denied it, and there were no other witnesses. But feelings had been running high on both sides since the PFs had refused to patrol the other side of the river or to help in rebuilding the compound. Sarge and Trung-si Nguyen had to step in to quell a near riot. We were more than ready to believe the worst at the time. From what I now know of the Vietnamese and their war, however, I can see it did not require that our PFs be in active collusion with the enemy for Papa Three to be ineffectual.

Our PFs had obviously made their accommodation with a seemingly unbeatable enemy that usually asked no more of them than that they stay on their own side of the river. From the provincial perspectives of our PFs, moreover, the other side of the river might as well have been another country. In later life, at an academic conference, I spoke to a Vietnamese woman who confirmed that assessment. She told me that the traditional associative village

23. The Way We Were

culture up through the 1960s was xenophobic and insular in the extreme. Even people living in neighboring villages, she said, would not trust and open up to one another.

Today, having the advantage of 20-20 hindsight, I suspect an enemy gearing up for the Tet Offensive had put out the word to all whom it may concern: "Stay on your own turf. Mind your own business!" Under the circumstances, our PFs probably simply saw no advantage in crossing the river, in effect going begging and borrowing after trouble. Likewise, they didn't have to alert the enemy of our coming. We saw to that, as we were hardly very subtle in our patrolling. It is certainly tempting to blame the PFs for all of Papa Three's shortcomings, but the truth is we came by our incompetence naturally and without any allied assistance.

One patrol in particular stands out in my memory as a shining example of just how inept we could be. The great irony is that, tactically, at least, we did everything right on this patrol. Operating without PFs, we spent the night in a remote ambush site on the far side of the river and set out before dawn for a nearby village. This village was a sullen place, seemingly devoid of military-age males—always a bad sign in Vietnam. Our plan was to hit the village at first light, catching the people off guard and searching for caches of weapons or supplies.

We found no such items. But, in the first house we came to, we did find a thirty-something man dressed in a khaki shirt and khaki trousers. There was no doubt that our sudden arrival came as a surprise to this man at least. He was visibly shaken, and his behavior was atypical.

By and large, most of the villagers in our area would affect a demeanor of stoical indifference, trying to ignore us and go about their business even as we rummaged through their possessions and tore their houses apart. This man, however, couldn't do enough to help us search. He even took the initiative, opening things and pointing out nooks and crannies we hadn't even thought to check, all the while protesting, "No VC, no VC!" Not finding anything, we wished him a good day and moved on. It would not be until that December, after we had taken a couple of Main-Force VC prisoners, that I realized our host of some two months before had been protesting too much. Our prisoners that day were wearing the same shade of khaki.

We had obviously surprised a VC on that previous occasion and had let him go—not out of compassion but rather inexcusable ignorance. At the time, we didn't even know that there were organized, full-time Main-Force VC units. No one had told us.

Like most Marines in Vietnam, we too aspired to kill VC, and we were exceedingly frustrated by our inability to do so. But, in my view, entirely too much has been written about the savage, racist character of the war, charging us with cynically inflating body counts with civilian casualties. The popular view persists that such practices were widespread and largely condoned—the rule was "If it's dead, it's VC." Perhaps other units did pursue a shoot-first-and-ask-questions-later policy. But I can testify that Papa Three, probably the least supervised of all units in Vietnam, exercised self-restraint.

The "If-it's-dead-it's-VC" proposition may have been debatable, but there was universal agreement in Vietnam that anything moving about during hours of darkness was VC, or at least could be presumed to be such. On another occasion, we must have done it right. It was my night to lead the ambush patrol. We left the compound after midnight, without PFs, set up at a trail junction just outside one of the larger hamlets on the other side of the river.

It was just starting to get light when we heard someone coming down the trail. We were sorely tempted to open up as soon as we could make out the shadowy figure against an even darker backdrop. Reaves, who had set in next to me, whispered, "Do you want to open up?" Something told me to wait, even though he seemed to be walking with something that could have been a rifle. "When in doubt, shoot" was the conventional wisdom in Vietnam, and as the patrol leader I almost acceded. But I realized that something was not quite right with this shadowy apparition coming steadily toward us. The gait was sprightly, even nonchalant, and we suddenly realized he was dressed all in white. "Hold your fire!" I shouted. "It's only an old man."

We took him into custody and turned him over to the village chief, who probably only warned him about the dangers of breaking curfew and sent him on his way. I have no doubt that, had we been of a mind to, we could have murdered that old man with impunity. Had it been raining that night, had we been cold and miserable, had this happened after December 4, there might have been a different outcome. And it would have been dismissed as one of the fortunes of war, an unfortunate accident occasioned by his own folly in venturing out before sunrise. Many of the so-called atrocities and the undeniable excesses of the war, I suspect, happened under similar circumstances, and I do not mean to imply that we always held the high ground morally.

On one other occasion, during a day patrol, we were walking down a trail alongside one of the tributaries to the Song Cam Lo. The creek was six or seven feet wide at that point, and was lined with high hedgerows on both sides. Suddenly, a short burst of automatic fire rang out. The rounds passed safely over our heads, but we responded in kind—and then some. We each emptied a magazine and threw a couple grenades.

At that point, we realized that no one was firing back, but we heard someone crying on the other side. We moved down to a shallow area where we could ford and doubled back to the area we'd been firing into. It was the edge of a hamlet, and an old woman was sitting inside the doorway of her house holding her breast and crying softly. She'd caught a piece of shrapnel from one of our grenades. Fortunately, our corpsman was able to extract the piece of shrapnel and to patch her up. We looked around but found no VC bodies or blood trails. Chalk one up as "collateral damage" due to Papa Three.

On the plus side, it was this incident that I would always look back on as first entitling me to wear the Combat Action Ribbon. That sniper round at Papa One didn't really meet the criteria. You had to be fired upon and fire back—and that I did for the first time on this patrol.

24

Puff the Magic Dragon Comes to Call

"Do you suppose he knows we're here?" That was the question of the hour.

"Of course," someone replied. "He has the location of all friendly units plotted."

As I look back on it now, it seems to me our PFs had long been looking to distance themselves from us and our cause. They finally found just the pretext they had been looking for one night in November when "Puff the Magic Dragon" came to call. "Puff" and "Spooky" both were popular nicknames for the AC47, an updated version of the venerable old C47 transport plane. A Vietnam variation on the theme of "something old, something new," Puff sported the latest in electrically driven Gatling guns capable of firing 6,000 rounds per minute. Puff also carried a seemingly endless supply of parachute flares and, in our area at least, was employed primarily at night against suspected North Vietnamese Army (NVA) troop concentrations.

Watching Puff in action could be an amazing spectacle, an awesome sound and light show that made you feel almost sorry for the other side. The extremely rapid rate of fire made the tracers blend into an unbroken stream of fire stretching between the plane and the ground, and the overlapping reports of the guns would meld into an eerie burping, tearing, or farting sound. Rumor had it Puff could put one round in every square foot of a football field with just one pass. We could believe it.

Puff had been a frequent visitor that fall to the hills west of our compound. Always before, however, he had appeared at least two miles away and had seemed to work his way away from us. On this particular night, however, he suddenly appeared less than a mile to the southwest and actually seemed to be working toward us.

We were naïve enough to believe that the Marine who had spoken up was right. Puff must have had the location of all friendly units plotted.

24. Puff the Magic Dragon Comes to Call

Confirmed in that faith, we had not been practicing light discipline. We never did, actually, as the location of our compound was no secret (to our foe, at least), and Puff's flares had lit up the area like daylight anyway. Puff continued making passes, moving within a quarter mile of the compound, until the flares he had dropped burned out. With the area again plunged into darkness, Puff's location suddenly became a cause for concern. But no one felt any real anxiety until the next flare appeared. It burst forth over the hills on the eastern side of our compound, within only two or three hundred yards of our wire.

It occurred to me later—much later—that Puff might have had the location of the original Papa Three plotted. But had anyone told him we had moved?

We heard the buzz and cracking of bullets before we heard Puff's distinctive report. We instinctively dove for a long, four-foot-deep trench the Seabees, with their backhoe, had thrown in free of charge. No trench, of course, would have protected us from the hail of fire we took that night had Puff been directly overhead. But, fortunately, he opened fire from out on our flank. The fire was angled and somewhat masked by the facing bank of the trench. Still, it was a very near thing. As I crouched at the bottom of that hole, I could feel the impact of the rounds hitting within inches of my head and was stung by fragments of rock and dirt.

Trite as it sounds, I remember lying there as the rounds hit thinking this is it; this is just like in the movies. I was scared, but I also felt a perverse pride at being in real and imminent danger at long last. My elation was short-lived, however. It suddenly occurred to me we could be in serious trouble with Puff's next pass. Mercifully, I didn't have time to dwell on the thought. Nordberg suddenly appeared at the edge of the ditch caterwauling that he had been shot in the ass.

Where he had been when Puff opened fire I don't know. I tried to tell him to get in the ditch and get down before Puff came back, but he was hysterical by then and was soon rolling around on the ground clutching his punctured behind. When he rolled over close to the edge, Reaves and I saw our chance. I grabbed him by the collar, Reaves caught an ankle, and we both yanked. Nordberg came tumbling in, landing squarely on his backside. His screams were pathetic, but he was at least as safe as the rest of us.

Fortunately, Mack Garrett had had the presence of mind to take a PRC-25 (a tactical radio) with him when he dove into the ditch. While we were catching Nordberg, he was getting through to our headquarters, and they managed to reach the fire support coordination center posthaste. Puff did not make a second pass. Instead, we heard the sound of his engines fading as Mack relayed to us the welcome news that Puff had gotten the word. Mack was destined to save the day once more before I left Papa Three. But to my knowledge, he was never recommended for so much as a Navy Achievement Medal.

In the immediate aftermath, we discovered that another Marine and two PFs had been wounded, one seriously. In Nordberg's case, the round had entered at the top of one buttock and exited at the bottom, just above the leg. Scotty, who had been asleep in our hooch at the time, had suffered a rude awakening, taking a round through the fleshy part of his thigh. One of the PFs had been shot through the forearm. The other had an exit wound the size of a half dollar in his abdomen just above and to the side of his navel. There was almost no blood, but I could see a loop of intestine protruding from the wound.

The medevac chopper was there in minutes. Nordberg made us carry him to it, along with the seriously wounded PF. The other PF walked aboard. Scotty walked, despite the round he had taken through the thigh.

No sooner had the chopper lifted off and the noise faded than a PF ran up to Sarge loudly proclaiming, "Nguy guyen chet!" (Nguy guyen, pronounced "neo-quin," meant government puppet soldier, the way PFs typically referred to themselves. Chet meant dead.) Leading us to a fighting hole out on the perimeter, this harbinger of death shined a flashlight on a figure slumped forward in a narrow hole, face against the dirt at the leading edge of the parapet. Of a morbid turn of mind, our guide pointed out that the thick black hair was even thicker with blood at the top near the crown of the head. Grabbing a shock of hair, he pulled the head back, illuminating the face. The bullet had exited below the nose, taking the upper lip and front teeth with it.

A dead PF, of course, did not rate a medevac. The PFs wrapped him in a poncho, and his relatives came and bore him away the next morning. I remember this sad delegation. It was soon after they left that we had the most bizarre confrontation we ever had with our PFs.

Since the reconstruction, we had been a house divided, physically as well as culturally. The PFs, in effect, had claimed one half of the compound and we the other. Combined action, in my experience at both Papa One and Papa Three, had never entailed complete integration. There had been a degree of segregation in the original Papa Three, with PFs claiming one strong-back hooch and bunker as their exclusive domain. But there had always been a healthy amount of interaction. Now we seemed to have an invisible boundary running through the middle of the compound, with emissaries from both sides making only occasional polite diplomatic forays across the border. On this particular morning, we were visited by a delegation of five or six PFs, who accused us of calling in Puff to get even with them.

We were initially dumbstruck at the accusation. Recovering somewhat, we tried to point out that two Marines had been wounded and all of us were placed in jeopardy, making their charge patently false and more than a little absurd. But in light of how much more heavily they had suffered, they refused to see our wounded as anything other than a miscalculation on our part. They could not, or would not, see their part in the incident for what it was, an unlucky accident of fate. Puff had fired from off their side of the compound, making for a steeper and more dangerous angle of fire on their side than ours—as evidenced by the PF killed in his fighting hole. We tried to show them what had happened by scratching diagrams in the dirt, but they seemed to remain skeptical. In the end, we asked them to trust us, assuring them that someone would be called to account for such a serious mistake.

As it turned out, no one came out to investigate, and we never heard a word officially. Nordberg and Scotty came back sufficiently healed about two weeks later, reporting that the pilot and copilot had visited them in the hospital and apologized, explaining how difficult it is to know exactly where you are in the air over Vietnam at night. To my knowledge, no one came out to apologize to the PFs or their families. But Nordberg and Scotty did receive Purple Hearts, which they said were officially listed as due to enemy artillery.

As I look back on it now, it seemed that I had always been at greater risk from our own side than the enemy.

25

Schism

It was shortly after Puff's visit that we received another delegation of PFs, this time headed by Trung-si Nguyen. He announced that, by order of their dai uy (captain), all PFs had to go out on an operation that would last about a week and that would exclude Marines. We should have seen it coming but didn't. Their "one-week" operation lasted nearly two weeks and would be followed by two more separate PF operations between early November and late December 1967.

Regardless of whether the PFs were out on a bona fide operation or not, I don't blame them for the next major event in Papa Three's sad saga. No one in particular was responsible; we were all responsible. It comes under the heading "Fortunes of War."

At some point in mid or late November—I don't recall exactly when—Sarge came back from a meeting in Cam Lo with some disturbing news. The captain was concerned that Papa Three had not made any significant contact with the enemy since the August attack on the compound. According to Sarge, the captain's orders were to become more aggressive. He wanted us to go so far as to "set a pattern on our patrols," if that's what it would take to lure the enemy into attacking us.

Our reaction was immediate and predictable: "Man, that's dumb; he just wants to get us killed," Heinie was heard to complain. But we complied, and after another uneventful week or so, we lapsed back into our old complacency.

Our captain, however, was no longer willing to leave us to our own devices. He sent us a new corporal. I don't remember his name. I do remember that he was arrogant and boastful. Within minutes of meeting him, we learned that he had had a lot of combat experience and that he had purposefully been sent to Papa Three to take charge and to get us on our game.

Of course, as a mere corporal, he couldn't displace Sarge, but within 15 or 20 minutes of his arrival he asked to meet with me and Sarge. The first thing out of his mouth was aimed at me: "What's your date of rank?" (I was the only corporal at that point. Sarge's Grand Rapids friend had rotated home.)

25. Schism

"October 1," I replied. "Mine's September 1. I'm senior. I'm taking your patrol team," he announced.

No doubt mindful of the pressure he was under, Sarge let him have his way. I suddenly found myself elevated to Sarge's assistant compound leader without much to do.

"Be careful what you ask for," as the old saying goes. To date, that brash young corporal stands as the best validation of that bit of conventional wisdom I've ever encountered.

26

Close Encounters of the Strange Kind

What I'm about to relate actually happened to me, although I've read about essentially the same experience in another Vietnam memoir. I suppose it concerns a kind of testimony that a number of soldiers and Marines in country were driven to give.

Just so that they could say they saw something of the war, I suppose, headquarters types—affectionately known as "Remington Raiders"—would often volunteer to ride along and help provide security for our supply truck as it made its rounds from compound to compound.

One day, a sergeant whom I had never met hopped off the truck as it was unloading and struck up a conversation with me.

"I'm short! I only have 33 days and a wake-up before I head back to 'The World,'" he bragged, while pulling his wallet out of his pocket.

Before I knew it, he was holding up for my inspection a wallet-sized black-and-white photo. "Look what I have waiting for me!"

The photo was a full-length view of an attractive, well-proportioned twenty-something woman standing totally nude in front of the camera. I remember that she had shoulder-length hair and a sort of Mona Lisa half smile. She had her hands on her hips so not as to obscure any of her charms.

"Wow! Nice," I said, or something to that effect. "You got that right!" he replied and climbed back onto the truck without another word.

Also, every now and then, a Marine from our headquarters would go out on patrol with us. One in particular stands out in my mind. I don't recall his rank, but he was personable and well-read. His father, he told me on one occasion, wrote for one of the leading television news personalities of that time. By way of bragging, he confessed that his father was always ragging him about his English. He also related that his father was a serious drinker. "I'll bet he spends $100 a week on booze. He says it helps him write."

On one occasion, this Marine was in a poetic frame of mind. It was

26. Close Encounters of the Strange Kind

dusk, and we were about to set out on a night ambush patrol, when he started reciting:

> Out of the night that covers me,
> Black as the Pit from pole to pole,
> I thank whatever gods may be
> For my unconquerable soul.

That much I had to look up and reconstruct years later. This much stuck with me:

> I am the master of my fate:
> I am the captain of my soul.

He had memorized and was reciting "Invictus" (1888) by William Ernest Henley. It may not have fit the occasion, but I was impressed and envious. I remember wishing I had a ready store of literature on which to draw.

I don't remember his name. I never saw him again. But, for me, at least, he validates the impression *Dispatches* author Michael Herr got of the soldiers and Marines he reported on: "The mix was so amazing; incipient saints and realized homicidals, unconscious lyric poets and mean dumb motherfuckers with their brains all down in their necks."

I met more than one of each during my time in Vietnam.

27

On Courage—Physical and Moral

To my mind, one of the true heroes of the Vietnam War died in 2006 without getting quite the recognition he deserved. He was Hugh Thompson, the Army helicopter pilot who rescued civilians from U.S. troops at My Lai.

Many of my fellow Vietnam veterans still have trouble coming to terms with the existential reality of the war we fought: It was a war that made anti-heroes rather than heroes in the traditional sense.

This is not to say that a lot of Marines and soldiers and sailors didn't do heroic things in Vietnam. They did, and they deserved the medals and the recognition they got. But the fact remains that they fought bravely and well on behalf of a dubious cause, and their heroism has to be viewed apart from the cause for which they fought.

One of the most celebrated heroes of the war, for instance, was a Marine officer who braved enemy fire to swing out, hand-over-hand, monkey-bar style, to plant explosives under the bridge at Dong Ha, halting the North Vietnamese advance during the Easter Offensive of 1972. It was an incredibly brave act, for which he was awarded a Navy Cross. Marines still argue that he should have gotten the Congressional Medal of Honor, and maybe he should have. But his heroism, ironically, helped prolong a war we were destined to lose anyway.

In all fairness, though, most of the heroes in Vietnam didn't view themselves as fighting for the cause. They were fighting for one another. For too many of us in Vietnam, survival became the only moral touchstone. As Vietnam novelist Larry Heinemann once phrased that existential ethic: "You cover me, and I'll cover you, and we'll all go home." The greatest heroes of the war were those few who, even in extremis, would not let go of the values and ideals that were supposed to have brought us to Vietnam in the first place.

Hugh Thompson was one of those heroes. Another one was the still unidentified soldier played by Michael J. Fox in the 1989 Brian De Palma film *Casualties of War*. He put himself at great risk by first trying to stop and later

27. On Courage—Physical and Moral

by reporting the brutal rape and murder of a Vietnamese girl. For doing the right thing, he still has to live under an assumed name.

In an interview with the *New Yorker*'s Daniel Lang, this anonymous hero remarked, "Just because we could die any minute, everybody is acting like what we do doesn't matter. I figured it was just the opposite." I imagine Thompson felt that way, too. What both men did required physical courage, but, more important, it required moral courage. In my experience, that was the kind of courage that was much harder to come by in Vietnam.

28

Winning Hearts and Minds

Just as I had been led to believe in my screening interview for the program, theft did indeed become a major problem and another area of division between Marines and PFs at Papa Three. It was one thing to pretend tolerance and sympathy during an interview, another to remain stoical or saint-like in suffering an actual loss. Most of us learned in very short order to safeguard major valuables. The real problem was a continual pattern of petty theft. Every morning we would awake to find that a few more barbed wire stakes or another roll of barbed wire had walked out of the compound overnight. C-rations practically had to be kept under guard 24 hours a day. But even more frustrating, things of only sentimental or purely personal value would disappear regularly.

I made the mistake one day of leaving an exposed roll of 35mm film unattended on the shelf over my rack. When I returned for it, less than an hour later, it was gone. In front of all the PFs there that day, I expressed my anger and did my best to explain that the film was of no value to anyone but me. Through pantomime and pidgin, I communicated that the film had already gone through my camera and therefore had no resale value. There was no reaction at the time, but I must have made my point. About a week later, after I had already despaired of ever getting my film back, a PF I knew by name approached me, offering to "souvenir" me a roll of film. It was, he explained, "number 10" that a PF or PFs unknown had stolen my film. He claimed that, wishing to make amends for his brethren, he had taken it upon himself to go to Dong Ha to buy me a new roll of film. I thanked him and accepted the film.

Noting that the leader had been wound into the cassette, indicating that it was probably already exposed, and noting that it was the type of film I had lost, I took a chance and sent it in for processing. It was my film.

This one incident stands out in my memory as perhaps the closest we ever came to winning anyone's heart or mind at Papa Three. We were told at CAP school that we would be able to interact with the Vietnamese people in ways the brutal French professionals, the legionnaires and the professional soldiers of elite paratrooper regiments, never could. We had rough edges, to be sure. But sooner or later, we were assured, the Vietnamese would warm to us. Our irresistible boyish charm, our irrepressible enthusiasm and disarming friendliness, would win them over eventually.

This, of course, was long before Lieutenant William Calley, U.S. Army, would disabuse us of such notions, creating in the popular mind, at least, a Vietnam where atrocities were both common and condoned. I know nothing of such a Vietnam. I can honestly write that, despite the admittedly lax supervision we operated under, I never witnessed anything remotely resembling an atrocity, nor even a single incident of abuse, during my tour with Papa Three. When it came to winning hearts and minds, however, I am certain we fared no better than the French. In fact, given the scale of our commitment, I suspect the Vietnamese liked us even less than they had the French.

We could read it in the studied indifference of the people as we passed, the way they ignored us even as we searched their houses and property; they considered us barbarians. Former Marine lieutenant Philip Caputo, in his Vietnam memoir *A Rumor of War*, first pointed out the historical irony of our conduct: We were those "bullying redcoats."

We couldn't even sell our civic action projects. At the insistence of our headquarters, we repeatedly asked the village chief what the village needed or wanted in the way of civic improvements. He would promise to think about it and get back to us, but never did. The only thing we ever did in the name of civic action was to present

An indication that the Combined Action Program was not well established in our area: I encountered these two brothers while on patrol with Papa Three in Cam Hieu. They were not used to seeing American Marines and were clearly afraid of me.

The teacher accepting the government-sponsored books we had forced on her. The accidental inclusion of the bayonet in the corner suggests her reluctance to accept the books.

the village school with new government-sponsored textbooks. But no one asked the schoolmistress whether or not she needed new textbooks. We simply showed up one day and delivered the books. The schoolmistress seemed reluctant to accept them at first. She did in the end, but she was less than profuse in her thanks. Later, it occurred to me that we may have put her in an awkward position with the local VC infrastructure.

Likewise, we never had any great call for our medical services. Occasionally, a mother would come by seeking help for a child suffering from cellulitis or some other infection. Children sometimes came on their own initiative. Once, a middle-aged man came in with a festering bullet wound through his hand. When he could present no satisfactory explanation for the wound, we turned him over to our headquarters for questioning. But, in general, most of the people who lived in the vicinity of Papa Three didn't want anything we had to offer.

I remember in particular an especially revealing conversation we once had with our PFs on the topic of why we were there. They were amazed and somewhat skeptical to hear that we weren't happy to be in Vietnam. They simply assumed combat was what we lived for. Why else would we seem so eager to prosecute a war they had long since learned to live with? It was evident they had made their accommodations with the other side. The practical effect of this arrangement was to place the other side of the river off limits. I

28. Winning Hearts and Minds

The village teacher after receiving the government-sponsored books we had brought. Her expression suggests that we had put her in a difficult position. The children too appear to be apprehensive.

Doc, our corpsman, treating a village child brought to him by his mother, as Reaves looks on.

judged our PFs harshly at the time. We all did. But I have since tried to put myself in their place. They stayed in our compound under our protection only every third night. They and their families were otherwise on their own and vulnerable. To their minds, I would imagine, we were not capable of toppling the existing order, only of bringing a part of it down on their heads. Consequently, I believed our PFs were always looking for ways to distance themselves publicly from us and our cause.

29

Boys Will Be Boys—
American and Vietnamese

This chapter could also be titled "Sex and the Single Marine—Unmarried or Geographically Single." The epigraph I would choose for it can be found in Tim O'Brien's *The Things They Carried*: "The average age in our platoon, I'd guess, was nineteen or twenty, and as a consequence, things often took on a curiously playful atmosphere, like a sporting event at some exotic reform school."

As I look back over my six months in CAP, I am struck by the irony that I never knew a Vietnamese person—not really. I knew five or six PFs by name and they me. But they were superficial acquaintances at best, not friendships. I could blame the language barrier, of course, none of us speaking more than a few handy phrases of Vietnamese, and they knowing only the usual French-English pidgin. But anyone who has ever been in such a situation knows that, with a little ingenuity, you can communicate amazingly well using little more than such all-purpose adjectives as beaucoup or petit and "number one" or "number 10." A little pantomime and a few universal gestures round out the process. In our early days, at least, and even continuing up to the strain of the reconstruction period, we managed to communicate well enough to engage in horseplay and mutual ribbing—always a good sign that the situation was perhaps not irretrievable.

I remember in particular one attempt to share with our PFs our view of the best in American culture, a newly arrived issue of *Playboy*. (We were interested mainly in the feature articles, of course.) The centerfold that month was especially buxom, and we signaled our appreciation in the standard manner, labeling her "number one." The PFs disagreed vehemently, however, denouncing the pride of American womanhood as "number 10." "Same-same water buffalo," one of their number explained, and a lively debate ensued on the relative merits of Vietnamese versus American women.

The sexual mores of the traditional Vietnamese are, of course, prudish and even puritanical compared to ours. But there seemed to be no harm in exploring our mutual feelings about sex so long as the topic remained abstract. It was when the issue became particular and pressing that we had problems.

Much of the goodwill we managed to build up through horseplay or drinking coffee together in the evenings was more than offset by such seemingly innocuous acts as greeting young girls with a familiar "Chao Co" (Hello, miss) as we passed on a trail. We had been told back at CAP school that this was definitely a faux pas, the Vietnamese considering it virtually an assault on a maiden's honor to address her so familiarly before being properly introduced. But we either forgot or didn't care. Young American men at that time were incorrigible in certain areas, and the PFs never failed to become visibly agitated and upset each time it occurred. Realizing this, I suspect, more than one Papa Three Marine continued to greet young women just to get a rise out of the PFs.

On the other hand, we never failed to become visibly agitated and upset each time we found our PFs engaged in what we considered homosexual conduct. Our CAP school instructors, as I mentioned before, had tried to prepare us for this aspect of Vietnamese culture. But it would be another 10 years at least before America would come out of the closet on homosexuality, and to a man, we couldn't transcend the prejudices and double standards of our culture.

We could understand in principle why a society that so rigidly prescribed and regulated the relations between the sexes, including an absolute ban against premarital and extramarital heterosexual relations, would condone mutual masturbation. Most of us were even large enough to feel that whatever two consenting PFs did on their own time was their business. It was when we caught them doing it on guard duty that we had a problem with this practice. Echoing Swift's immortal Gulliver, "Strange effect of ill breeding and narrow principles," some may charge. But we just couldn't see how the participants could remain vigilant while caught up in the business at hand. To make matters worse, the PFs caught in such a compromising position didn't seem in the least embarrassed. To my knowledge, no Marine ever became the object of such advances. Ironically, some would point to that as evidence we never found acceptance among our PFs. But, as we were well aware, one can expect an average group of young Marines to go only so far above and beyond the call of duty, not to mention the Uniform Code of Military Justice.

And, then, there was the problem of prostitution. Vietnam's practitioners of the world's oldest profession were commonly referred to as "boom-boom" girls. I have been told that the term derives from the Vietnamese word for "butterfly"; the idea was that these girls flit from customer to customer just as a butterfly flits from flower to flower. The reality, however, was not nearly so romantic.

If films such as *Pretty Woman* and television sitcoms such as "Two and

29. Boys Will Be Boys—American and Vietnamese

a Half Men" are to be believed, today's high-price prostitutes specialize in the "girlfriend experience." They will pretend to be making love, and all that implies, and will even pretend to be enjoying the experience. That's not what Vietnam's boom-boom girls, circa 1967, offered. They offered two categories of service, "short time" and "long time," each priced accordingly. The only difference lay in the number of ejaculations they would facilitate. In either case, it was copulation devoid of foreplay—not even kissing. It was perfunctory and impersonal, with the girl taking no more active role than presenting her vagina—after collecting her fee, of course. And the experience certainly belied the usual come-on: "You beaucoup handsome. I love you longtime."

They were certainly enterprising. We had to give them that. The kind of trolling I described above typically happened in the towns and cities. It couldn't happen in a traditional village, such as we were in. But they knew when payday was, and we could always count on one to take the bus from Dong Ha and to arrive soon after pay call.

The going rate at the time was $10. That price was the result of the runaway inflation the great influx of American troops had caused. "I used to be able to get it for $5," one of the old salts who had been in country nine or 10 months was heard to complain. But we didn't have much else to spend our money on, and since a boom-boom girl had gone to all the trouble of traveling out to us…

Confession being good for the soul, I have to admit that most of us partook—as many as 12 of us on at least one occasion. A sandbag bunker became the girl's boudoir, a poncho on the hard ground her bed. We would put our names in a hat and go in whatever order our names were called. One Marine, who shall remain nameless, had phenomenal bad luck. He placed last two months in a row. "Ah, come on, guys. This just ain't right!" He would complain, but no one would trade with him.

With the festivities concluded, we would have to walk the girl down to the road and wait with her for the bus. Otherwise, our PFs would steal her money.

Eventually, we paid a price for our adolescent concupiscence and recklessness—and not just in monetary terms. We didn't have condoms, and we paid no attention to the wild and crazy rumors about an incurable venereal disease that could get you permanently quarantined on a remote island somewhere. And the VD strains we knew about back then were curable. Add to the mix that sense of invulnerability young men are famous for: "Ah, that only happens to the other guy!" Five of us soon found ourselves disabused of that misplaced confidence.

About a week after our third or fourth payday visit, five of us came down with the stinging urination and pus-like discharge symptomatic of gonorrhea. Our corpsman offered us a Hobson's choice: "I can send you guys to

Delta Med in Dong Ha, but it will go on your record that you've had VD. Or, I can treat you. I have penicillin, and a few shots should do it."

Worse than the prospect of having a VD entry in my health record was the thought of taking a doctor's time and attention from the wounded. As I've already related, it was that consideration that had induced me to allow the corpsman back at Papa One to put five stitches in my head without benefit of anesthetic. Also, a few shots of penicillin in the rear wouldn't be so bad, I reasoned, whether administered by our corpsman or one at Delta Med. I was wrong about that one.

"There is a catch," Doc mentioned. (There was always a catch.) "I only have potassium penicillin, and it does sting a bit."

Again, that seemed the lesser of the evils, so we all went for it. Doc wasn't lying; he was understating. I can still see us hopping around, holding our buttocks, for 10 or 15 seconds after each injection. Served us right, I suppose. But it worked. We were all cured. And that boom-boom girl lost our business from that point forward.

30

The R&R Experience

One of the great regrets of my Vietnam experience is that I never went on "R&R"—short for "rest and relaxation." Every serviceman and woman (and there were very few women in country in 1967) was entitled to at least one week-long break from the war at an approved R&R destination. The possible destinations I remember were Okinawa, Japan, the Philippines, Thailand (Bangkok), Malaysia (Kuala Lumpur), Hong Kong, Hawaii, and Australia. Hawaii was especially popular among married men, as their wives could get there. Bangkok, for reasons I'll relate, was the hands-down favorite among single men or married men who were not too seriously married.

Australia had just opened up as an R&R location during my tour, and that's where I really wanted to go. But it never seemed to open up; rumor had it that Australia was limited to officers. Before I left 3rd Engineers, I finally relented and put in for R&R in the Philippines. I did that because a Marine I had known at Camp Lejeune had been assigned to the Marine Barracks at Subic Bay. I'll call him Don. I wrote to Don, and he responded, offering to show me around.

Before I could take that scheduled R&R, however, I was transferred to CAP, and my orders couldn't go with me. By the time I was eligible in CAP, I was reasonably short. I decided just to tough it out and to live vicariously through the accounts of those returning from R&R.

Among the troops, "R&R" had been relabeled as "I&I"—short for "intercourse and intoxication." And the most popular destination for that, bar none, was Bangkok, Thailand. Reportedly, all you had to do was to go into virtually any bar, where you would find 10 or 12 girls in various stages of dress and undress. You could then see the barman to rent whichever one appealed to you, for the day or the entire week. The rates were quite reasonable—or so I was told.

The wonder of it was that every Marine who went to Bangkok seemed to have had the same exceptional experience. I heard essentially this same story at least three times: "My girl was brand new in the business. She didn't want to do it, but she had to in order to help support her family. I was her first customer, and she fell in love with me. She still writes me letters."

The cynic in me assumed that the girl was writing with a number of possible outcomes in mind: If the Marine got a second R&R in Bangkok, he might hire her again. Perhaps he would become so smitten with her that he would marry her and take her home to the "Land of the Big PX." And if he got killed, there could be a consolation prize. Maybe he had been so foolish as to name the girl the beneficiary of his G.I. insurance. It paid $10,000—a lot of money at the time.

To be sure, some of those girls left their customers with a going-away gift they hadn't counted on. How many, I don't know. But Bangkok was commonly referred to as "Bang-Clap" during my time in country.

As for me and my aborted R&R trip to the Philippines, chalk it up to the thoughtlessness of youth, but I never thought to write Don to tell him that I wouldn't be coming. I ran into him again when I was back at Camp Lejeune. He assumed I had been killed.

31

The Fire Next Time—
December 4, 1967

There is a literary device, often employed in romantic literature, called the pathetic fallacy. The works that employ this device are fallacious in that they humor our egocentric expectation that nature should mirror our moods and respond sympathetically to our predicaments. A dastardly deed, in other words, should take place on a "dark and stormy night."

On the other hand, there are stories that employ an extreme form of realism termed naturalism. Such works illustrate how, in reality, nature is supremely indifferent to us and our problems. "Deal with it!" is what these works tell us.

But I didn't know much about literature on December 4, 1967. That would come later, when I went to college.

I remember that the day dawned sunny and bright. Ever since that brutal, but short-lived preview of the things to come earlier that fall—the typhoon that led to the flood—we had enjoyed a largely unbroken spell of good weather. The clouds were beginning to build dramatically, a promise of the impending monsoon. But, for the time being, the sun was shining, and by South Vietnam's standards, it was actually cool and balmy.

There had been warning signs, however. No matter what time of day we came through the village on the northern side of the river, it seemed strangely deserted, although people clearly lived there. The odd person we would encounter—usually an old man or woman, rarely a man of military age—would hurriedly pass by, eyes fixed firmly on the ground. Still, nothing had ever happened there.

Of course, our PFs had tried to warn us. As I recounted earlier, when they first refused to cross the river, the leader of that little sit-down strike had said, "Beaucoup VC." Still, without PFs, we had patrolled the northern side of the river several times since then—and if there were "beaucoup VC" over there, we hadn't found them.

As I recounted earlier, however, our CO was determined that we would find them. Talk about setting a pattern: He ordered not only that we continue to run the same patrol but that we leave at the same time, that we cross the river in the same place, and take breaks in the same places.

Over the years, I had forgotten—or repressed—the role I had played in launching the patrol that morning. Sarge remembers that he had charged me with planning the patrol and that he had approved my plan. Ron Parks recalls that I actually got the patrol organized before they set out.

As Parks remembers it, I was concerned that the new corporal didn't know the area. I believe it was his very first Papa Three patrol. I suggested that he may want to allow someone else to lead. Reaves, however, had run that same patrol before, and he volunteered to go along to help guide the new corporal.

Again, as Parks remembers it, Reaves was short by that time and, because his rotation was imminent, he hadn't been going out on patrol for the previous two weeks. Parks also remembers me talking Reaves into going. I very much doubt that was the case. But I probably did acquiesce in his decision to go along. I wish I hadn't.

This time around, faithful to the CO's charge, the new patrol leader was intent on running the same patrol we'd run several times through that northern village without incident. The plan was to cross the river and to skirt along the perimeter of the village, turning south at the northeastern edge, proceeding back toward the river. Just as we'd always done, the patrol would use well-worn paths for the entire route. Using established paths was always considered one of the "no no's" of patrolling, but again, the idea was to antagonize and tempt the enemy into making their presence known.

The PFs were out on one of their "operations," and one member of the patrol team had gone to sickbay. That left the new team leader, Reaves, Heinie, and Yost. The team leader approached Mack, who agreed to join the patrol as long as he didn't have to carry the radio. Yost volunteered to do it.

As the patrol entered the village, Mack was struck by how quiet it seemed. Not even the birds and crickets were stirring. This time, there were people around. But, as Mack would later realize, there was an air of expectation. People were gathered by their houses, holding back their children and dogs, "like sprinters in their starting blocks."

There was one particular house, set off by itself, along the path at that far northeastern corner of the village where we had stopped before for a break. A dense hedgerow ran along the trail back toward the river but cut in at this house, surrounding it on all four sides, with an opening only on the side facing the trail. The side opposite the hedge opening must have been the front. Two large wall sections on that side were propped open with poles and served as the doors.

As the patrol approached, they noticed that an old woman was standing

31. The Fire Next Time—December 4, 1967

out front chaffing rice. The new team leader told Mack to ask for her I.D. card, which she immediately pulled out of her pocket.

"Hey! I don't like this!" Mack said. "These villagers don't usually carry their I.D. cards with them when they're just out in front of their own houses."

"Okay. We'll search this house," the team leader replied. "Reaves, you and I will keep watch out front. Mack, Heinie, Yost—you three go in and see what you can find."

After a few minutes of rummaging through the house, Heinie yelled, "There's nothing here!"

"All right. Quick smoke and water break!" the team leader declared.

Reaves remained standing near the front of the house, serving as a lookout. The new team leader and Yost sat down in the middle of the house. Heinie and Mack sat down on a low table near the left rear center of the house. As luck would have it, between the front legs of that table was a row of sandbags filled with rice about three tiers high. Near the table, there was also a bunker of the sort most villagers constructed in hopes of staying out of the way of the war. It was dug about two feet below the floor, with about a foot of earth piled up around the edges. It measured only about two-feet by three feet—just large enough for one person. That old woman was probably the only one left living there.

Looking up and staring through the holes in the loosely thatched roof, Mack noticed a pigeon landing just above his head.

"I'll bet I could put a round right up that pigeon's ass," Mack boasted, raising his M16. If he was serious about that, he never got the chance.

In the aftermath, just as Mack was considering bagging a pigeon, Heinie would claim to have seen the old woman running down the trail. "She knew what was up. I wish I had shot her," Heinie later said.

It must have been what's called a "hasty ambush," not one that was planned out and set up in advance. Just as the patrol went inside the house for its break, the enemy sneaked up behind the hedgerow along the left (the south) side of the house.

The initial burst of fire caught everyone by surprise. Whether Reaves saw the enemy before they opened fire, we'll never know. He was hit first, in the torso. The new team leader reached out to grab and pull Reaves inside, taking a round in his own thigh for his trouble.

Heinie and Mack dove for that one-person bunker. Heinie managed to get in first. Yost hit the deck under the table and behind the row of rice-filled sandbags. Mack settled for whatever cover he could get behind Yost. The new team leader was out in the open, lying prone to the right of the table. Reaves ended up flat on his back against the north wall of the house.

Yost was frantically trying to get through on the radio and having no luck.

"Let me try," Mack hollered. Heinie, remembering Mack's success in calling off Puff, shouted, "Let Mack do it!" Crawling over to Yost, Mack replaced the short antenna with the longer whip antenna and got through to "Grasshopper," our "upcom" air support unit. "Grasshopper Six," the CO himself answered. "Tiger Papa Three, what's going on?"

"We're pinned down in a house taking fire, and we have wounded. We need some help out here."

"Switch to frequency … and give 'Birddog' [a spotter plane] your coordinates. Help's on the way!"

Mack gave the spotter plane pilot the coordinates, and within a minute or two, he was on station and had marked their location with white smoke. Two helicopter gunships followed close behind.

In the meanwhile, the new team leader, lacking adequate cover, caught another round—this time in the groin and exiting from his right buttock. He was obviously in a lot of pain and unable to continue returning fire. Mack crawled over and stuffed his battle dressing into the gaping exit wound. "I'm sorry. That's all I can do for you," Mack said before crawling back behind Yost and continuing to return fire.

Early on, Heinie would later claim, he hollered over to Reaves to ask if he was all right. "I'm okay, but my hand is busted," Heinie said he replied. He must have caught another round through his hand. Maybe he was in shock and didn't realize he had sustained a much more serious wound.

With the arrival of the gunships, the enemy's hasty ambush instantly turned into a rout with the attackers scattering in all directions.

It was amazing to watch the gunships do their thing. They took turns performing a deadly aerial ballet. The first one came in firing rockets into the area behind the hedgerow before breaking off in a steep climb and turning back in a steeper bank than any of us thought a helicopter could do. While the first chopper was going around, the second one would swoop in on its attack run, firing rockets. They repeated the cycle several times. All the while, the door gunners were seizing every opportunity to fire on the fleeing VC.

Listening to the cool, collected professional banter on the radio between the pilots was equally impressive.

"There's one running on the dike to the west."

"Okay. Got him!"

Would that the gunships had arrived 15 or 30 seconds earlier. As the enemy was scattering, Heinie hollered back to the new team leader: "How's Reaves?" "He's dead, man!" the new team leader replied. Just before the enemy broke off contact, as the medevac chopper was radioing in, asking for the number and types of casualties, Reaves had caught a round through the head.

Mack too caught one of the last rounds fired—in his foot, costing him the tip of a toe.

31. The Fire Next Time—December 4, 1967

Meanwhile back at Papa Three.... Only four men had been left back in the compound when the patrol set out that morning—Sarge, Mike Fink, Ron Parks, and a Marine whose name I can't recall. I'll call him Harper. Much of what follows I owe to Ron Parks, who filled me in on this part.

Ron was monitoring the radio that morning when a call came in indicating that Reaves should pack his gear. A chopper was on its way to pick him up; he would be heading home. Knowing that Reaves was then on patrol on the other side of the river, Parks wasn't sure what to do.

About five minutes later, Parks heard the firing across the river followed by a radio call from the patrol reporting that they had been ambushed and were taking heavy fire.

Fink, Harper, and Parks threw on their gear and set out running toward the ambush. Sarge stayed back to monitor the radio.

Crossing the Song Cam Lo was always a dicey proposition, but especially on this day, when a firefight was taking place only a few hundred yards from the northern bank of the river. If the enemy had set out a rear-security element, Parks realized, they were heading out on a "suicide mission." One volley of automatic fire and all three members of their ad hoc reaction force would never have made it across the river. But, much to their relief, they got safely across.

They landed at the edge of the village next to a trail that led to the backside of the ambush site. A helicopter was already on station, the door gunner firing steadily into the hedgerow where the enemy had set up. Parks, Fink, and Harper ran up the trail toward the ambush, hoping to catch any VC fleeing the firing from the chopper.

Encountering some houses on the way, Parks decided that they should search for any VC who might be hiding in the bunkers all Vietnamese families had. They demanded that the families come out, and one Marine would hold them at gunpoint while the other two would search the next house and bunker. They moved on this leap-frog method until they got to the last house before the ambush site.

By this time, as Parks remembers it, a helicopter gunship was firing rockets, door gunners were firing steadily, and women and children were crying. At that last house, after pulling the people out of the bunker, Parks thought he saw someone still hiding inside. He pulled the pin on a grenade. That set the women to wailing and to begging him not to throw the grenade. As Parks remembers that scene: "Not sure what to do, I looked up and Mike and Harper were gone. There I was, standing around about a dozen Vietnamese with a grenade in my hand and with enemy and friendly fire going on all around me. I just was not sure there were no women or children in the bunker, and I could not force myself to throw the grenade as much as I believed the VC were there." Parks replaced the pin in the grenade and ran to catch up with Fink and Harper.

Coming around a corner, Parks saw a small one-engine spotter plane flying over and marking the ambush area, and the area where Fink and Harper were, with smoke bombs. When this pilot/aerial observer ran out of smoke bombs, he started flying over shooting at VC with his .45. He was flying so low that Parks could have thrown a rock and hit him.

Through the smoke, Parks saw that Fink was lying on a Vietnamese grave mound, using it for cover. Parks did likewise, claiming a grave mound about 75 yards behind Fink. Harper was to his right on a small hill. The ambush was to the left of Parks—at 10 o'clock and about 150 yards away.

Gathering his wits about him, Parks noticed that a VC was crawling through a rice paddy, behind a dike that rose only about a foot above the water level. Parks immediately began firing at him. He hunkered down in the mud and the muck, with only his helmet showing above the dike. At the same time, a chopper gunner was firing at some VC out beyond Fink's position.

After about a dozen tries, Parks was certain he had hit him. "Like deer hunting, you just know" is how Parks put it.

Parks then turned his attention back toward Fink. In the confusion, Parks realized, the door gunner was firing right at Fink. At that very moment, he noticed that a VC was coming around the burial mound toward Fink. The door gunner was obviously trying to get that VC, but he was firing danger-close to Fink and had actually hit him in the elbow.

The VC tried to come out from behind the mound three or four times, with Parks just missing him each time. Parks was firing over Fink's shoulder, with the door gunner continuing to fire short bursts. Parks realized that he had to get that VC before he or the door gunner killed Fink. Timing the door gunner's bursts, after the third, Parks got up and started running toward Fink and the VC. Again, as Parks remembers it: "At first I heard four or five rounds go by close to me and then it was just quiet. It seemed all [time] stopped almost. The water was about knee deep and the mud came up over the ankles about hallway up the calf. I could only hear the gunner. He was doing just what I hoped he would. He wasn't firing in bursts any longer. He was letting it go while I ran so as to cover me. God, thank you! God, thank you! How many times have I prayed like this? Under fire! Church can be anywhere, I learned in 'Nam. And any time. Running with all that gear and through that muddy rice paddy like a halfback was not an easy task. Running through deep mud! I thought I would never get there. It really did seem half an eternity as I look at it now, but at the time it seemed like, and was, all eternity."

Seeing Parks approaching the burial mound, the VC immediately threw down his AK47 and put his hands up. Keeping his prisoner in front of him, Parks moved toward the VC he believed he had shot. He found him floating face up. Seeing no rifle and no blood, Parks' first thought was that the VC could be faking. As a deer hunter, he had learned never to walk up on an an-

31. The Fire Next Time—December 4, 1967

imal he had shot without first checking to make sure it was dead. As he was pondering what to do, Harper walked up with another prisoner.

Harper told him that Fink had been shot through the elbow and that he was lying on a burial mound with a grenade in each hand. His M16 had jammed. Telling Harper to guard both VC, Parks proceeded to check on the one he had shot.

He approached slowly and nudged the body with his rifle, checking the area around him to ensure that there were no booby traps. He noticed a small mark in front of the ear on one side before rolling him over. That's when he knew that this VC was unequivocally, irrevocably dead. The exit wound opened up about a third of his head, exposing his brain.

The next thing Parks remembers is seeing the two patrol members who had not been wounded in the ambush, Heine and Yost, walking along the rice paddy dike toward him. (Only later did Yost realize that a bullet had creased his left ear.) They were obviously shaken by what they'd been through and announced their intention to kill the two POWs.

Parks understood that that couldn't happen. They were wearing what he took to be NVA uniforms, and he explained that they could yield valuable intelligence about the enemy's organization and activities in the village, perhaps enabling us to root them out once and for all. Still, Heine and Yost were adamant. But so was Parks. He told Heine and Yost that they would have to kill him first if they were going to kill the prisoners. That defused the situation.

The two main-force VC prisoners taken on December 4, 1967.

Concerned that he had not found the dead VC's weapon, Parks asked Heine to search the paddy while he helped guard the prisoners. Heine found it. It was an AK47 with a 30-round magazine, and it was caked with mud. Heine picked it up and fired all 30 rounds without a stoppage. It was, Parks reports, a "sickening" site, knowing that Fink had been wounded while his rifle had been jammed.

Parks no longer remembers how they managed it, or who did it, but somehow they got the prisoners tied up and blindfolded and led them back to the Papa Three compound for interrogation by both our intelligence people and Vietnamese officials.

It had been too beautiful a day for people to fight and die. Something there is in human nature that just won't allow us to let go completely of that pathetic fallacy.

32

Confession Being Good for the Soul…

So where was I when all this was going on?
I was at the PX in Dong Ha.
There, I admitted it. Confession is indeed good for the soul—if not the reputation.

I was no longer a team leader; as I already related, the new corporal had demanded, and was given, my patrol team. I could have, I should have, I wish I had volunteered to join the day patrol that day as a snuffy—just another rifleman. But I didn't want to follow that new corporal's lead. It wasn't that I lacked confidence in him. Truth be told, I'm sure he was no more incompetent than I was. I just didn't want to give him the satisfaction. And, insofar as I knew, I really wasn't needed that day, either on patrol or back in the compound.

As the photos I've included might suggest, I've always been a frustrated photojournalist. Photography had been my passion ever since I was 12. That was the year my absentee father sent me an adjustable Edixa 35mm camera. A nice salesman at a camera store showed me how to use it, explaining the interplay between F-stops and shutter speeds as well as film speed. That same year, for Christmas, I received one of Kodak's elementary developing and contact printing kits, and I set up a darkroom in our basement.

Lincoln Camera, the best camera store in Wilmington, became my Mecca. It was there that I bought my chemicals and photo paper as well as my first decent enlarger for $50. I had to buy it on layaway and pay installments, but eventually it was mine. And I became fairly proficient in black-and-white developing and printing.

I became an avid reader of *Popular Photography, U.S. Camera,* and *Camera 35*. My grand ambition back then was to become a photojournalist like the ones celebrated in those magazines—men like Henri Cartier Bresson, Alfred Eisenstadt, and Robert Capa. In enlisting, I was hoping against hope that the Marine Corps would recognize my talent and potential and make me a combat photographer.

They didn't, of course. But I thought I would go on to a career in photography after the Corps. Hence, everywhere I went, a 35 mm camera went with me, and I tried to take advantage of every opportunity to add to what I hoped would become a portfolio of interesting photographs.

That was challenging, to say the least, in Vietnam. I fancied myself a black-and-white purist at the time. But black-and-white film was hard to come by in Vietnam, and decent processing and printing even harder. And there was the problem of how to store and care for prints and negatives in that humid, tropical climate.

But, as Shakespeare's Hamlet would say, "even in that was heaven ordinant." The PX at Dong Ha carried rolls of Kodachrome slide film complete with Kodak pre-paid processing mailers. I decided to document my Vietnam experiences with Kodachrome color slides. And, for once, I made a wise decision. Rather than worry about storing and protecting my slides in country, I addressed the mailers to my home address in Delaware. I never saw any of the color-slide photos I took in country, but they were there, waiting for me in perfect condition when I got home.

There were at least two other benefits I hadn't anticipated: First, don't believe what you may have heard in a popular song about Kodachrome. Ektachrome is famous for vivid, saturated colors. Kodachrome's color palette is subdued and realistic. Second, the dyes used in Kodachrome last. If stored properly, and not subjected to frequent projection, Kodachrome slides don't fade.

Most of my Vietnam slides are still in excellent condition despite having been processed 52 years ago (as of this writing).

December 4 found me on my last roll of film, so I asked Sarge if I could hitchhike into Dong Ha to buy some more. He agreed, and off to Dong Ha I went that morning. I don't think I tarried. On at least one of my trips to Dong Ha, I had to run for the shelter of a bunker. Dong Ha was in range of North Vietnamese artillery by late 1967. December 4 may or may not have been the occasion when the NVA was nice enough to treat me to an artillery barrage. I just don't remember.

But I do, of course, remember buying that Yashica 35mm camera from that Marine at Papa One. I wish I hadn't.

33

Innocents Abroad

In the aftermath, a squad of Marine intelligence-types and Vietnamese officials descended on us to interview the two prisoners. I helped guard them and later witnessed their interrogation conducted by an intelligence team that came out to our compound. Underneath a liberal coating of rice paddy mud, both prisoners were wearing plain khaki uniforms of a sort I found vaguely familiar but couldn't quite place at the time. It would be a day or two before I would make the connection. Under interrogation, one prisoner remained stoically silent, refusing to give even the proverbial name, rank, and serial number. The other wept and talked profusely.

They were main-force VC, members of a psychological operations company that shared our tactical area of responsibility and competed with us for

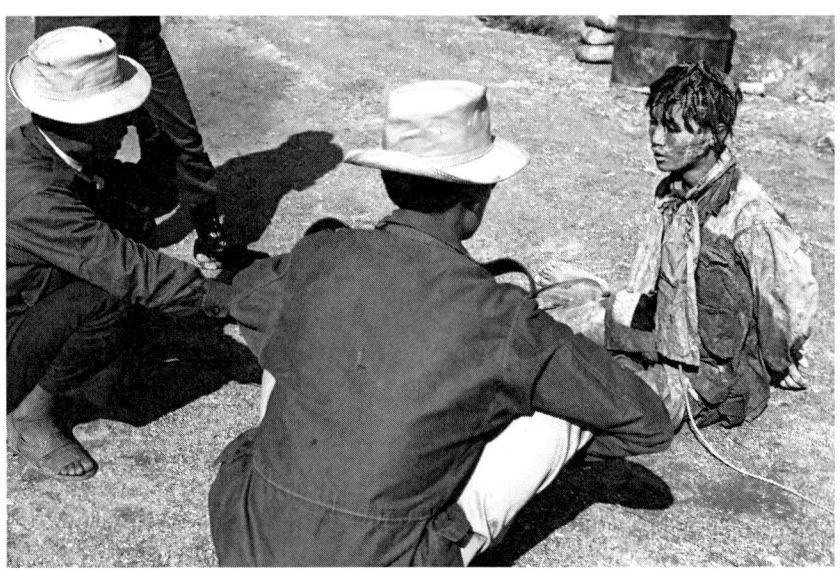

The cooperative VC prisoner being interrogated by South Vietnamese officials.

the hearts and minds of the people. Just as our PFs had us, this VC company had North Vietnamese advisers. Their modus operandi, however, was to disperse throughout the area, hiding in groups of two or three by day and regrouping at night. Hence, to a group of innocents abroad such as we were, they remained virtually invisible, often hiding in plain sight. That man dressed in khaki who had seemed so eager to help us search his house some weeks before had no doubt been one of their number. Interpreting such ineptitude as arrogance perhaps, the local VC reportedly had wanted to hit us for some time, but the NVA advisers had opposed it, arguing that the time was not right. By 4 December 1967, however, the locals had obviously won the debate, and it was thanks only to American air power that they didn't win the day—quite possibly with a shutout.

Yost after the ambush—holding a captured AK47 rifle and showing the bullet crease along his ear.

It was no thanks to our PFs, of course, that the patrol hadn't been wiped out. They were out on an "operation" at the time. But our bitterness at our supposed allies was eclipsed this time by a complaint nearer and dearer to our hearts. For the Marine Corps, at least, these were the early days of the M16, and true to form for that time, every rifle had jammed when it was needed the most. I remember Heinie in particular melodramatically throwing his M16 on the ground and denouncing it as a "piece of shit."

Ironically, through practical experience, some of us by that time had come to suspect what would later be confirmed through official inquiry. The principal cause of the problem was the ammunition. We had noticed that our M16s seemed to work fairly well with ammunition made by Remington, but would consistently fail to extract every third or fourth round with ammuni-

33. Innocents Abroad 137

tion made by other suppliers. Remington ammo wasn't always available, however, and a few Papa Three Marines were too skeptical of the M16 to believe the brand of ammo really could make a difference.

Heinie, for instance, had his father send him a .38-caliber pistol, and Reaves consistently volunteered to be the grenadier, carrying the M79 grenade launcher. Another Papa Three Marine would carry only a shotgun. They probably considered those of us who tried to load only with Remington rounds superstitious.

The fact remains that even this precaution wouldn't guarantee flawless operation. In 1967 all M16s occasionally failed to extract spent rounds and jammed. The enemy's AK47, on the other hand, may have been heavier and not nearly so aesthetically pleasing, but it was a marvel of reliability. I watched Heinie test fire an AK47 he had captured that day. One of the prisoners had had it with him in the rice paddy, and it was caked with mud. Heinie only made sure the chamber and barrel were unobstructed, otherwise firing it as is. It operated flawlessly, emptying a 30-round banana clip on full automatic without a stoppage.

As I've already related, later that afternoon, the company gunnery sergeant came up on the radio. He needed someone from Papa Three to go with him to identify Reaves's body. It was the least I could do. Everyone else had been through enough on that day.

The next day, another Marine and I helped Sarge inventory and pack up Reaves's gear. When we got to a Marine Corps ring recovered from the body, the other Marine—whom I remember well but won't name—spoke up, claiming that Reaves had said he wanted him to have this ring should anything ever happen to him. Sarge and I both realized it was a bald-faced lie. The two had never been close friends. But it was not a valuable ring, and I didn't think Reaves's family would want it under the circumstances. Sarge asked me what I thought. I said I thought it would be okay. (After all, I had broken up with that girl back home without thinking of trying to reclaim the ring I had given to her, my high-school ring.) But before handing over the ring, I stopped to take a good look at it. It was the standard model available in any PX—a gold alloy with a red stone and carving on the sides. There seemed to be something unusual about the carving, however. It appeared to have been done in some sort of rough red inlaid material. All at once, I realized what it was. Grabbing a canteen, I washed the blood off Reaves's ring, handed it to the man who had asked for it, and together we finished the inventory.

A week or so later, a disconcerting rumor reached us: The Vietnamese had allowed the two prisoners to escape. Whether that was true or not, I'll never know.

Years later, in 1982, when I was a Marine officer serving as a battalion adjutant, I had a young lieutenant as my assistant. He was from the South and happened to be an avid hunter who couldn't get over the fact that I had never been hunting in my life. I told him I grew up in the suburbs without a father, uncles, or friends who were hunters.

"Seriously, you've never gone hunting for anything?" he asked more than once.

"Well," I finally conceded, "in 1967, I did go hunting for Viet Cong, but that didn't go so well."

"Hey, whatever's in season," was his reply.

Viet Cong had long gone out of season by then.

The VC prisoner who remained stoical and silent.

34

A Way You'll Never Be

The best writer the Vietnam War wrought, Tim O'Brien, in *The Things They Carried*, reflects on the genre of war stories: "True war stories do not generalize," O'Brien writes. "They do not indulge in abstraction or analysis…. A true war story, if truly told, makes the stomach believe."

Here is a war story I heard while I was in Vietnam. At the time, it stood out as the funniest war story I ever heard.

A Marine in another unit was really angry to learn that the postal inspectors had opened a package of souvenirs he had sent home. So he decided to get a little payback. He packed an old sea bag halfway full of rags and put a grenade on top. He pulled the pin and carefully held down the spoon while he tightly packed more rags on top and closed the bag. Then he addressed it to his family and mailed it home.

What he didn't count on was that the postal inspectors couldn't open every package. This one made it home, and Mom shook the contents out onto the living room floor in front of the whole family—all of whom were promptly blown away.

Not so funny after all? Well, I guess you had to be there, with me and my squad in Vietnam—and that is my point. Hemingway had a phrase for it: "a way you'll never be."

In reality, this little war story probably never happened. But it sure rang true at that time and in that place. We really thought it was funny. Clearly, the things we had witnessed and the conditions we had endured had warped our sensibilities and embittered us—and, except for Sarge, none of us, at that point, had been in country more than nine months, nor were we facing the prospect of being sent back to Vietnam within a four-year enlistment. Is it any wonder that we are hearing so much about PTSD and suicides among today's troops, many of whom have endured two, three, four, or even more combat tours?

But even before the Department of Defense upped the ante, the Iraq war brought us Haditha. Readers may remember that a group of Marines were accused of killing at least 15 innocent civilians in that city after a bomb blast had killed one of their own. The case eventually fell apart for lack of evidence, but as I related earlier, I certainly understand how these things can happen.

The problem with the war in Afghanistan, I suspect, is the same as the basic problem with my war. When the commitment is not shared by the country at large, and the strategy and tactics no longer make sense, behavior has a way of becoming relative to the goal of personal survival. The constraints of civilized society, the old norms and moral absolutes, no longer seem to apply, especially when one cannot tell friend from foe.

It didn't surprise me, therefore, when I read that four Fort Lewis soldiers had been accused of killing innocent civilians. Admittedly, I only know what I read in the papers regarding what any of these soldiers did or didn't do. I trusted the military justice system to determine that. Nor do I have firsthand knowledge of their war. But I do know how and why a war can turn even a "good American kid" into someone his own mother wouldn't know.

35

Life Goes On

In the end, there was nothing to do but resume our routine. Probably the saddest thing about losing someone you have lived and worked closely with under such circumstances is how rapidly you adjust to the loss.

Those who haven't been there seem to find this aspect of the experience especially troubling or distasteful. I remember a bitter argument I had a couple of years later with a non–Vietnam veteran friend of mine over My Lai. He pronounced me "shallow" because I didn't agree that the casualties Calley's men had previously taken in the area somehow mitigated what they did at My Lai. That is posturing, not honest emotion. Never having experienced it, my friend couldn't grasp the sad truth and the existential ambivalence of the experience as reported on by Michael Herr in his book *Dispatches* and many others. A man feels many things when someone he is close to is killed in combat, but paramount among those feelings is generally relief that it wasn't him. We are just constituted that way.

There was one final scene to be played out between us and our PFs that December. Less than two weeks after we were ambushed, while Marines and PFs were still going their separate ways, the PFs were ambushed under circumstances very similar to ours. They managed to break off contact without air power, however, making their way back to our compound with one dying and two lightly wounded PFs.

After we evacuated their casualties, they shocked us with the announcement that they were going back out to settle the score with the VC. What is more, they asked us to come along. We couldn't quite believe this latest development. It was so out of character for our PFs that I am not sure I understand it yet. The VC must have broken a longstanding covenant, perhaps unfairly holding them responsible for what our helicopter gunships had done on December 4.

Whatever the motivation, our PFs seemed gung-ho at last, and many of us were thinking that we had perhaps given up too soon on combined action. Filled with renewed hope and confidence, we eagerly radioed for the required permission. After several minutes, the answer finally came: "Permission denied." I don't know why our commanding officer wouldn't allow us to go. Perhaps it was more than petty revenge at the way our PFs were treating us. Whatever the reason, I believe it was a mistake. We missed a golden opportunity to reestablish some semblance of solidarity, and I don't know when, if ever, a similar opportunity presented itself. I was short by then, and Marines and PFs were still going their separate ways when I rotated only a couple weeks later.

36

The Shape of Things to Come

My last days at Papa Three, in retrospect, now seem portentous.

On two consecutive nights in late December the compound was raked with short bursts of automatic fire from the general direction of the village. No one was hurt, but our attention was diverted—just long enough probably to move troops across Highway 9 west of our compound. A few nights later they repeated the process, this time firing a single rocket at us as well. I actually saw it take off from somewhere within the village. Fortunately, it overshot us, exploding harmlessly on a hill about 200 meters behind our compound. On another night, the bridge only about 200 meters east of us came under attack. Using our 60mm mortar, we fired illumination for the Army of the Republic of Vietnam (ARVN) platoon guarding the bridge, and it held. An ARVN lieutenant came over the next morning and thanked us all personally.

On Christmas day, because of the usual truce, we were forced to watch an NVA platoon brazenly cross an open area with impunity. They were less than 1,000 meters away, and Heinie, who had been practicing with our mortar, was just dying to reach out and touch someone.

Sarge radioed for permission to go after that NVA platoon, and we proceeded to get ready. Knowing I was "short"—that I would be rotating home soon—Sarge told me I didn't have to go. I was scared, but having missed the events of 4 December, I felt I had to go. Frankly, I was relieved when the answer came back: "Permission denied!" We were to stay in the compound. We were allowed to fire only if fired on that day.

Clearly, all these incidents now seem to portend the momentous Tet Offensive just around the corner. It was evident that something was coming, but none of us could have foreseen the scope of the coming offensive. It just didn't seem possible in late 1967 that the enemy could rise up in force and challenge us openly throughout most of South Vietnam.

And that brings up one of my longstanding criticisms of the Combined Action Program. If some CAP units, particularly those in the South, really won the confidence and support of the people, why didn't they turn up solid intelligence of what was to come? Villagers in or around CAP units, as well as PFs, had to have been aware that supplies were being stockpiled and that NVA troops had infiltrated and were hiding in their areas. We reported the harassing fire we took in late December. Perhaps other CAP units provided additional pieces of the puzzle, but those on high didn't fit the pieces together until it was too late.

37

Coming Home

By late December, I was "short—down to the single digits," as we used to say. I had my own interpretation of the harassing fire we had taken. The enemy had simply stepped up efforts to get me while they still had the chance. And I was beginning to suspect some complicity on the part of our headquarters by then.

It was the last day of December 1967, New Year's Eve. By my calculations, I should have been out of the field several days earlier when a radio call came in for another Papa Three Marine to pack up and catch the supply truck to Dong Ha. I knew I had been in country a couple of days longer than this guy, so I had Sarge get on the radio and ask about my orders. "Not in yet," came the discouraging word. We had all said our goodbyes, and the truck had come and gone, bearing away the lucky Marine, when we got another radio call. Someone had double-checked, discovering that my orders were in after all. If I could get to Dong Ha in time to catch a 1300 flight to Phu Bai, I could leave that day.

It was already 1000, but it didn't take me long to pack what I needed and to give away the rest. I was out on Highway 9 hitchhiking by 10:30. Ironically, Rodney, the man we had all denigrated as the "Reverend Mr. Black," was the only one to come down to the road to wait with me.

Within 10 minutes, a jeep stopped to pick me up, and suddenly Papa Three and six months of my life were receding behind me. I didn't know what I was heading toward. I was only 20 years old, and I had no definite plans or ambitions at the time. I had no one special waiting for me. As I related earlier, I had broken up with my first serious girlfriend soon after being assigned to CAP.

Of course, I was happy to be heading home—back to "The World," as we called it. But I wasn't as happy as I had imagined I would be, and I was surprised to find myself feeling strangely ambivalent at the prospect of actually leaving at long last. I think I realized even then that, wherever I was going and whatever I would do, very little of my subsequent life back in the States could ever match the intensity and poignancy of those six short months as a combined-action Marine.

Much has been written about the abrupt transition from combat to stateside suffered by many Vietnam veterans. A former Army helicopter pilot I know, for instance, found himself back in Miami walking his mother's dog only 24 hours after flying his last medevac mission in country. After all he had done and seen, he found it hard to fathom that he was suddenly, really safe at home. Such was not my experience.

I arrived at Phu Bai too late to turn in my gear and to make the last flight of the day to Da Nang. I flew out the next morning, New Year's Day.

After arriving at Da Nang, I learned that I had about 30 hours to kill before beginning the next leg in my journey back—a flight to Okinawa. I got to spend that night in a nice cinderblock barracks complete with indoor plumbing—the first I had enjoyed in 13 months. In the middle of that first night, however, the airbase got rocketed, and I got to spend a half hour in a muddy trench adjacent to our nice clean barracks.

Having no obligations the next day, I went to the new PX and recreation complex on Marble Mountain. I was amazed at how nice it was. The PX was larger than some I had seen in the states, and the movie theater was a well-appointed permanent structure with plush seats rivaling theaters back in the states. I saw the Dick Van Dyke film *Fitzwilly*. Van Dyke plays a highly educated and sophisticated butler who resorts to crime to support and keep his elderly employer from learning that she is no longer wealthy. It wasn't a great film, but it was a good way to kill a couple hours. After it was over, I treated myself to a cheeseburger, an order of French fries, and a Coke before heading back to the transient barracks.

The next afternoon, I found myself, along with a couple hundred other Marines, boarding a government-contract airliner—complete with "round-eye" stewardesses, as we unreconstructed male chauvinists used to refer to them back then. Next stop: Okinawa. I still remember how, as soon as we lifted off, the entire plane erupted in a resounding cheer!

I still have my original orders. One of the endorsements indicates that I reported to the transient facility on Okinawa at 0130 on 3 January. The main thing I needed to do was to pick up the Class A winter green uniform I had boxed up and turned in there 13 months before. Knowing Marines as I did, I half expected my box to be missing. But a supply clerk retrieved it right away, and everything was still in good shape. My one disappointment was that the PX had run out of Vietnam service ribbons. But I soon found that an enterprising Okinawan woman was selling the standard three-ribbon set—National Defense, Vietnam Service, and Vietnam Campaign—by the front gate.

From Okinawa, I flew directly to Norton Air Force Base, near San Bernardino, California. I'd been lucky compared to the Marines who had to go to and from Vietnam by ship or even by an Air Force plane. I got to go via government-contract civilian airliners both ways. On the way to Vietnam we

37. Coming Home

had had to stop for refueling in Hawaii and on Wake Island before stopping over in Okinawa. But our flight from Okinawa to the states was non-stop. I remember wondering why. Perhaps it was a bigger and better plane than the one that had taken me from Travis Air Force Base to Okinawa.

I was also fortunate to have a window seat. I was struck by the beauty of the California coast and the coastal range as we flew over them. It seemed somehow surreal that, after 13 months, I would soon be landing back in the United States. The announcement came to "put your tray tables up and your seats in their upright position for landing." There were no cheers when we touched down, only thoughtful silence. I suppose that, like me, everyone was reflecting back on where we'd been and what we'd done or failed to do, and above all, wondering what it all meant.

Again, an endorsement on my orders indicates that I reported to the Marine Liaison Section at Norton Air Force Base at 1430 on January 5. Thanks to the miracle of the Internet, I've learned that it was a Friday—still my favorite day of the week.

After picking up our luggage, we were ushered into a large hanger and told to line up, with our orders, before five or six tables, each manned by an enlisted Marine. The line moved quickly. When I got up to the table, the clerk stamped my orders, told me I was assigned to the 2nd Marine Division at Camp Lejeune and that I needed to report by midnight January 31. That was it. I was on my own.

Somehow, I don't recall how, I learned that there would be a bus leaving for the Los Angeles International Airport in a couple hours but that there were also cabs available. I went in with three other Marines on a cab. I think it cost us $15 each.

At LAX, I learned that there would be a direct flight to Philadelphia later that evening. In those days, you could fly military standby, in uniform, for half price. And the flights were seldom full in those glory days of federally regulated airlines. As I recall, half price was only about $70. I bought my military standby ticket, and I must have had a lot of time to kill there at LAX. I think I went to the airport's USO and read magazines and watched TV until it was time to board my flight.

I do remember that we landed in Philadelphia early in the morning on January 6.

The myth persists that Vietnam veterans were roundly spat upon in returning home. That myth lies behind what West Point professor Elizabeth Samet has termed our "mantra of atonement." It is our perceived obligation to make up for vilifying the troops in Vietnam by thanking any and all of today's troops for their service at every opportunity. And the myth of the spat-upon veteran is just that—a myth. Sociologist Jerry Lembcke, in his book *The Spitting Image* (1998), established that there is no documentary evidence, no news reports or film footage, of antiwar protesters spitting on returning veterans. This is not to say that it didn't happen in isolated cases, but it certainly was not widespread. To the contrary, there is documentary evidence of pro-war demonstrators spitting on antiwar demonstrators.

I know I wasn't spat upon. Far from it. I'd been sleeping when we landed, and I was feeling the effects of not enough sleep and too much traveling over the last 24 hours. I was also suffering from a bad attitude by then. I got off the plane with my uniform "blouse" (the coat) unbuttoned as well as my collar unbuttoned and my tie down.

These were still innocent times. Anyone, not just ticketed passengers, could go anywhere in an airport back then. As I was walking up the concourse, I noticed that a forty-something man had stepped out from an airport bar on the right. He seemed a bit buzzed, but not seriously drunk. He stuck out his hand and asked, "Are you coming back from Vietnam?"

I acknowledged that I was and shook his hand as he said, "Welcome home." But then he leaned in toward me, almost whispering in my ear, "But, you know, you are a Marine. How about buttoning up your blouse and cinching up your tie." I was in no mood for a confrontation. I did as he suggested and walked on. He didn't offer to buy me a drink. I suppose supporting our troops in early 1968 only went so far.

After picking up my luggage (a sea bag), I found a telephone and called home. My mother seemed genuinely happy to hear from me. Within 45 minutes my mother and her boyfriend Joe pulled up to the curb, and I was on the final leg of my journey home.

I remember that it was a typical gray winter day, weather that matched my mood as we drove home in silence. I felt strangely let down and more than a little ambivalent now that I was finally back. The character Michael in the film *The Deer Hunter* probably put it best. Like Michael, I was feeling "a lot of distance."

I also remember three dreams I had in those first days home.

In one of the dreams, we were under attack. An NVA soldier was charging toward me, and in a frantic effort to shoot him before he could shoot me, I raised my M16. But it suddenly seemed that an inordinate amount of strength was required to pull the trigger. Try as I might, I couldn't get my M16 to fire.

In the second dream, I would find myself saddling up with my M16 and all my combat gear, setting out on patrol from my mother's house in New Castle, Delaware.

In that third dream, I would be unpacking my sea bag only to discover that I had inadvertently brought home a live grenade. Not knowing what else to do, I went out to the field behind my mother's house, pulled the pin, and threw the grenade as far as I could. It was midday, with most people at work, so I had assumed that this was a good time to get rid of the grenade. But the

37. Coming Home

explosion was louder than I expected and rattled windows throughout the neighborhood. I was worried that someone would report it—and then I woke up.

I suppose you don't have to be an expert in the interpretation of dreams to know what those three dreams signified. I hadn't come home. Not really. And it would be some time before I did.

An enduring part of the legend and lore of my war holds that World War II veterans viewed us as wimps and whiners who had let America down by not winning. I'm sure that some members of that so-called "greatest generation" did feel that way, but I never met one. To the contrary, what stands out in my memory is the reaction of my Uncle Al—who had served in Italy during the war.

I'd only been back a couple of days when my mother invited the family over to welcome me home and prevailed upon me to show my slides. I dutifully set up my slide projector and screen and went through much of my collection, unedited. When I got to a slide of Reaves, I made the mistake of letting the family know that he had been killed.

"I can't see this goddamned war!" Uncle Al exclaimed. "Just kids killing kids."

I couldn't say he was wrong. I still can't.

38

Looking Back on Leaving

One of the few things my father and mother ever agreed upon was that her parents and her siblings were all "wonderful people." That's how my father described them when I visited him and his new family at K.I. Sawyer Air Force Base in the summer of 1966. Only in later life did I fully appreciate just how wonderful they were to me.

As I've already related, my grandmother Masarik tried to run interference for me with my mother, as did my Aunt Rose and her husband, my Uncle Bill. He was especially good to me. As I've also related, my Aunt Jo—who never had any children of her own—paid my tuition to Salesianum. Not trusting my mother, she would send the money to my cousin Doris, 10 years my senior, who would go to the school to pay my tuition in person.

Another measure of how good they were to me was how they reacted when they learned I was on my way to Vietnam.

My Uncle Jule (short for Julius)—who was an excellent marksman and a prize-winning competitive shooter—had heard from a friend that our military didn't give troops nearly enough live-fire practice with their weapons. Knowing I would soon be leaving for Vietnam, Uncle Jule and his friend insisted on taking me to the State Police shooting range, where they had me practice with a .45 pistol until they were satisfied that I was reasonably proficient. It would have been better to have gotten some practice with the M16, but they didn't have access to that weapon. Still. their hearts were in the right place.

Uncle Jule also took me to the "Polish Library," which may or may not have had a book or two. It was actually a private after-hours club in Hedgeville, a Polish neighborhood in Wilmington. I wasn't much of a beer drinker then, but I appreciated the time and attention.And then, the weekend before I was to leave for Vietnam, the whole family descended on me and my mother to say goodbye and to wish me well. The latter took the form of monetary gifts. As I recall, I wound up with at least $120. To this day, I love them for it. To this day, I'm still angry with myself for what I did with that money.

I gave most of it to my mother. "Are you sure?" she asked. But she obvi-

38. Looking Back on Leaving

ously had no qualms about taking it. I realize now that she didn't really need it. As it turned out, I did.

Silly me! Ever since that close call with getting back on time from that visit to my father at K.I. Sawyer Air Force Base, I had been neurotically determined not to overstay leave or liberty. Accordingly, I flew out a day earlier than I had to and found myself with over 24 hours to kill in San Francisco. I don't recall how much money I had kept for myself out of my family's largesse. I do remember that, after buying my bus ticket to Travis Air Force Base (where I was to board my flight to Vietnam), I barely had enough money left to eat dinner at a cheap chain steak house and to pay for a flophouse room with bathroom down the hall. I got to Travis in the late afternoon without having eaten all day. I found myself borrowing $5 from a Marine I barely knew so I could buy a barbecue sandwich at the snack bar.

I'm pleased to report that we got paid when we got to Okinawa, and I paid that Marine back. But it still galls me that I was stupid enough not to keep the money my family had given me and that my mother was selfish enough to take it.

39

A Siren's Spell

The club's DJ happened to be playing Frankie Valli's "Can't Take My Eyes Off of You." And indeed I couldn't when she said, "I want to have sex with you. Is there someplace we can go?"

To my everlasting regret, I missed the summer of love. I was in Vietnam for all of 1967, and I could only marvel at how sexual politics had changed in only 13 short months. This was only our second date.

Soon after arriving home, I had reconnected with my best friend in high school, whom I'll call Josh. Josh was a junior at the University of Delaware at the time, and he volunteered to set me up with a blind date.

I was one day short of my 21st birthday when we went on that date. I'm not a superstitious man, but perhaps I should have been on this occasion. It was January 13. But, in all fairness, it wasn't Friday the 13th. It was a Saturday.

The four of us—Josh and his date, me and the girl Josh set me up with—met at a movie theater in Newark. Josh introduced us. I found myself facing a small (5'2"), trim, and pretty young woman with short dark hair and brown eyes and glasses. I'll call her Amber. I can't say I was immediately smitten, but she impressed me as definitely a cut or two above Erin. And, even better, she fit the profile that Betty said I should aspire to—an intelligent college girl.

We saw Lee Marvin in *Point Blank*. The film was clearly ahead of its time. I've seen the film any number of times since then and have come to appreciate its challenging non-linear narrative and editing. At the time, I was mostly impressed with the tough-guy character Marvin played. He was relentless and brilliantly resourceful in getting even with the man who had double-crossed him and in getting the money he believed he was owed. For his part, Josh couldn't get over the fact that we'd been treated to a glimpse of Angie Dickinson in the nude. What was the big deal? I thought, despite having missed the summer of love.

We capped off the evening by going back to Josh's house. But, first, Josh thought we should stop at a liquor store and buy something with which to lubricate the evening. "None of us is 21 yet," I protested. Josh, however, was of the impression that there was a 24-hour grace period, and since I was within less than one day of my birthday, I would be good to go. The liquor store clerk didn't see it that way. After examining my driver's license, he said, "Come back tomorrow."

Of course, I got Amber's phone number and made a date with her for the following Friday night. I was definitely lacking in *savoir faire* in those days, and not knowing what else to do, I took her over the bridge to Pennsville, New Jersey, to a night club that was especially popular among young people back then.

Over whisky sours (I hadn't yet developed a taste for scotch or beer), and unbidden, she had just finished telling me what she thought I needed to know about her past. The first great love of her life had joined the Navy while she was still a senior in high school and, in the course of one of his weekend trips home, had impregnated her.

"I know exactly when it happened," she said, telling me more than I really wanted to know. "Just after he finished, I said, 'You didn't use anything this time, did you?'"

Buttressed by the Navy, he refused to take responsibility for what he'd done. She, in my estimation, did the right thing: She put the baby up for adoption. It was a girl. She only got to hold her briefly, and she claimed that leaving the hospital without her was the hardest thing she'd ever done or would ever have to do.

I wasn't put off by that. I wasn't looking to lay siege to another maidenhead. Thanks to Erin, I'd been there and done that. My one concern was that I would come off as inexperienced and unsophisticated in her eyes. I'd only had one lover. (Perfunctory couplings with a few Vietnamese prostitutes didn't count in my estimation.) I found Amber's lack of inhibition and apparent sophistication refreshing and took both as a promise of good things to come. Still, I was taken aback by her blunt proposition that we go somewhere and have sex.

She proceeded to tell me that the great thing about our generation was that we had freed ourselves from the Victorian inhibitions and the prudery of the past. We were "demystifying sex and declaring our right to enjoy it freely," she said. "I mean, if I like a guy," she went on, "why shouldn't I have sex with him?"

And, then, she really did say it: "For our generation, it's really just the next step up from shaking hands."

I can't say that I agreed with that analogy. I still thought sex should be meaningful and special, not an experience to be entered into lightly with "the proper stranger," as the title of a popular '60s film would have it.

On the other hand, part of my seduction strategy with Erin had been to convince her that sexual compatibility was crucial to a good marriage. The bad marriages among our parents' generation, I argued, could be traced to the fact that couples were naïve and overly idealistic. They had bought into the romantic ideal that Erin had been clinging to—that marriage is essentially a spiritual union and that only virginal women were marriage material. As a consequence, too many members of that so-called "greatest generation" really didn't get to know one another before marrying, especially in that all-important biblical sense. Sexual incompatibility, I believed, had led to many a miserable marriage. I still believe that, my ulterior motives in Erin's case notwithstanding.

"I'm on the pill," Amber reassured me. "So you don't have to worry. Where did you used to go parking when you were in high school?"

The question made me feel like a phony, a nerd in a cool guy's clothing. The fact is that I really didn't know of a good place. I knew that New Castle's Battery Park, where I had first taken Erin to the "submarine races," was heavily patrolled and not nearly private enough for what Amber had in mind. Erin and I had once made it on a dirt road below Thompson's Bridge, but that was too far away, and I wasn't sure I would remember how to get there. (The fact of the matter is that most of our serious coupling had occurred at my house, when my mother wasn't home. I wasn't about to admit to that uncool reality.) Amber and I ended up cruising around Collins Park until I found a reasonably secluded and dark spot next to a baseball diamond behind the ranch-house section.

I had misgivings about the spot not being private enough, but Amber was ready to go for it and reassured me that one of her requirements would make it somewhat safer.

"I need to be totally nude for this," she said, sliding down on the bench seat of my mother's Chevy II and beginning to strip off her clothes. "But you don't have to be. It's safer for the guy to keep most of his clothes on in a situation like this." True to her word, soon she was nude, except for her coat, which she draped over her shoulders and left unbuttoned.

"Also, you should know that I don't have to have an orgasm to enjoy sex. That's just icing on the cake. The act itself is pleasurable enough for me."

So having been duly instructed and reassured, I went for it.

By that time, I still had about 10 days left before I would have to report to Camp Lejeune, North Carolina. I'm sure we had sex a few more times over the span of those 10 days, but those liaisons seem to have faded from my memory. What I do remember is that finding a time and place was a strain. I think we did it once at her house when no one was home, and I'm sure we did it at least twice at my mother's house when she was at work. I know we did it enough. I was smitten.

I can't say I wasn't warned. It must have been the first time we went to my mother's house during the workday for a tryst. We were getting dressed,

39. A Siren's Spell

when the phone rang. It was Josh, the friend who had arranged the blind date with Amber.

"I'm glad I caught you at home, buddy," Josh began. "A friend just told me that Amber is bad news. Don't get involved with her. I'm sorry I didn't check her out before I fixed you up."

"What do you mean? How is she bad news, Josh?" I asked, with Amber next to me overhearing my end of the conversation. She moved next to me, placing her ear next to the receiver.

"My friend says she's pretty loose, man."

"Well, thanks, Josh, but it's a little late," I said, without expounding on why the warning had come too late. "I'm a big boy. Don't worry about it."

"Okay, buddy, but don't say I didn't warn you."

For my part, I put it down to the kind of prudery Josh had displayed at the theater in reaction to Angie Dickinson's nude scene. I was intent on showing Amber that I was getting with the '60s program, that I didn't have any puritanical hang-ups about sex and that I was above being bothered by her sexually active past. For her part, Amber was not nearly as upset as I expected her to be about being maligned as a slut. She dismissed it as the kind of gossip she had come to expect from a former friend whom she didn't identify. I wouldn't have known him or her anyway. Josh's call was quickly forgotten in the afterglow of that afternoon.

Before I left for Vietnam, I used to travel home to further my campaign of seduction against Erin on the average of one weekend a month. We referred to such trips as "swooping"—as in "Are you swooping this weekend?" There was even a "Swoop Circle" where, on a Friday afternoon, drivers could solicit Marines willing to chip in for gas for a ride to wherever they were going.

Driving from Lejeune to New Castle, Delaware, took between eight and nine hours. The good thing was that "Delaware"—as a Marine friend from New York used to say—"is one of those places you have to go through to get there." I could usually catch a ride with a driver bound for New Jersey or New York who would agree to pick me up again on the way back. I would be lucky to make it home by 1 a.m. Saturday and would have to leave by 4 or 5 p.m. on Sunday. That would put me back at base in the wee hours of the morning, often only an hour or two before reveille. I stumbled through many a Monday short on sleep but with erotic memories to sustain me.

Thanks to Amber, I lapsed back into the same pattern post-Vietnam. Only this time I had two advantages I hadn't had before. I bought my first car, a 1967 Pontiac Tempest, while still home on leave from Vietnam. And I started working a swing shift as a military police desk sergeant, giving me one long weekend a month—from Friday morning until Monday morning, I think it was. That made it easier.

From the start, I was aware that our relationship was an uneven one. Before I left for Camp Lejeune, I had gotten the impression that Amber wanted a monogamous relationship, but I was wrong. The contemporary classification "friends with benefits" comes to mind. That's how Amber saw our relationship.

There was also the fact that she was better educated, more articulate, and more sexually experienced than I was at that point in my life, leaving me understandably insecure. She was a college student, an English major; I was only a high-school graduate and an enlisted Marine. I took her family to be solidly middle class (a misapprehension I'll address later). I was working class. I always worried that she might be looking down on me.

The topic even came up once. Apropos to nothing we were discussing at the time, she confided that a good friend of hers was unhappy in her marriage because she had found her husband to be her "intellectual inferior." Perhaps I should have let it pass, but I couldn't help but ask if this was a parable directed at me. She reassured me that she didn't consider me her "intellectual inferior." Looking back on it today, I think that telling me about this mismatched couple may have been her way of warning me not to get too attached.

But that troubling conversation occurred relatively late in our relationship. Soon after reporting to Camp Lejeune, I resolved to come off as a man of the world during my next trip home to see Amber. I was determined that we would no longer flail around like horny teenagers desperate to find a place to park. Before going to the university to pick her up, I rented a room at the motel where I once worked as a bellhop, the Gateway Motor Inn.

This was perhaps the one and only time I got one up on Amber. She was initially shocked when I first showed her the key. "This is illegal, isn't it?" she said. "No," I reassured her, and we had a great uninhibited night.

That night set the pattern for the rest of our relationship. Late in our relationship, we had an idyllic weekend in North Carolina, but for the most part, I came to her. On the average of once a month, I would swoop home to Delaware, check into the Gateway, take Amber out to dinner, and then on to the Gateway where we would spend the night. After treating her to breakfast in the morning, I would check out and we would go somewhere and do something until I had to begin the eight-hour drive back to base. From my point of view, the frustrating thing was that we rarely found a place to have sex on a Sunday afternoon. Clearly, that wasn't as much of a problem for her. Comparing me to the sailor who had left her pregnant, she once said, "I really appreciate how you don't try to spirit me off for one last copulation before you have to leave." The truth is that I would have if I could have.

As the phrase "spirit me off" would suggest, Amber was nothing if not articulate and well-read. Looking back on it today, I don't believe she meant to make me feel insecure and inadequate. She always reassured me that the

39. A Siren's Spell

sex was great. I choose to believe her on that point. Her family, however, was a different matter.

Her father, Amber told me, had been "an executive on his way up with Blue Cross and Blue Shield" (the major health insurers in Delaware back then). He had given up that supposedly secure career to join his brother in saving the plumbing business their father had started. But the business had failed. I never got the whole story, but Amber showed me a gold-plated faucet, implying that the business went under due to the unreasonable demands of the wealthy woman addicted to such bling.

On our first meeting, Amber's father made sure I knew that, while only a high-school graduate, he had qualified for OCS and had served as an officer during the war (but in a support capacity). He even showed me his officer's uniform, which he had proudly preserved over the years.

Amber's father, moreover, had the same propensity for troubling innuendo that Amber had displayed in telling me about her intellectually superior friend burdened with the intellectually inferior husband. On one of my visits, unbidden, he brought up one of Amber's former admirers, whom he roundly satirized and declared to be "going nowhere." Perhaps I'd been overly sensitive, and he didn't intend his remarks as a veiled judgment of my potential. But I found it ironic that he could be so judgmental when he himself was "going nowhere." His business had failed, and he was sitting at home unemployed and drinking heavily.

As Amber freely admitted, her father had developed a drinking problem that her family could no longer ignore. Amber had been the driving force in getting her mother and older sister to acknowledge the problem and to stage an intervention. As Amber related it, she told her mother and sister, "We have to stop pussy-footing around. Let's face it: Dad is an alcoholic."

One good thing I can say about Amber's father: He thought I was foolish to spend so much money on her. His attitude, as Amber confided, was "you can get her so much cheaper." He, of course, didn't know the half of it.

Just as they still do, the Marine Corps used to keep expeditionary units—consisting of battalions reinforced with air and other support units—afloat in the Caribbean or Mediterranean and the Western Pacific at all times. The difference is that back then spending six months afloat on one of these "cruises" didn't count as overseas time. I had been back from Vietnam less than six months when I learned that I would be floating around the Caribbean for six months as the NCO in charge of a military police detachment. I did take a week's leave before I had to deploy, and Amber and I made the most of that. But I was gone from early June until early November, and absence doesn't always make the heart grow fonder.

Before I left, Amber's father had implied that I had lucked into a real boondoggle. Life aboard a Navy ship as an enlisted Marine, however, is no holiday. And liberty ashore left a lot to be desired. We did hit some good liberty ports, but we had not been allowed to bring civilian clothes. We had to go ashore in our sloppy starched khaki uniforms, and we didn't have much money. Worse, drugs were rampant and racial tensions high.

At one point, black and white Marines had squared off against one another at an outdoor theater on Vieques, Puerto Rico. The colonel threatened to cancel all liberty for the rest of the cruise if there were a recurrence. Later, we spent an unscheduled week in Panama, much of it, locked below decks while the Naval Investigative Service conducted a thorough investigation of drug trafficking and use throughout the cruise. By the time the cruise was over, I realized that I would rather have gone back to Vietnam for six months.

One of the first things I did after reporting to Camp Lejeune was to request a change of MOS from supply to infantry. I was determined not to sit out my remaining time in the Corps in a supply office. I, of course, cited my CAP experience as a rifleman and patrol leader, and I got my wish. I was still undecided about my future, however, and the 2nd Marine Division was not short of infantry NCOs. Thinking I might want to join the Delaware State Police, I volunteered to be an MP.

Despite being an MP, somehow—I'm not sure how—I managed to navigate my way safely through that Caribbean cruise. One of my most vivid memories was watching a large black Marine casually walk up to and punch another Marine, only to walk calmly back past me, greeting me with a cheerful, "Hey, how're you doin,' Sarge?" As a member of a six-man MP detachment among 1,200 grunts, you learn to pick your battles.

That cruise marked a turning point in our relationship. Before I left, Amber had given me a book that meant a lot to her, Kahlil Gibran's *The Prophet*. I wasn't much taken with it. Much of it, I didn't understand, and the parts I did understand impressed me as sentimental. Still, I would occasionally turn back to it, trying to determine just what Amber saw in it—until one particular letter arrived. She gushingly told me about a weekend she had spent in New York City with another guy. We were docked at San Juan at the time. I threw *The Prophet* into the harbor.

For most guys, that would have been the end of it. But I hadn't exactly remained celibate throughout the cruise, and I was always conscious of not wanting to appear provincial and prudish in what I took to be her sophisticated eyes. We had an initially angry confrontation when I got back. She acknowledged that the trip to New York had not been a platonic one and reminded me that we had never really agreed to be exclusive. Somehow, we smoothed it over and resumed our desultory relationship. I didn't have anything else going, and the truth is I was hoping to move to the next level.

The beginning of the end came in early 1969. I was initially scheduled to be released from active duty on August 10 of that year. Early that spring—hav-

39. A Siren's Spell

ing found that a little police work can go a long way and realizing that, above all, what I wanted was an education—I had applied to and been accepted at the University of Delaware. At some point soon after that acceptance, the Marine Corps had decided to cut back and invited Marines in certain military occupational specialties (MOSs) to apply to be released early. My MOS, which I had gotten changed to infantry, was eligible, and I applied. I was given a new release date of April 18.

I wrote to Amber giving her the good news and expecting an enthusiastic response. I didn't get it. As it turned out, her senior year at Delaware would coincide with my freshman year. That was more proximity than she could handle.

During my last weekend trip home before being released from active duty—in early April, it must have been—she made it clear that it was time for us to disengage, to become merely friends. And she explained why "it" would never work between us. She had long been in love with someone she couldn't have. I never found out who that was, but she indicated that it was not the father of the child she had given up for adoption.

I would run into her occasionally on campus, and she would always greet me like a long-lost friend and pretend to be in awe of the good grades I was getting—especially since, like her, I had decided to major in English. The last time I saw her was near the end of her senior year. She was particularly full of herself on that occasion. She had just been accepted to train as a flight attendant for a contract commercial airline. I'm sure she excelled at it.

It wasn't love. Amber had made that clear. I had merely been filling a niche—more literally than figuratively. Looking back on it all today, I'm reminded of the phrase that once set Erin off: It was "an affair to remember." I can certainly say that about it.

I've never been one to moon over what might have been. I certainly have my share of regrets, especially about roads not taken, but I try to be philosophical about them. "Would I really want my life to have turned out markedly different than it now is?" I ask myself. I always come back around to the same answer: "No." For the most part, I wouldn't want to trade what I've learned in that proverbial school of hard knocks for some missed opportunity or advantage. Still, whenever I think of falling under Amber's spell, I can't help but think of something I'd been missing all along.

I suppose I've always been slow on the uptake. I didn't spend much time on patrol as an MP. I was promoted to sergeant before leaving on that Caribbean cruise, and I became a desk sergeant upon my return. The counter I sat behind while on the desk faced out into the vestibule of the building, and the base's pet registration desk faced the front door, within my line of sight. Whenever I was working the day shift, I couldn't help but notice that the pet registration desk was staffed by a Woman Marine PFC who certainly didn't fit the stereotype. Forget the stereotype. She was young, cute (even smaller than Amber), and demure. I'd seen at least one of our MPs try to make her acquaintance, and he hadn't seemed to get anywhere.

Occasionally, when our pet registrar wasn't busy—which was most of the time—I'd seen her looking my way. But I didn't think anything of it, and I never bothered to try to talk to her—until my last day on duty before I would begin checking out. I don't know why, but on that day I approached her and told her I'd gotten an early out and that I would be heading home to begin college under the G.I. Bill. Something about the way she said, "Aww" told me she was genuinely sorry to see me go and that I should have struck up an acquaintance long before that day. That too might have been an affair to remember instead of one of my roads "not taken."

But, then again, the closing lines of Milton's *Samson Agonistes* have always resonated with me: "All is best, though oft we doubt what the unsearchable dispose of highest wisdom brings about, and ever best found in the close." I keep telling myself that. Someday, I may actually believe it.

40

"All the way with LBJ!"

Maybe I'm just idiosyncratic, but when I think of all the momentous events I've witnessed in my 70-plus years, I always come back to one that probably didn't have as profound an effect on most people as it had on me.

I'll always remember where I was—psychologically and physically—and what I was doing on March 31, 1968, when I heard President Johnson announce that he was falling on his sword over Vietnam.

I was having dinner at the NCO club at Camp Lejeune. Barely three months back from Vietnam, I was still grappling with my demons, trying to make sense of that experience. And there was LBJ, on TV, saying, "I shall not seek, and I will not accept, the nomination of my party for another term as your president."

I was especially feeling conflicted about my astoundingly good luck; I had rotated back to the States, at the end of a full 13-month tour, about three weeks before the Tet Offensive.

The myth persists in some quarters that the troops were all on board and that morale was high in Vietnam before Tet. That must have been some other Vietnam War. The one I went to in late 1966 was already seeing a breakdown in good order and discipline. I witnessed pervasive drug, discipline, and racial problems when I was "in the rear with the gear," as we used to say.

And, as I've already related, when I went out in the field, as a rifleman and patrol leader with the Marine Corps' Combined Action Program, I found myself expected to train and inspire a group of Vietnamese Popular Force soldiers who clearly had no interest in fighting a war they viewed as ours and not theirs.

I learned firsthand that the only people who were really committed to their cause were on the other side.

Just to make matters worse, for three years, I had been hearing our political leadership and our command structure cheering us on from the sidelines with seemingly little appreciation of what they were asking us to do.

President Johnson, in particular, I found galling. "I do not find it easy to send the flower of our youth, our finest young men, into battle," I remember hearing him say. "Yeah, but it's a hell of a sight easier than going yourself!" I remember thinking. My hatred for him was visceral in those days.

Outwardly, I was still wearing the uniform, but inwardly, my heart was already with the college kids who used to shout, "Hey, hey, LBJ, how many kids did you kill today?"

There he was, on that early spring night in 1968, at least acknowledging the possibility he may have been wrong to keep staying the course in Vietnam. Something about his demeanor that night convinced me that he was sincerely feeling the weight of the war and that I may have been wrong to assume that people like me were merely expendable to people like him.

I suppose that speech made such a strong impression on me because it was the first time I felt as if I had indeed come home to the America in which I had grown up. I remember feeling reassured that our leaders do listen to the American people.

As it would turn out, of course, Johnson's sacrifice only opened the door for President Nixon, whose secret plan for ending the war involved expanding it to Cambodia. Getting out of Vietnam would take five more frustrating years.

But that wasn't Johnson's fault, and for that "one, brief shining moment" in March 1968, I really felt that America was going to be all right.

I wish I could feel that way again.

41

Shelter from the Storm

T.S. Eliot, in a fit of poetic pique, once declared April to be "the cruelest month." Someone should probably have told Eliot to lighten up. Still, I remember how April of 1969 turned out to be a cruel month for me, and it has lately occurred to me that how I felt back then may just help explain why we've lost so many veterans to suicide in recent years.

When I returned from Vietnam in January 1968, I still had nearly 18 months left on my enlistment. As I've already confessed, without benefit of formal training, I became a military policeman.

It was a stressful job. Too many Marines had returned from Vietnam with drug habits and bad attitudes. Racial tensions were high. PX cashiers had been robbed at gunpoint.

After only a few weeks of patrol experience, moreover, I made sergeant and soon found myself assigned beyond the level of my incompetence. I became a desk sergeant responsible for everything a dozen patrolmen did or failed to do. There were days when I would rather have been back in Vietnam.

I had already made up my mind that I was going to use my G.I. Bill to go to college. August 10, 1969—the end of my four-year enlistment—couldn't come fast enough.

Then, in early 1969, deliverance beckoned. As I mentioned in a previous chapter, the Marine Corps was cutting back and offering "early outs" to Marines in certain noncritical fields. One of those fields was infantry, the MOS I happened to have despite my MP assignment. I applied and received a new release date: April 18, 1969.

I still remember how elated I felt all throughout the process of packing and checking out during my last few days. The final hurdle in the checkout process was disbursing—where on the morning of my release I was in for a rude awakening. A patient clerk explained that I was in arrears on my leave balance, and that accounted for the difference between what I was hoping to get and what I actually got. I walked away with only about $300 and an outlook that was beginning to cloud.

Then, in driving through the front gate, it hit me: I really had nothing to go back to. That long-distance relationship with Amber—on whom I had spent too much leave time and money—had fizzled out. My mother and I were not on good terms. It would be over four months until I could start college, and the best I could do, I suddenly realized, would be an interim job of menial monotony. I had no good friends I could count on reconnecting with, much less ones who would understand what I had been through. I've never felt lonelier in all my life.

I would bet that many of today's young soldiers and Marines experience the same sense of letdown that I felt upon getting out of the service. The fact that many of those of who committed suicide had never seen combat is not puzzling to me. In my experience, the overriding motivation for enlisting is often a need for validation.

We all have a basic need to belong, to feel respected and accepted. Today, as in my day, many a young man with only a marginal high-school diploma—and who feels undervalued by teachers, misunderstood by family, and put-down by peers—joins the military primarily to prove to himself that he is somebody. What if such a young man finds that respect and acceptance have eluded him in the military as well? It may not take a touch of PTSD or a failed marriage to drive such a soldier or Marine to despair.

A friend recently asked me what veterans really need. Veterans need jobs, to be sure, but not just to earn a living. They need meaningful jobs or pursuits that make them feel that they belong, that they are capable and respected. The last thing veterans need is to feel patronized or pitied and singled out for special treatment. Contrary to popular belief, the indifference that the country displayed toward returning Vietnam veterans was not necessarily a bad thing. When I started college, I found myself accepted and treated like any other college freshman, and that was exactly what I needed. I began to feel normal again.

As for that depressing interim period between the Marine Corps and college, fortunately, my father and his family took me in. He was still on active duty at the time, stationed at the Lockbourne Air Force Base just outside Columbus, Ohio. I got a 700-hour temporary civil-service appointment and spent that spring and summer helping with hot-tar roofing on the depot roofing crew at the Defense Supply Agency in Columbus.

It was miserable work, but being part of a family and looking forward to the start of college got me through. And my father used to delight in telling people that his son had a "high-up job in the government."

Previously, I mentioned a regret that I still can't let go of—giving my mother most of the money my family had given me shortly before I left for Vietnam. Another regret I still feel is a request for help and an opportunity I spurned soon after joining my father and his family in Columbus.

Another officer's wife called Betty and asked if we would come over for drinks that afternoon. The reason she was inviting us, she confided, was that their son had recently gotten out of the Army and seemed to be having difficulty getting over his Vietnam experiences. She was worried, and through the grapevine, I suppose, she heard that I was a Vietnam veteran. She was obviously hoping I would befriend her son and help him exorcise his demons.

Air Force bases are tightknit communities. On the officer side especially, everyone seems to know or at least know of everyone else. Clearly, Betty was not close to this family, and she seemed to find the invitation to be an imposition—on me especially.

This was before post-traumatic stress disorder—PTSD—was widely recognized and publicized. If anyone at that time had asked me if I was suffering from PTSD, I would have emphatically denied it. There was still a stigma attached to any form of depression. People tended to view depression as a form of self-indulgence and self-pity. I was intent on showing that I had put Vietnam behind me, and my own denial left me unsympathetic to those who couldn't get past it. I also wanted to show Betty that—like my father, who seemed to have taken combat in stride—I was made of sterner stuff.

Hence, on that afternoon, that other veteran and I never got past a superficial comparison of where we'd been and what we had done. My impression is that, unlike me, he had seen heavy combat and would have liked to tell me more about it. But I made no overtures toward getting together again. I wish I had. He needed a friend, and the truth is, so did I. And it would have made for a much more pleasant summer. I assume he knew other young people on base and that he knew his way around Columbus. As it was, my social life throughout that summer was limited to taking my half-brother Brian, seven years my junior, to the movies.

As I look back on it now, there is at least one example of my actual psychological state that summer. Before I left Columbus, I gave Brian that Yashica camera I'd bought from another Marine at Papa One. Later, at the University of Delaware, I would learn a literary term for what that camera represented. It was my own personal "objective correlative." It symbolized why I hadn't been there when it counted at Papa Three.

42

A Chance Encounter with the Third Kind—of Girl

Even after all these years, I still marvel at how an offhand remark can change your life.

It was my second semester at the University of Delaware. Starting college that fall was the first thing that had made me feel normal again. I'd become a born-again student. I'd finished the fall semester with a good GPA, and I was resolved to live like a monk, if that's what it took to see it through. I hadn't taken a vow of poverty, but I might as well have. As a G.I. Bill student, I didn't realize that financial aid would have been available to me, and I had sold my car in order to pay for the spring semester. A single room in Delaware's "Rodney C" dormitory had become my monastic cell. I used to joke that I was translating the Bible back into Hebrew and Greek.

The medieval history course I was taking that semester met twice a week in a large lecture hall with the professor and once a week in a small quiz section conducted by a graduate student. The quiz section I had registered for met at 4:00 p.m. on Friday afternoons. I challenge any college to try to fill a Friday afternoon class today. But I was high on academics back then and had nothing else to do with my Friday afternoons. I was so academically gung-ho, in fact, that I would get to most of my classes early, that quiz section included.

Having arrived early one Friday in late January, I was trying to go over the reading assignment but found myself distracted by two young women sitting in front of me. They were commiserating and complaining bitterly to one another about what a disappointment the freshmen boys had turned out to be. To hear them tell it, all the freshmen boys fell into one of two categories, with no shades of gray in between: Either they were aspiring to be fraternity wolves or they were nerds who giggled.

I ignored this diatribe as long as I could. Assuming that my superior standing as an older—four years older, to be exact—former Marine and man of the world was apparent, I decided to speak up: "Well, some of the freshman girls haven't lost their baby fat either!"

42. A Chance Encounter with the Third Kind—of Girl

That must have shocked them into silence. They didn't say another word.

I don't remember how, but after class, one of the girls struck up a conversation with me, and I ended up walking her back to her dormitory. Her name, I learned, was Andrea. She was from Smyrna, Delaware, a small town I'd never heard of—although I had to have passed through it on family trips to Rehoboth Beach. (Smyrna is in central Delaware—"South of the Canal," to fall back on the geographic and cultural line of demarcation I introduced in Chapter 9.) She would later confide that her first impression of me had been, "Well, there's at least one freshman boy who has some spunk!" Before I knew it, we'd made a date for the following Friday night. Marshaling my meager resources, I walked her to a theater in Newark, where we saw Dustin Hoffman and Mia Farrow in *John and Mary*.

Andrea, I soon learned, was one of four valedictorians at her high school. She was an honor graduate and, along with her best friend, Paula, she was offered a full scholarship to Brandeis University, which at the time was committed to diversifying its predominantly Jewish student body. But her father, who had grown up in New York City, wouldn't let her go. He told her he used to see those Jewish girls coming home from school and that they were "round shouldered from all the books they carried home." He led her to believe she wasn't smart enough for Brandeis. I suspect his real concern was that because Andrea wasn't Jewish she wouldn't fit in. Paula's experience at Brandeis lends credence to that suspicion. As a gentile, she found herself snubbed by all but the foreign students, one of whom she married. He was a Dane, and she moved to Denmark to be with him. Andrea went on to the University of Delaware, where she met me. Hence, initially, at least, Paula's parents were probably sorry they let her take her scholarship. Andrea's parents were definitely sorry they didn't let Andrea take hers.

There was no question that Andrea was smart enough to make it at Brandeis. Articulate, literate, and well-read, she was also a whiz at math. She was majoring in computer science when I met her—largely because she had been told it was the wave of the future. But she found it boring and soon realized she had no ambition to become a computer scientist. As she readily admits, she was majoring in pinochle with friends in her dorm. I was majoring in English and had always been hopeless in math. We soon realized we complemented one another. We still do.

Aided and abetted by Delaware's decision to go to open dorms that very semester, our relationship quickly escalated. We spent all our spare time together. Her mother, unfortunately, never approved of her going with an older former Marine, and when she learned that our relationship had proceeded to the tie that binds, she delivered an ultimatum. She demanded that Andrea break up with me, drop out of the University of Delaware, and enroll at Delaware State College in Dover. The ultimatum went unheeded.

The author and Andrea in the fall of 1970.

We eloped. We were married on August 8, 1970, by a justice of the peace in Elkton, Maryland. I wish I could say I've been a perfect husband. I haven't. Early on, I wouldn't admit that I had even a mild case of PTSD. Andrea would beg to differ. While I was never physically abusive, I suffered from frequent dark moods and unreasonable fits of anger. I could be passive-aggressive and hypercritical in ways that tested Andrea's patience. When our son came along, I proved to be an inept father. But through it all, Andrea wouldn't give up on me, and I eventually realized how lucky I had been. Wives don't come any better. As of this writing, we've been together for 50 years. Not bad for a starter marriage!

The moral of this story is this: Weigh your words wisely. An offhand remark may just change your life in ways you never anticipated.

43

Palm at Penn

It had been a bad day at the U Penn. I mean Ben Franklin's Penn, not Joe Paterno's Penn. The University of Pennsylvania was founded in 1740 by Franklin, and they never let you forget it. It's on all the building signs.

I suppose that it wasn't any one thing. An accumulation of things had gotten to me that day. I was a post–M.A. graduate student in English and a teaching fellow and was only a little more than halfway through my first semester. I'd gotten there through the good graces of my undergraduate adviser at the University of Delaware, Professor Donald Mell, who had earned his PhD at Penn and still had friends there. (Mell was also a Yale undergrad, and I would come to realize how that sort of background made the difference in his ability to fit in at Penn.) Mell had tried to warn me: "Penn is going to make Delaware seem like a pastoral idyll." And indeed it did.

It had been my good fortune to earn my B.A. and M.A. degrees at Delaware while it was still in transition from a good state university to the major research university it is today. Professors were still accessible and interested in students. You could drop by and talk to them, even outside of posted office hours. Three professors in particular had taken an interest in me: Don Mell, who had inspired me to major in English; Franklin Newman (deceased), who had shown me that Shakespeare mattered; and George Miller, who had turned me on to Milton. It was Miller who had also turned my head. It was during my junior year that he told me he considered me PhD material and that I could have an academic career—if that's what I wanted to do.

I wasn't sure at first. I had hoped to work my way into journalism, especially photojournalism. (I had gotten over my photographic setback at Papa Three.) A career in photojournalism held the promise of travel and adventure. But the academic life impressed me as an even nobler calling—and a freer one. To think that I could get paid to study whatever interested me, regardless of how irrelevant it was to the world's commerce!

Before making up my mind, I decided to visit the *Evening Journal*, the paper of record in Delaware. What I didn't realize was that the field of journalism was aspiring to recognition as a full-fledged profession and not just a craft. The *Evening Journal*'s personnel director told me, in no uncertain terms, that they would not even think of hiring someone without a master's degree in journalism or photojournalism.

I knew I could get a fellowship to go to graduate school in English. As far as I knew, no such support was available for graduate study in journalism. And, truth be told, I was seriously infected with youthful idealism about the importance of preserving and transmitting our literary heritage.

Ironically, it wasn't my idealism that had convinced Miller that I had the right stuff to make it in academe. My timing was especially bad. The academic job market was dismal and getting worse year by year. Miller once told me that he had finished his PhD in the last year that the market was good, 1969. By the time I was contemplating jumping into that Darwinian fray, the forecast was that only three of every 10 newly minted PhDs would get academic jobs. Miller thought that because I was older, more mature, and more pragmatic I would stand a better chance at getting an academic job than my younger and overly idealistic competitors. It was a matter of convincing a hiring committee of senior professors that I would not be a prima donna—that I could fit in and be counted upon to do my share of academic drudgery.

Miller did give me one bit of very good advice: I should not stay on at Delaware for the PhD. Earning three degrees in a relatively small—and, as of then, relatively undistinguished—English department would smack of academic incest. He also may have steered me in the wrong direction. I had an excellent offer from the University of Illinois. They admitted me to their PhD program and offered me a teaching assistantship in their Department of Rhetoric. More importantly, in their acceptance letter, they indicated that they were enthusiastic at the prospect of my joining them. Miller, however, told me that, the job market being what it is, Penn's name would give me an edge. But, as I would soon discover, there is a world of difference in having a graduate program express enthusiasm in getting you and one that merely allows you to join them.

I found myself just another one of 75 graduate students in English at Penn. My fellow graduate students, for the most part, impressed me as arrogant, snobbish, pretentious, and unfriendly. Most had come from name schools. Few could claim the sort of working-class roots that I had sprung from, nor would they admit it if they had. That peculiar nose-in-the air mumbled diction known as "mainline lockjaw" seemed to be a popular affectation among the women. I remember one in particular who seized every opportunity to boast of her erudition, making comments such as, "For years I advocated *Critic X's* point of view, until I encountered *Critic Y*." This from a young woman who was all of 22 or 23 years old.

I also found myself put off by the students I taught in my freshman literature class. They were certainly bright enough, but most seemed to be spoiled

43. Palm at Penn

trust-fund babies who took admission to an elite university for granted and whose principal complaint was that they hadn't gotten into Harvard, Yale, Brown, or Princeton. Later in my graduate work, I would find myself standing in line to buy my books at the campus bookstore and hearing a young woman telling her friend, "I didn't want to go to the Bahamas over our Christmas break, but Mummy and Daddy insisted. They said I'd been working so hard and needed a good vacation." That conversation spoke volumes about the cultural and economic divide between me and my students.

And, then, there was the graduate faculty. One of the few faculty members at Penn who took an interest in students, and who didn't take himself too seriously, turned out to be the Director of Freshman English, Peter Conn. He put it best: "Teaching doesn't even make the top ten on the list of things a faculty member must do at a school like Penn if he or she wants to earn tenure." (The Ivy League universities are Darwinian places. They're notorious for hiring 10 assistant professors to do the drudge work that senior professors don't want to do, with the understanding that maybe one will get to stay. Conn, I would later learn, had been the first assistant professor to earn tenure at Penn in a long time.) Conn also told me something else that would certainly ring true in my experience of Penn: "Parents will spend a lot of money to send their children to a place like Penn so that they can study under the people who are exceptionally well-prepared to teach in their fields—which is not to say that they are prepared on a day-to-day basis."

A case in point was a professor who had made a name for himself in the scholarship of one of the major figures in English literature. I will call him Professor Norton. (He is now deceased, but I'll assume an officer-and-gentleman stance rather than name him.) In addition to teaching one class a semester, I had to take three graduate classes. I knew that I was weak when it came to Norton's specialty, and when I saw that this famous professor was offering a class in that literary lion, I jumped at it. As a colleague of mine once observed, however, "The world of academic publishing moves at a stately pace." I hadn't stopped to consider how long it must have taken to become such an eminent scholar.

I'm not a great judge of age, but the professor who walked into our Chaucer seminar on that first day of class was obviously over 70. (At this point, I plead innocent of ageism. I'm well aware that some people remain lucid and capable well past 70. Having gotten past 70 myself, I think I'm still with it.)

"Hello, I'm Professor Norton," he said and sat down at the head of the seminar table. After a few more perfunctory words of introduction, he passed out the syllabus, picked up his ancient, battered briefcase, and dumped the contents onto the table. Out came a profusion of note cards, article offprints, a book or two, miscellaneous papers, and what seemed to be a laundry slip.

He then proceeded to sort through the pile, commenting on whatever he found in no particular order.

"Oh, here's an interesting article by one of my former students. Frankly, I never thought he'd amount to much, but this article is rather good. He makes the point that…"

And that's the way it went for the rest of the two hours that week and for the next two or three weeks.

Then, the following week, instead of Professor Norton, in walked the chair of the graduate program. "Ladies and gentlemen," he began, "I have some bad news. Your professor has had a stroke. I'll be taking over the class for the time being and perhaps for the rest of the semester."

The graduate chair was not an inspired teacher, but he did attempt to follow the syllabus. For that week and the next, we were starting to get something out of the course. But on the third week, in came our professor, leaning on a cane and otherwise no worse for wear than when we had first met him.

"I had a bit of a scare, ladies and gentlemen," he said, "but I'm okay now." Up came that old, battered briefcase, and out came that profusion of relevant and irrelevant materials. He began to sift through the pile, and off we went again.

That's the way it went for the rest of the semester. There were two requirements for the course, a midterm exam and a term paper. We dutifully took the exam, but two weeks passed before one brave soul spoke up, asking if we were ever going to get our exams back. "No," he replied, "I like to hold on to those and to compare them to your term papers." Later, in speaking to a fellow graduate student, I would learn that our esteemed professor was notorious for giving one of two grades—an "A" to those students whom he knew to be working toward a dissertation in his field and a "B" to everyone else.

In all fairness, there were some professors at Penn who took their teaching seriously. Roland Frye, a nationally noted Miltonist, was one. It was George Miller back at Delaware who first turned me on to Milton. I too wanted to contribute to justifying "ways of God to men," but in a secular humanistic sense. I wanted to write a dissertation on Milton under Frye's direction, so I was eager to impress him—too eager, as it turned out. I got only a C+ on the first hour exam. I had overreached; I spent too much time on the first part, trying to show that I knew a lot about Milton, and I ran out of time. I went to see Frye to explain what happened, and I eventually redeemed myself with a good term paper. I went on to take two more courses with Frye, earning A's in both. And in my last year on campus, Frye got me through my comprehensive exams on Shakespeare, Milton, and didactic writers of the English Renaissance. But it was on a day like the one in which I had gotten that C+ that I came to a crossroads.

43. Palm at Penn

Somewhere—probably at the student center—I had come across a brochure on Marine officer programs. Listed on that brochure was the phone number of the Marine Officer Selection Officer, the recruiter for officers. On a lark, I decided to call him.

I introduced myself. I told him that I was a former Marine and a Vietnam veteran who had been honorably discharged as a sergeant. I explained that I was 27, that I was a graduate student at Penn, and asked if it was too late to become an officer. He said, "No, it's not too late," and asked if I had some time to come down to the Philadelphia Navy Yard to talk to him about it. I replied that I did, and he asked where I was at Penn. I told him I was at Bennett Hall, at 34th and Walnut. He said he would send a corporal around in a sedan to get me.

Before I knew it, I was signed up to report to Officer Candidate School at Quantico on January 6, 1975.

I'm not a religious man, but as I admitted before, I do think that Hamlet may have been right in proclaiming, "There is a divinity that shapes our ends, / Rough-hew them how we will."

I really thought Andrea would divorce me when she found out I was going back in the Marine Corps. I had certainly given her cause. But she didn't. She wondered why I wasn't seeking a commission in some civilized service, such as the Air Force or even the Army. They have better bases and more bases, she reminded me. She also asked me if I really believed all the hype about the Marine Corps being the best. I sheepishly admitted that I did. The fact of the matter is she had never liked the life of a working wife supporting a grad student. She too found my fellow grad students pretentious and snobbish. But the real selling point for her was a chance at making a decent, middle-class living that would give us the opportunity to have a baby. She signed on, and it was her weekend visits to Quantico that sustained me.

But, above all, I owe my commission to my sergeant instructor (the OCS title for a drill instructor) at Quantico, whom I'll call Kenneth Leonard. He was a staff sergeant at the time, and he was the real thing. He had won the Navy Cross—the second highest award—in Vietnam. It was rumored he had charged a bunker and actually killed two North Vietnamese Army soldiers with his entrenching tool (his small shovel). Whether or not that part was true, he had certainly proved to be a genuine hero.

Early in the program, we'd been required to write our biographies, and Leonard took an interest in mine. As I would discover, his devotion to his six-month-old son and his wife belied the brutality the war had brought out in him, and he believed the Marine Corps needed officers whose moral and intellectual horizons extended beyond the institution they would serve. Leonard worked with me and got me through a demanding physical regimen I was not prepared for.

Leonard was meritoriously promoted to gunnery sergeant at the end of our OCS program and went on to retire from the Marine Corps as a sergeant major—the top enlisted rank. I went on to serve my two years and nine months of required active duty as a lieutenant at Camp Pendleton, California. By the end of that stint, I had decided to go back to finish what I had started. I had taken a leave of absence from Penn, and much to my surprise, they took me back—even reinstating my teaching fellowship.

I'd be lying if I said my readjustment to graduate school had gone smoothly. It was a difficult time for me and for Andrea—all of which was my fault. I was distracted and once again having second thoughts. I had hit rock bottom in the spring of that first year back. I failed a qualifying oral exam to go on to the next year. I would have just one more chance to pass it. I came home thoroughly depressed and thinking I had let myself and Andrea down. I was even thinking of dropping out altogether.

But before I had gotten off active duty at Camp Pendleton, my executive officer at the time gave me some good advice. Knowing I was going back into academics, he told me that Headquarters Marine Corps was always looking for reserve officers available for temporary active duty in the summer to work on special projects. Knowing I was going back into academics, my XO urged me to write to Headquarters to tell them that I would be available for temporary active duty in the summers. I wrote and sent in that letter before I left Camp Pendleton, and I thought no more of it until that dark day when I failed my oral.

That very afternoon, the phone rang, and it was a major from Headquarters Marine Corps asking me if I would be willing to come back on active duty to teach in a special program in San Diego. It was called the Marine Enlisted Commissioning Education Program, or "MECEP" for short. Each year, the Corps selected promising enlisted people to attend college at their expense and to go on to become officers. Wanting to leave nothing—or as little as possible—to chance, the Corps ran a special prep program every summer, the purpose of which was to ensure the selectees were ready for college. I would be assigned to teach English in the prep program. I jumped at the chance. And it worked out wonderfully well. The reserve colonel who ran it was a physics professor and department chair at Montana State. We clicked, the students were great, I found a good friend in a fellow instructor, and I had a great summer.

The MECEP prep school had left me little time to study, so when I got back to Penn, I went into that last-chance oral exam fully expecting to have to find an alternate career. But much to my surprise, I passed! I went on to teach in that special program for two more summers, and I believe it was that program that kept me in the Marine Corps' good graces.

I did nothing for the Marine Corps in between those active-duty stints

43. Palm at Penn

in San Diego, but in the early spring of 1980, I received a letter informing me that I had been promoted to captain. Later that spring, a letter arrived from Headquarters Marine Corps offering me three years of active duty. That too came as an act of grace.

I had gotten through my course work and exams and had even started my dissertation, but my teaching fellowship had run out. I had a son as well as a wife to support. I really needed an ABD (all but dissertation) job to sustain us. By that time, however, the academic job market was flooded with PhDs looking for work; schools didn't have to settle for ABDs. I wasted a lot of time and money applying for jobs I stood no realistic chance of getting.

Andrea and I talked it over and agreed that life back in the Marine Corps was certainly better than continuing to live hand-to-mouth with her working to support a struggling graduate student. I took the offer, and off we went to the 2nd Marine Aircraft Wing at Cherry Point, North Carolina. Back at Camp Pendleton, because I was one of the officers who excelled at reading and writing, I had become an adjutant—the personal assistant to a commanding officer. I became an adjutant again at Cherry Point.

After a year at Cherry Point, I was offered a regular commission, meaning that I was in with the in-crowd. I became "USMC" instead of "USMCR," giving me a degree of job security. At that point, Andrea and I agreed that we would see it through to a 20-year pension, after which I would restart my academic career.

There was one drawback. Along with that regular commission came a one-year unaccompanied tour of duty at the Marine Corps Air Station in Iwakuni, Japan. It was now or never. A sympathetic executive officer allowed me to take a 30-day leave, during which I finished my dissertation.

I had started graduate school with the thought of specializing in Milton—becoming a "Miltonist." I passed comprehensive/PhD qualifying exams in Milton, Shakespeare, and didactic writers on the English Renaissance. But, in the end, I opted for a brand-new field—imaginative representations of the American experience in Vietnam. Much to my surprise, my dissertation—"American Heart of Darkness: The Moral Vision of Five Novels of the Vietnam War" (255 pages)—was accepted without revision. Looking back on it today, I still wonder how I managed to clear all the hurdles and earn the right to claim the title doctor of philosophy. I finished in time to receive the degree at Penn's graduation in May 1983. (Andrea insisted I wear my Marine officer white uniform under my academic garb.) I left that June to attend the Public Affairs Officers Course at Fort Benjamin Harrison, Indianapolis, and then on to Japan for a year.

I wish I could say that my Marine Corps career went smoothly from that point forward. There were problems and missteps aplenty along the way. But I can't complain. The Corps made good use of my idiosyncratic accomplishments and ambitions. They assigned me to be the Marine Officer Instructor with the Naval ROTC unit at Berkeley, an assignment I loved; and they let me finish out my career teaching English at the Naval Academy, an assignment I loathed but which served as my halfway house back to civilian academe.

44

Men Without a Country

We'd all been told to report to the Hawkins Room at 1600. We didn't know why. Saigon had fallen just two days before, finally marking the end of the war in which several of us had served. I was hardly the only former Marine Vietnam veteran who had decided to come back to the Corps as an officer. But I doubt that any of us surmised that this summons had anything to do with the events of April 30, 1975.

The Hawkins Room was a bar located on the first floor of O'Bannon Hall, the BOQ complex for the Marine officers' basic school—formally called The Basic School, or TBS. It had been my weird luck to start OCS in the winter of 1975 and to go through TBS in the spring and summer of that year. The TBS program, I discovered, was low stress and was more about socialization than training. As we liked to joke, TBS offered three months of training crammed into six.

We'd been cordially commanded to report to the Hawkins Room before, but it had always been for a mandatory happy hour. The Corps felt it was important to get to know, and to form personal relationships with, your fellow officers. I suppose I was a bit of a stick-in-the-mud in those days, but I looked with disdain on one of the camaraderie building customs of the Hawkins Room. It was called "Dead Bug."

The way it worked was this: Suddenly, without warning, someone would shout out, "Dead bug!" Everyone would immediately drop to the floor on their backs with their arms and legs up and pointed to the ceiling. The last lieutenant to assume the dead-bug position was then required to buy a round of drinks for his group.

But alcohol-fueled fun and games, we soon learned, was not the order of the day on this occasion. We entered to find our company commander, a major, standing at the bar flanked by six South Vietnamese exchange officers who had been going through TBS with us. They had suddenly become men without a country.

Calling us to attention, the major explained that, given recent events, our Vietnamese allies would be leaving us. He didn't say where they were

177

going. I don't recall his exact words. But I do recall that his speech was succinct. He said something on the order of our joining him in wishing our allies well. What else could he say, except "dismissed"?

I suppose he could have fallen back on the Vietnamese phrase xin loi, which we took to mean, "Sorry about that." But the sardonic spin we generally put on it—adding "ric tic," as in "xin loi ric tic"—suggested anything but sorrow. And I have no reason to believe the major was feeling anything like schadenfreude over the uncertain future these young South Vietnamese officers were facing.

Dispatches (1977) author Michael Herr long ago put it best: "There's nothing so embarrassing as when things go wrong in a war."

We all filed out, and that was that. The war in which I had served, and which America had bowed out of in 1973, was finally over. And here I was back on active duty as an officer.

45

Vietnam and Modern Memory

Back in the mid-'80s, an Army officer of my acquaintance succinctly summed up the mood of the post–Vietnam military: "It's okay to be a Vietnam veteran in today's military," he observed, "so long as you don't dwell on it or refer back to it." He was right. He had intuited the largely unspoken but widely understood politically correct attitude toward our humiliating defeat: Vietnam had been an aberration, the kind of war we would never fight again. And the less said about it, the better.

Ironically, this same spirit of denial and revision has spread to American society in general in recent years. It's okay to be a Vietnam veteran in today's America, so long as you remember that war the way President Reagan portrayed it, as a "noble crusade," and so long as you profess utter admiration for our Armed Forces and unwavering support for our current crusades.

The Vietnam War I remember was anything but a "noble crusade." It was a profoundly existential experience. Survival was the only moral touchstone and getting through to our rotation tour dates the only goal we cared about. All the Marines I knew in country were profoundly skeptical of the official rationales for why we were there and increasingly embittered by the reluctance of the South Vietnamese to fight their own war.

So many of my fellow Vietnam veterans seem to have forgotten how traumatized we were about all this. We have been co-opted, bought off with belated handshakes and glib expressions of gratitude. We have forgotten what really occasioned all the bitterness and fueled the post-traumatic stress of our generation.

It wasn't that the country failed to welcome us home or to honor our service with parades. It was the discovery that our leaders had lied to us about the nature and the necessity of the war and that the conduct of the war put the lie to the ideals and values in which we had all been raised to believe.

Would that we all knew then what we know now. Ho Chi Minh was first and foremost a nationalist. Early on, he had appealed to us to help dissuade France from reclaiming its former colony at the end of World War II. But we needed France's help in blocking communist expansion in Europe—or thought we did—and the ensuing Cold War clouded our judgment. We feared falling dominoes. By 1950, we were mired in Korea and bankrolling France's Indochina War. With the fall of Dien Bien Phu in 1954, we took over. We sent in intelligence operatives to subvert the Geneva Accords, especially the plebiscite that would have reunited North and South Vietnam under whichever form of government the majority chose—communism or democracy. Having defeated the French, Ho Chi Minh was the hands-down favorite to win. The South Vietnamese president we had installed, Ngo Dinh Diem, was almost as alien to his own people as we were. Ho Chi Minh had cornered the market on Vietnamese nationalism, and out in the countryside, most of the people seemed to want no part of what we were selling.

What's worse, once we had taken over in our own right, we began to take that indifference personally. Contrary to popular belief, we weren't forced to fight with one hand tied behind our back. We unleashed a greater tonnage of bombs on Vietnam than we did in all of World War II. We declared free-fire zones. We defoliated large areas with Agent Orange. We made liberal use of close air-support and indirect fire weapons with little regard for the so-called "collateral damage" such weapons inevitably inflict. Racists that we were, we dehumanized the Vietnamese as "gooks" and "slopes." Unable to distinguish friend from foe, we viewed them all as potential threats. Hence, the worst atrocity of the war—the My Lai massacre. Hell hath no fury like a country scorned, especially one that considers itself to be exceptional and eminently deserving of admiration and emulation.

This not to say that, because we were wrong, the other side was wholly righteous. They resorted to terror. They mistreated our POWs. They were hardly magnanimous in victory. But the irony is that we seem to have won after all.

Vietnam today is what we had tried to make it—a free-market consumer society. The tragedy of it is that over 58,000 Americans and some two million Vietnamese had to die just so that Vietnam could get there on its own timetable rather than ours.

In an especially resonant scene in Tim O'Brien's surrealistic and metafictional novel "Going After Cacciato," a squad of hitchhiking soldiers who had walked away from the war in Vietnam are picked up by a member of the counterculture, a San Diego State dropout, driving a VW van. The soldiers are actually on a mission to bring back the deserter Cacciato, but she assumes they are taking a principled stand against what she characterizes as "The Evil": "Children getting toasted, the orphans, atrocities," as she characterizes it. "God, the guilt must be awful," she concludes. After stealing her van and leaving the girl by the roadside, one of the soldiers concedes that "sometimes I feel a little guilt."

That scene encapsulates what to my mind was the most troubling aspect of the antiwar movement. As I related earlier, forget the myth of the spat-upon Vietnam veteran. Sociologist Jerry Lembcke, in his 1998 book *The Spitting Image*, argues that there is no documentary evidence that returning veterans were literally spat-upon. To the contrary, it has been established that pro-war demonstrators spat on antiwar demonstrators. Personally, I don't doubt that, in isolated cases, it may have happened, but it never happened to me. What I did experience, however, was the pretentious moral empathy of those who, like O'Brien's San Diego State dropout, presumed they understood what we had been through and how we should feel about it.

As Daniel Ellsberg—who leaked the secret history of our involvement in Vietnam, the Pentagon Papers—once put it, "We didn't intervene on the wrong side; we were the wrong side." What's worse, the means we employed were all out of proportion to the ends we sought in Vietnam. At times, we seemed intent on destroying the country in order to save it.

So how then should those of us who served in Vietnam feel about participating in such an unnecessary, misbegotten and misguided war? And how should our country feel about us?

Should we feel guilty?

The fact of the matter is that our cause was not "noble," but it wasn't "evil" either. As I've already related, former Marine Phillip Caputo, in his Vietnam memoir, *A Rumor of War* (1977), likened our day-to-day conduct of the war to "those bullying redcoats" of our own revolution. But history is not likely to rank us among the German Wehrmacht, much less the SS, in World War II or even the Army of the Confederacy during our own Civil War. We were not out to subjugate or enslave the Vietnamese. Neo-imperialists that we were, we just thought we knew what was best for them.

Also, like many of us who went to Vietnam, some who fought on behalf of the Third Reich or the Confederacy may have questioned whether their cause was just. But, from time immemorial, soldiers haven't fought for the cause so much as for one another. As a character in another Vietnam novel puts it, "You look out for me, I'll look out for you, and we'll both go home."

Like O'Brien's San Diego State dropout, the ideological purists of my generation—most of whom were risking nothing—would argue that "you've just got to separate yourself off from evil." But, like another of O'Brien's characters, we would have asked, "What's evil?" And having grown up where and when we did, for most of us, it was unthinkable to turn our backs on the country that had nurtured us and where we still hoped to make a good life.

The answer, it seems to me, comes from a Marine veteran of the war in Iraq, Phil Klay, who has published a collection of stories inspired by his experiences titled *Redeployment* (2014). In one of the stories, "Prayer in the Furnace," a chaplain has an epiphany about what the Marines he has counseled are going through in Iraq. Despite the insanity and the horrors of the war, he senses that "this place is holier than back home. Gluttonous, fat, oversexed, overconsuming, materialistic home, where we're too lazy to see our own faults."

While so many of our contemporaries sat in self-indulgent safety and comfort, we put ourselves on the line. Some of us went in believing. Others suspended judgment or, like O'Brien, even went in against their better judgment. But the great majority of us served honorably and proved ourselves to be better than the muddle-headed politicians who had sent us. That's something to be proud of.

Epilogue

Graham Greene was wrong about Vietnam. Not in the main, of course. *The Quiet American* (1955) still stands as not only the inaugural novel of the American intervention in Vietnam but also as a brilliant exposition on why we were destined to fail. Greene's portrayal of Alden Pyle, the earnest young American CIA operative blinded by the cultural constructions of the Cold War and armored in his good intentions, captures the essence of the dilemma we would face throughout our involvement. Greene was there at the beginning and understood better than most that we were "trying to make a war with the help of people who just aren't interested." When it came to just what the people were interested in, however, Greene seems to have known the Vietnamese no better than we did.

Greene obviously romanticized traditional Vietnamese culture and held it to have been largely impervious to Western ideas and values, a position he articulates through his narrator, Alden Pyle's worldly wise and reluctant mentor Thomas Fowler. At a key point in the novel, Fowler dismisses the American obsession with falling dominoes, expressing a conviction that seems to speak for the author as much as the character:

> If I believed in your God and another life, I'd bet my future harp against your golden crown that in five hundred years there may be no New York or London, but they'll be growing paddy in these fields, they'll be carrying their produce to market on long poles wearing their pointed hats. The small boys will be sitting on the buffaloes.

It is a view that certainly struck a resonant chord in me the first time I read it. I have returned to it often over the years in trying to make sense of my own experience as a patrol leader and rifleman with the Marine Corps' Combined Action Program throughout the last half of 1967 in a traditional Vietnamese village.

Our mission, as I've already related, was not to search and destroy but rather to win those elusive hearts and minds out in the countryside. Our attempts, however, were largely rebuffed, a failure I have always attributed to the nearly insurmountable cultural gulf across which we were trying to operate. In the summer of 2002, for the first time since I left Vietnam on January 3, 1968, I went back to find the village in which I served. What I found there, and throughout Vietnam in general, convinces me that Graham Greene and I were both wrong about the resiliency of the traditional Vietnamese culture. But, in all fairness, neither of us could have foreseen the power of mass media and of consumer capitalism to make even Vietnam over into America's image.

A man lying dead in the road seemed to sum it up for me. He had met his fate at the intersections of Highways 1 and 9 in Dong Ha. He was so much like the dead men I'd seen in Vietnam before—young, no older than his early 20s, maybe still in his late teens. This time, however, there was no obvious gore, not even any blood. The injuries must have been mostly internal, but instantly fatal nevertheless. He was lying on his stomach, with his head turned toward us, both eyes closed, and with one hand in front of his mouth, as if he were trying to stifle a burp. He looked rather peaceful actually, as if he had suddenly succumbed to the urge to take a nap. But who takes a nap in the middle of an intersection between the front and rear wheels of an "IFA" dump truck? A small crowd had gathered, but it was evident that there was nothing to be done except to wait for the police and to stare at the dead man or his motorbike, which lay on its side some 20 or 30 feet past the intersection. It was a "Honda Dream."

If only that young man had stayed back in the village "growing paddy." If only he hadn't succumbed to Honda dreams.

Obviously, the body count continues in Vietnam today—only this time, a young Vietnamese man had become a casualty of western-style consumerism instead of communism or what we used to characterize as democracy.

It's not that I have a quarrel with capitalism or with western civilization. I was happy to see that all throughout Vietnam today people have electricity and television and even internet cafes. I am at the age at which I didn't find it especially reassuring to see that the kids are growing up watching MTV-Asia, but people were also watching the World Cup soccer matches and films and television programs from America and Europe. And even a relatively poor family in Vietnam today, we would learn, could save up and buy a motorbike. But early in the trip I found myself feeling depressed by the ironic realization that so many had had to die on both sides just so that Vietnam could westernize according to their timetable instead of ours.

We came across the accident scene three days into a seven-day "trip back." The "we" in this case was myself; Bill Cooke, who had been my sergeant the first time around; our Vietnamese guide, and our Vietnamese driver. About three years before this trip, Bill found me through photos I had posted on the Internet. We hadn't seen or communicated with one another since my rotation from Vietnam in January 1968. I remembered him well, but ironically, neither of us could remember the other's name until that day in 1999, when, surfing the net for CAP photos and stories, he realized that he was looking at a photo of himself. He e-mailed me, and we've since gone on to become fast friends.

A former small business owner, Bill spent most of his working life as an insurance adjuster based in Grand Rapids, Michigan. He is retired now. He and his wife have come to visit us, and Bill and I even flew out to California together to meet with and interview Mack Garrett when I was first thinking about writing a book-length version of the story of Papa Three. Bill and I had spoken about the possibility of going back someday to retrace our steps and to see what the area was like now, but it just didn't seem practical or even especially desirable to me at first.

Then, in March of 2002, I landed in the hospital. Fortunately, it was nothing serious—just a minor problem with my heart rhythm—but it made me realize that I had reached the age at which I could no longer make all the old assumptions about my health and even my continuing mobility. At about the same time, Bill discovered that he had a hernia that needed surgery. I suppose there's nothing like a stay in the hospital, especially your first, to put you in a carpe diem frame of mind. My old "Sarge" must have been feeling the same way. "If we're ever going to take that trip to Vietnam," he wrote, commiserating with me by e-mail, "we better do it soon, before we have to carry too many meds."

Again, as I've already recounted, I had spent my entire 13-month-tour in what the U.S. command designated as "Northern I Corps," the most significant part of it in Quang Tri Province. I was 19 when I got to Vietnam, 20 when I left. Then, at age 55, I was doing something I had once vowed I would never do, professed to have no need to do. I had come back.

I had come back, mainly, to revisit the site of the most significant set of experiences I had had in Vietnam. Again, as I've already related, I served most of my Combined Action tour with the third platoon of Papa Company—or "Papa Three," as we called it—located about halfway between Dong Ha and Cam Lo alongside Highway 9. We were only about 10 kilometers from the DMZ. We were in "Cam Hieu" hamlet, a part of a larger village complex called "Thon Vinh Dai." But, as I've already admitted, I didn't know these names, or their significance, until much later in life. To us, the quasi-ugly young Americans assigned to Papa Three, all Vietnamese villages looked alike. Ours was simply the "ville" for the whole time I was in Vietnam.

Back in 1988, when I first told the story of Papa Three in the pages of *Marine Corps Gazette*, I won an award—the Colonel Robert D. Heinl Jr. Award—for the best contribution that year to Marine Corps history. I also attracted quite a bit of attention, especially since I seemed to be the lone iconoclast when it comes to the Combined Action Program. My fellow veterans and the leadership of the Corps both have invested heavily in promoting combined action as one of the few things we did right in a war gone wrong. For my part, I still think CAP Marines bore the brunt of friendly folly as well as enemy fire.

Our one consolation, unlike the Marines and soldiers in conventional infantry units, was that we got a good, firsthand look at the culture that seemed to be defeating us. Their principal weapon, throughout my time at Papa Three, at least, had seemed to be a studied indifference, a kind of passive aggressive insistence on holding to their values and their traditional rhythms of life no matter what. Along with Greene, over the years, I had imagined it would always be so. Now, along with Bill, I had come back to see for myself.

Our guide throughout most of this adventure was Nguyen Chanh Trieu—or "Tango," as he liked to be called. He had been an interpreter with the Marines throughout our war. Hence, the nickname "Tango," the phonetic alphabet designation for the letter "T"—the phonetic alphabet being a simple system aimed at ensuring the accurate transmission of information despite the vagaries of radio reception and individual pronunciation and accent. Trieu was a university graduate who had studied French and English literature and who had planned to be a teacher. For reasons he never divulged, he enlisted in the Army of the Republic of Vietnam (the "ARVN") and was assigned as an interpreter to the Marines and, apparently, went on to accommodate himself to the Marine sensibility.

Trieu was 59 years old when we met him. We found him to be a pleasant, cheerful man who seemed to be doing well at that time as a licensed freelance tour guide, but he had paid a high price over the years for his association with Americans. Within an hour of meeting us and ascertaining our own USMC backgrounds, he was showing us his scars. He had been shot twice, once through the face and again through the upper arm. Because he had never become an officer—he never wanted to be one, he said—he hadn't qualified for the "Orderly Departure" program. He'd spent three years in a reeducation camp, working in the fields and being told every day that he was "a mother fucker" for siding with us. The constant taunting, he said, inevitably came back to the same cruel, rhetorical question: "Why didn't you leave with the Americans so that you could eat butter in America?"

I can't speak for Bill, of course, but Trieu's story impressed me as just one of a number of depressing reminders of all the sadness that lay just beneath the surface in the new Vietnam. Trieu himself, however, hardly seemed consumed by bitterness or self-pity. He said he had a wife, five children, and 13 grandchildren, several of whom still lived with him and his wife in a small house in Da Nang. After learning what I did for a living—I was college dean and professor at the time—he told me the highest paid professor in Vietnam makes about $40.00 a month. Trieu, I realized, must have been doing fairly well by Vietnamese standards. Bill and I tipped him $50.00 for only five days' work. (We spent our first couple days in Ho Chi Minh City, where we had had

Bill and Trieu at the Citadel in Hue.

a different guide.) Other tourists probably ended up even more moved by his history than we were.

We had flown from Ho Chi Minh City to Da Nang. It was there that we had met Trieu and our driver. Our vehicle was a battered, older American car with a broken air conditioner. From Da Nang, we drove over the Hai Van Pass and up Highway 1 to Dong Ha. Before taking us to our hotel, Trieu had the driver turn into a residential neighborhood with two-story American-style houses. Trieu had us get out of the car and walk into one of the backyards, where an oddly familiar-looking building stood.

Trieu asked us if we knew where we were. We didn't, of course, and Trieu revealed that we were standing in what had been the middle of the airfield of our sprawling base at Dong Ha. That odd-looking building had been the hangar for a helicopter or airplane, and up near the roof, shell damage was still visible. It was the only remnant left of our presence, and it was being used as a carpentry shop.

I was reminded of Shelley's poem "Ozymandias" (1818). A cautionary tale about the vanity of earthly ambition, Shelley's poem begins, "I met a traveler from an antique land" [Egypt?] who describes finding the fragmented ruins of a once-great statue in the desert. Only the legs were still standing on the pedestal, and the inscription on the pedestal read, "My name is Ozymandias, King of Kings; / Look on my works, ye mighty, and despair." "Nothing beside remains," the traveler reports. "Round the decay / Of that colossal / Wreck, boundless and bare / The lone and level sands stretch far away."

Epilogue

Some of the happy children who thronged us on the site of our former combat base in Dong Ha.

Before we left, we were thronged with happy neighborhood kids who were growing up with no knowledge of war.

Trieu proved to be a good guide—personable, thoughtful, and well-informed. He was also a prudent man. He did a great job showing us all manner of things that the authorities want tourists to see, and even a couple more—such as that Dong Ha neighborhood. But, as Bill and I would learn, when it came to the one thing we had specifically come to see, our old "ville," his hands were tied.

Early on, Trieu had hinted at problems in doing what we had ostensibly come to do, to revisit the village where Bill and I had tried to win hearts and minds as Combined Action Marines. We would have to get the permission of, and be escorted by, the local "policeman," as Trieu called him. This is required, Trieu explained, any time a tourist wishes to go anywhere but the established tourist spots where "they sell tickets"—which, judging from other places we went, wasn't quite accurate but was probably as good as Trieu could do in designating anything unusual or anywhere off the beaten path. In return for the policeman's trouble, Trieu added, we would be expected to tip. Trieu told us that five dollars would be plenty.

Personally, I suspected that something was not on the up and up when, in setting out that morning, we pulled up not at a police station or other government building but at the office of DMZ Tours located within a rundown hotel across the street from ours in Dong Ha. The "policeman" we were going to meet turned out to be the deputy manager of DMZ Tours. His name was Nguyen Thanh Duy, or "Duy" (pronounced "Dwee") as Trieu would later introduce him. Duy was a short (even by Vietnamese standards), mild-manner, pudgy middle-aged man with a pleasant demeanor that seemed to belie whatever authority or clout he had. His dress too—a white polo shirt and red ball cap—suggested that he was no more than the tour promoter that his business card proclaimed him to be. If indeed he was one of the "intelligent police" that Trieu had earlier said were everywhere throughout Vietnam today, he was well-chosen to fit the bill.

Later in our trip, back at Da Nang, I mentioned to Trieu that I hadn't seen a single policeman. "You won't see them until they want to see you," he replied. No one would have singled Duy out as an undercover policeman. Looking back on it, I suspect that Duy was just the local Party hack who had the state-sponsored monopoly on tourism in that area. But whatever he was, Duy seemed to have the power to keep us from doing what we had come to Vietnam to do, and he probably had the power to make life difficult for Trieu. For both reasons, we went along with him.

Trieu went into Duy's office first, telling us to wait in the lobby. They were in there at least 15 minutes, suggesting that, contrary to what our travel agency had led us to expect, no prior arrangements had been made. Bill and I were finally summoned in, and, after brief introductions and handshakes all around, Trieu instructed me to show Duy an album of photographs I had brought and to explain to him our purpose in wanting to visit the village. Duy didn't say anything or seem to react at all as I was showing and explaining the photographs. The only indication we had at all that our trip was approved was when, after a brief exchange between Duy and Trieu in Vietnamese, Trieu said that Duy knew where the village was; and the next thing I knew, we were heading out the door to the car. Later, Trieu would confide that Duy expressed two concerns during their initial interview: First, he told Trieu that the people in the countryside were not supposed to become too familiar with Americans; and, second, he asked if we were good tippers.

Bill and I had really thought that our village would be easy to find. After all, it was located right alongside Highway 9, about halfway between Dong Ha and Cam Lo, and could be distinguished by at least three prominent landmarks. The river, the Song Cam Lo, cut in close to the highway in our area; there was a major tributary and a bridge just east of where our compound stood; and a well-established trail ran north-south into the village and began just across the highway from the prominent hill our compound was on. Also, a fairly large one-room schoolhouse stood only a couple hundred yards down (or so I had remembered), and to the left (west) side of the trail that led into the village. From looking at maps, we even knew the name of the overall village complex, Thon Vinh Dai, and of the actual hamlet we were in, Cam Hieu. Finding the area, however, turned out to be tougher than we expected.

Highway 9 was just a dirt road in our day. Now it is completely paved. We expected that. We didn't expect the area to be so heavily built up, especially along the southern side of the road, nor did we expect the vegetation to have grown up so high that it makes the river hard to see from the highway. We especially didn't expect that the major tributary that used to bisect the highway just east of our compound would have dried up into a small stream or that all the bridges now would be even with the roadbed and thereby easy to miss even as you were driving over them. In short, all our prominent landmarks were gone, and we began by overshooting our old village by at least five kilometers.

The first place we stopped looked like it could have been it. There was high ground on the southern side of the road and a prominent trail leading down into a village on the northern side. There was also a small store at the trailhead, alongside the road. We stopped in, and Trieu showed a man there my photos and asked him if this was the place where Marines had been stationed. The man replied that, no, this was not the place, and that the village we wanted was about five kilometers back to the east. He did, however, profess to recognize some of the people in my photos.

We turned around and set out back the way we had come. After what seemed like four or five kilometers, we stopped again at a place that seemed likely. The people there, however, said we were still about a kilometer short of our destination. Third time is a charm. Sure enough, about one kilometer farther east, there was a prominent hill on the southern side of the road and a trail leading off into a village on the northern side. Suddenly, Bill and I both realized that we were there.

What had thrown us, I think, was the proximity of a large brick factory that now sits along the southern side of the road on the high ground just east of the bridge and of the hill where Papa Three had once stood. Somehow, Papa Three's immediate environs still haunted my imagination as a place of the pastoral. It had proved impervious to western influences back then. I never imagined that industrialization could encroach upon it, but it has. The dislocations that industrialization can bring, moreover, further seemed evident in our old village. On the hill, where only our compound had stood, now sits a shantytown of sorts, a collection of improvised cinder block and tin buildings, many of which are open to one side, suggesting a cross between traditional Vietnamese houses and a squatters' camp.

People who go back in adulthood to revisit their childhood haunts typically report finding places to be much smaller than they had remembered. Bill and I both, I think, had the opposite experience. One of the prominent landmarks we were looking for was a one-room cinderblock schoolhouse, with a tin roof, that had stood, as I remembered it, on the left side of the trail only a couple hundred yards north of the highway. The school building was gone, but as we would discover later, its foundation was still there, and a new family had even built a house on it. But that site turned out to be at least five hundred yards, if not a little more, down the trail from the highway. Similarly, as I recalled, splitting off from that main north-south trail there was another trail that led off to the east, down to the main part of the village and to the river. I had remembered that trail as relatively short. It too turned out to be at least three hundred yards long. In fairness to myself, I had remembered that rice paddies lined both sides of this trail, leading up to the tree line and the edge of the village proper. The area was still open, and the indented squares were still visible, but the rice paddies long ago seem to have dried up and been overgrown with grass.

(At some point in our tour, Trieu had told me most of the rice was being grown by large Japanese-run collectives. Agri-business had come to Vietnam.)

The original Papa Three (before the flood had forced us to relocate on the high ground to the south) had stood in an open area north of the highway; just to the west of the trail and within a stone's throw of the schoolhouse to the north. That much I knew was true; one of my 1967 Kodachrome slides confirms it. But I also had thought that our pre-flood compound had stood only a couple hundred yards from the highway. When I saw the house that now stands on the schoolhouse site, I realized my mistake. The original Papa Three had stood at least five hundred yards from the highway, and the school was less than a hundred feet beyond that. As for that original Papa Three site, a large copse of bamboo and elephant grass had reclaimed the area. Our guides made it known that we were not to walk off the trails and into the bush. (It would be bad for the tourist trade if one of us were to step on one of the mines or trip one of the booby traps either side forgot to remove.) But even if our guides hadn't objected, the brush looked virtually impenetrable, and the heat and humidity were winning out over any sentimental attachment I may have been feeling. Hence, we walked on by with nary a backward glance.

Our first stop was the site of the former school. The foundation and concrete floor of the old schoolhouse building were still evident. An older woman, her two grown sons, and the wife and baby of one of the sons were living there. They built their house on one end of the foundation and were using most of the old floor as a kind of patio. They seemed unfriendly and even apprehensive at first, perhaps because they didn't have a clear title or even permission to build on that site. After a few minutes of explanations about who we were and why we were there, however, they seemed to relax and even consented to show us around a bit.

Apparently, one wall of the original structure had still been standing when they arrived, and they built onto it, using it to form the back of their house. Taking us around back, they showed us where one of the original blackboards had been. Fragments of it were still affixed to the wall. They either couldn't or wouldn't tell us what had happened to the original schoolhouse building. They had only been living there three years, they said, so they also professed not to know anyone in my photos. But they did point us toward one of the few remaining houses in what had been the village proper. It stood at the end of the east-west trail, near the edge of the village. A long-time resident, an old woman, lived in that house, they said.

As I've already related, the people of Cam Hieu and Thon Vinh Dai had seemed aloof and largely indifferent to our presence in 1967—the result, we learned, of a well-entrenched VC infrastructure. A few of the children and some of the PFs, who had no choice but to associate with us, were the only real exceptions. One of the principal lures that tour promoters, ideologues, and even Vietnam's National Administration of Tourism dangle in front of us these days is the image of a warm, friendly, and outgoing people who especially like Americans.

That longtime resident, the old woman we visited next, was the only one to live up to that billing. Everyone else we visited, including the other members of the old woman's family, seemed standoffish and more than a little

An ironic juxtaposition: One of the North Vietnamese tanks that overran the Lang Vei Special Forces Camp on February 6, 1968, across the street from a billboard promoting tourism in Vietnam.

Epilogue

The old woman who still lived in Cam Hieu greeting Duy, as Bill looks on.

suspicious of us and our motives. In short, I found myself feeling the way I had felt when I was there the first time—unwelcome.

But not at that one woman's house. She reacted with exuberant delight to our presence. After Duy explained who we were, she literally danced from one of us to the other, chattering excitedly in Vietnamese, and squeezing our arms. She seemed to live with two middle-aged daughters and a slightly younger son in a traditional Vietnamese house, one of the few we saw without electricity. The daughters were reserved. The son may have actually been hostile.

While I was off to the side taking pictures, he came up to me. Pointing in the direction of the hill on which our compound had stood, he said, "You *leave* here," or "You *live* here." I'm still not sure which. (Bill didn't witness the exchange, but he thought the guy had been friendly.) In an effort to show my appreciation, I offered to take some Polaroid snapshots that the family could keep. The old woman insisted on first changing into her best blouse. I offered to take a Polaroid of the son. He refused.

Before we left, of course, we showed the old woman and her family my photos. They recognized only one person, Trung-si Nguyen, the PF leader and, ironically, the only PF we had really known by name. They pointed over toward the northern corner of the village and said he was still there. The next day, Trieu confided that, as soon as he heard that Nguyen was alive and still living in the village, Duy reached up and pinched him on the back of the arm, a gesture Trieu interpreted as meaning that we were not to go looking for our old ally. We said our goodbyes and moved on.

I had thought that Bill would ask to go see Nguyen. As the Marine compound leader, Bill had been closer to him than any of the rest of us. Many an evening, as Bill remembered it, he and Nguyen had gone down to a little café in the village and had drunk "33" beer together. Right after we set out from the old lady's house, however, Bill dropped back to where I was hanging back, still taking pictures, and told me that Trieu had taken him aside and said we had to keep moving. When I asked him if it was because the old lady's son didn't want us there, Bill said, no, that it was because Duy didn't want the people out in the countryside becoming too familiar with Americans. Perhaps we should have balked at Duy's lead, but our concern for Trieu and his position, the heat, and the realization that this is indeed *their* country now all kept us in check.

Since that day, I have given a lot of thought to why the authorities were trying to discourage contact between Americans and people out in the countryside. The answer, I've decided, may have less to do with any residual bitterness toward us, or even toward Vietnamese who supported us, than something we had learned about the former Saigon, Ho Chi Minh City. The official population is set at six million, we were told, but the actual population is about eight million. Our old village, on the other hand, had clearly lost population since 1967, and more than one of the people in my photos, we would learn, had long since moved to Dong Ha or Ho Chi Minh City. I have to wonder whether other villages, too many villages, had suffered the same fate, especially since electricity and television had begun bringing images of a wider world and a different way of life to a receptive younger generation. The authorities were probably hoping to stem that tide, or at least to slow it down. Then there is also the question of embarrassment.

Governments everywhere want to impress tourists, and depressed, half-emptied villages project an image of a country uncomfortably caught between two worlds—a pastoral world the Vietnamese have clearly outgrown and a world of western-style progress that, as of 2002, still seemed "powerless to be born."

Duy himself, probably hoping to get us away from people, suggested that we walk down to the river to see the spot where we used to have to cross in small boats. The tall, thick hedgerows that I had remembered as lining the path down to the river were still there. As we walked along the path almost 35 years later, still unable to see what lay beyond the bamboo and the brush on both sides, I found myself wondering if it were indeed really safe. Finally, we found ourselves at our old crossing point, a set of concrete steps that led down into the river. We found the steps fairly well covered with dirt, leaves, and other debris. Also, the brush had grown up dramatically on both sides. We

Epilogue

were clearly the first to walk down those steps in a good while. The small-boat ferry service no longer exists. There is a nice new suspension bridge now, just a few hundred yards east of the village.

From the river, we doubled back the way we had come, retracing our steps back to Highway 9. I stopped just long enough to photograph a small group of kids who had gotten the word and were following us by then. Forewarned by the travel agency that we should bring something to give the kids, I had brought some pairs of inexpensive sunglasses (three for a dollar at our local dollar store). I gave each kid a pair and photographed the kids wearing them. Duy, I could tell, didn't like that. He asked if he could have one for his daughter. I told him I had plenty and continued with my give-away.

Duy, for some reason, didn't seem to mind our visiting and mixing with the people who live in the shantytown that had grown up on the hill where our compound had been—perhaps because he thought these people were newcomers. Most were, but when, at my insistence, we showed my photographs, a man in his 30s claimed that one of my photos was of his mother and younger brother. Another man, who looked to be old enough, claimed that he had been a PF. He took us over to the eastern side of a row of buildings and pointed up a blind alley, where a new building now sat, perpendicular to the others, indicating that that was where our compound had been. Walking up through that alley would have involved trekking through some

Village kids sporting the sunglasses I had brought.

formidable-looking mud and brush and what, ostensibly, were people's back yards. Unlike in our day, when we acted as if we owned the whole country, the Papa Three hill looked and felt like private property now. We did try walking up the hill on the right, the western side, but likewise found our way blocked, this time by heavy brush—and going off trails and roads, of course, was supposed to be a "no-no" for us. We were at least on the periphery of the old compound, perhaps even within the perimeter we had marked out with barbed wire. That was enough, all things considered.

Over the years, I've always assumed that I had little or no exposure to Agent Orange. The dramatic contrast in foliage between now and then, however, has left me wondering. In 1967, for whatever reason, the hills south of Highway 9, including our own hill, had had only low scrub—rather like what is found in arid areas such as Southern California. The hills behind our compound even seemed eroded and were crisscrossed with a lot of small gullies and ravines, most of which had little or no vegetation. In 2002, the entire area seemed lush with vegetation.

My first thought was the difference may have been due to Agent Orange; perhaps the hills south of the highway had been sprayed long before we got there. Soon after I got back to the States, I mentioned this theory to a Vietnam-veteran friend. He told me that he had researched this issue long ago, when he and his wife were first considering having children, and that he had found records indicating that the Marine Corps didn't use defoliants in I-Corps until 1969, long after both of us had left the area. Also, I asked a biologist whether anything short of chemical defoliants could have accounted for such a dramatic difference in the foliage between 1967 and 2002. He said that heavy bombing, leading to extensive brush fires, could have left the area looking arid and eroded. Still, I have to wonder if the records my friend consulted were complete or if the Army command structure—the Army was in charge, after all—had indeed sprayed the area without the Marine Corps' knowledge or consent.

Regardless of when we actually started using defoliants in Quang Tri Province, the effects, according to Duy, have been horrendous. The statistics Duy trotted out made me realize that underneath his mild-mannered tour guide exterior lurks the heart of a party loyalist. At least 16,000 people in Quang Tri Province remain affected, he said. He further claimed to know one family in which five of seven children are paralyzed as a result of Agent Orange contamination. Similarly, according to Duy, there have been 5,500 land mine casualties throughout the province since the war's end. The numbers may be exaggerated, but the problems themselves do put an ironic spin on Duy and Trieu's translation of "Thon Vinh Dai," our village's name—"large village of tranquility and long life."

It had certainly not turned out to be an area of tranquility or even of longevity for us. As I've already reported, in the short six or months I was there, we were flooded out and had to rebuild on the high ground to the south of Highway 9; we were strafed by one of our own gunships—wounding two Marines and two PFs, and killing another PF outright; we took sniper and harassing fire, both out on patrol and in our compound; we fished a dead, badly decomposed Marine out of the river; we witnessed a truck hit a command-detonated mine almost in front of our compound, much to our embarrassment; we fought with our PFs, who had rebelled, refusing to go out on patrol with us, especially on the northern side of the river; and we were ambushed, on December 4, 1967. Four Papa Three Marines had been wounded and one had been killed. Another Marine had been medevaced for amoebic dysentery. Most of us, in visiting the Papa Company "rear" in Dong Ha, had had to run for the bunkers because of incoming artillery. And, on Christmas day 1967, we had suffered the indignity of having to watch an NVA platoon saunter along unimpeded, out in the open less than a "click" (1,000 meters) to the north of our compound; it was the Christmas truce after all.

The ironic thing was that I had had to fight to get to see some of the war; and, when I finally left Papa Three, I felt that I had indeed seen as much as I cared to see. As I would later write in that first version of "Tiger Papa Three," recalling the words to one of the old "Jodies" we used to chant while double-timing, "Got what I asked for, got what I came for;/I got Marine Corps!"

And then I was back, after a hiatus of 34 years. I found it all difficult to fathom. I had expected it all to be terribly moving and to be swept with waves of nostalgia for the "way we were." Instead, I felt numb and even strangely dissociated from the experience. I suppose that was because I had always felt that we just didn't belong there in the first place; and the way things worked out, I really didn't feel any more welcome the second time around. There was that. And, also, the place we had been to in 1967, I realized, was more existential than physical. Everything had changed in the interim. But, most importantly, we had too. Talk about not being able to go home again! Thomas Wolfe had nothing on us.

No trip back to greater Thon Vinh Dai would have been complete, of course, without at least setting foot on the northern bank of the Song Cam Lo, the river of our discontent. Over half of our Tactical Area of Responsibility (TAOR)—the area we were supposed to patrol regularly and thoroughly—lay on that northern side. As we learned on December 4, 1967, there were indeed "beaucoup VC" over there. And here we were, in the summer of 2002, walking calmly and peacefully across a new steel suspension bridge into that same area. It was like stepping through the looking glass in more ways than one.

In our day, our village, on the southern side of the river, had been the more prosperous and the more heavily populated of the two. In 2002, the reverse was true. Our old village had clearly lost population, while the village on the other side of the river seemed to have grown and even to have prospered. There had been a Catholic church over there, but in its place stood one of the new two-story stucco schools a foreign construction firm was building all over Vietnam. There seemed to be more houses. There were also several shops, including a small photo shop complete with a one-hour processing machine. Did the relative prosperity of the northern village have anything to do with their steadfast commitment to the communist cause? Maybe, maybe not. Perhaps it is just an accident of demographics.

But journalist David Lamb, who has lived in Vietnam for several years, in his book *Vietnam, Now* (2002), does decry the obstinate refusal of the victors to forgive and forget in Vietnam. That same obstinacy certainly kept us from Trung-si Nguyen. I suspect that it also played some role in the relative fortunes of the villages to the north and south of the river. The irony is that the people to the south, in my experience, were never more than nominally on our side, and most were probably sitting on the fence. But insofar as the other side was concerned, I suspect, if you weren't for them, you were against them.

Duy didn't seem to mind our loitering on the northern side of the river. We took a leisurely stroll along the river to the west. When we got to the new school, we noticed that one of the concrete posts to the fence that had surrounded the old churchyard was still standing. The top, however, was rough and had a couple of twisted iron rods sticking out of it. A crucifix had no doubt adorned it. The communists don't like religion, Trieu explained.

Bill asked me how much farther I wanted to walk. We had come there with the half-baked idea of trying to retrace that December 4 patrol route. Once we were there, both of us realized that too much had changed; we would never find the site of the ambush. Besides, it was hot, and wandering around in search of our past suddenly seemed a lost cause and an imposition on Trieu and even Duy. I told Bill that I was ready to go if he was.

Later that day, after we got clear of Duy, Trieu volunteered the opinion that Nguyen must have been a "good man" or Bill and I would be dead. He said that because, in his experience, 90 percent of Popular Force soldiers were VC sympathizers or active VC. Trieu was probably overstating the case. But I've always suspected that our PFs had at least worked out a modus vivendi with the other side, and I have long known that we owed our survival at Papa Three to dumb luck rather than tactical competence.

I suppose I had greatly romanticized my CAP experience over the years, even going so far as to think of it in Conradian terms as the "farthest point of navigation and the culminating point of my experience." It seemed, as Conrad's Marlow says, "to throw a kind of light" on my subsequent life; or, to paraphrase a passage from Vietnam novelist Tim O'Brien, whenever I would try to account for how I got from "*there* to here, it was to that village and to my CAP experience that I inevitably returned. But to say it the way we would have said it back then, the truth is that 'it didn't mean nothin.'" I think it was that realization that ultimately made the trip so depressing.

On our last evening in country, Trieu, who lives in Da Nang, took us to a little outdoor café where he often spent his evenings. It was there, his tongue loosened by our second or third round of beer, that Trieu told us how unhappy he was about how the Americans, in the end, had simply abandoned the Vietnamese who had helped them. He urged us to write to former Marines like Chuck Robb and Oliver North. I didn't have the heart to tell him that neither Robb nor North had the influence to right the wrongs of the past. Still, it was pleasant sitting out on that sidewalk, talking and drinking beer and watching people coming home from work.

Later, at the airport, I slipped Trieu and the driver envelopes containing their tips. Trieu hugged us both and wished us a safe trip back. We checked in and passed through security. As we were taxiing away from the terminal in the dark, I looked out at the lights of the terminal receding in the distance. It can't be the same terminal building, I realize, but something about it all seemed eerily familiar. The lights looked the same. The mixed feelings were similar. Just for a few seconds, 34 years seemed to slip away. I imagined that this was still Da Nang Air Force Base and that I was still young and leaving to go find my future.

The chills hit on the last leg of our trip, the flight from San Francisco to St. Louis. Suddenly, I began to shiver and to shake, almost uncontrollably. I grabbed one of the thin airline blankets, but I couldn't get warm enough. Malaria crossed my mind. But I had been taking an antibiotic as a preventative, and it seemed too soon for something like that to show up. Fortunately, the chills seemed to ease up within an hour. I felt wrung out when we landed, but I rationalized that as just the effects of jet lag and not enough sleep. I tried to tell myself that whatever had caused my chills was only transient and that I would be fine after a good, long nap.

But the chills started again after I got home, and the diarrhea began. My wife took my temperature. It was 103-point-something. The diarrhea never became bad, but my temperature kept cycling up and down. At one point later in the day, I must have been mildly delirious. My wife asked a question, and even I realized that my answer wasn't making much sense. But I couldn't seem to make it come out otherwise. When, the next morning, the diarrhea and fever were still there, we set out for the emergency room. A round of the antibiotic Cipro fixed me up in short order, although I continued to feel out of sorts and generally tired for fully two weeks. As it turns out, I had contracted campylobacter, a bacterial form of food poisoning commonly caused by fecal contamination. According to my wife, it had been a statement of sorts. Once again, Vietnam had told me to "eat shit and die." She had a point.

I have known, ever since my undergraduate days, that we intervened on the wrong side and that, by all the traditional standards, Vietnam could not be called a just war. The means we employed were horribly disproportionate to the ends we sought. To the world, it really did look as if America, a modern industrial society, was unleashing all its technological might to destroy the last vestige of the pastoral world, largely because we thought we could and because it was there.

The terrible irony is that Vietnam in the '60s probably was the closest realization of that pastoral myth left in the modern world. But Vietnam is not that way now and it never will be again. We couldn't prevail militarily, but culturally and economically we've won. We didn't win with B52s, Huey gunships, M16s, or Agent Orange. We won with MTV, the Internet, and Honda Dream Motorbikes. A bit of alternative Shakespeare comes to mind: "Rightly to be great/Is not to stir without great argument,/But greatly to find quarrel in a straw/When [markets are] at the stake."

Not long after I got back, two developments helped me put my return to Vietnam and my war in some perspective. The Ken Burns *Civil War* series was being rerun on PBS, and our country was about to embark upon yet another war, this time in Iraq.

Our Civil War, of course, was a horrible bloodbath; Vietnam pales in comparison (in terms of American casualties, that is). But watching bits and pieces of the *Civil War* series again, I found myself envying the soldiers of that war in at least one respect. Lincoln found a way to ennoble the Civil War and to make it about a universal principle and not just about states' rights or preserving the union.

Because of that, I found myself wondering if some of the veterans, the northern ones, at least, in later life didn't find themselves feeling the way that Shakespeare's Henry the Fifth predicts that his soldiers would someday feel— that they had indeed cohered into a "band of brothers" and that together they had served in a cause more important than themselves. The World War II generation certainly felt that way. I could wish that the current generation of young soldiers and Marines are coming away from Iraq and Afghanistan feeling that way again and not like they have merely assisted in the dirty work of empire. But I doubt they are.

Graham Greene and I were wrong about Vietnamese culture being impervious to change. But Greene was indeed right about the American neocolonial tendency to meddle in situations we don't fully understand. The Vietnamese have changed; we haven't.

Index

Afghanistan 200
Agent Orange 180, 196, 200
AK47 rifle 132, 136, 137
Alzheimer's disease vii
ambush (4 December 1967) 125–132, 197
American literature 11
Anikowski, James 79, 90, 108
anonymous hero 112–113; *see also Casualties of War* (film and article)
Armed Forces Radio 97, 98–99; *see also* Cronauer, Adrian
Army of the Republic of Vietnam (ARVN) 143, 177–178, 186
Arnold, Matthew: "Stanzas from the Grande Chartreuse" 194
Arsenic and Old Lace (Capra film) 7

B52s 200
baby boom generation 10
Baltimore 45
Bangkok, Thailand 123
The Basic School (Marine officers) 177–178
Battery Park 65
Battle Cry (Uris) 34, 76–77
Black, Mark 82
Blake, William: "The Tyger" 67
boom-boom girls 120–121; *see also* prostitution; venereal disease
Boorman, John: *Point Blank* (film) 152; *see also* Marvin, Lee
Brandeis University 167
Burns, Bob 25
Burns, Ken: *The Civil War* 200

Calley, William 115, 141; *see also* My Lai
Cam Hieu 68, 77, 115, 185, 190–192, 193
Cam Lo 40, 59, 67, 69, 81, 89, 189
Camp Lejeune 41–44, 147, 154, 155, 156, 161–162; mentor GySgt. Flores (pseudonym) 42–44; Mount Out Project 42–44
Camp Pendleton 174, 175
campylobacter 199–200
"Can't Take My Eyes Off of You" (Valli) 152
Capra, Frank: *Arsenic and Old Lace* (film) 7

Caputo, Philip: *A Rumor of War* 10, 115, 181
Caribbean Cruise 157–158
Casualties of War (De Palma film) 112
"Casualties of War" (Lang article) 113
Cimino, Michael: *The Deer Hunter* (film) 148
Civil War 181, 200
The Civil War (Ken Burns) 200
Clinton, Pres. Bill 66
Close Quarters (Heinemann) 112
Cold War 11, 180
Coleridge, Samuel Taylor: "Rime of the Ancient Mariner" 88
collateral damage 180
Collins Park 12
Columbus, Ohio 164–165
Combined Action Program (CAP) 1, 3, 48–51, 67, 183–186; badge 49; CAP school 57–58; staffing 50; *see also* Papa One; Papa Three
Conn, Peter 171
Conrad, Joseph: *Heart of Darkness* 198–199
Cooke, William ("Sarge") vii, 2, 27, 73, 76, 78, 79, 90, 91, 94, 96–97, 98, 99, 106, 108–109, 129, 145, 184, 186, 187, 193, 194, 198
Corson, LtCol. William R. 49
Cronauer, Adrian 99

Da Nang 5, 53, 186, 187; Air Base 199; Marble Mountain PX complex 146; rocket attack 146
Death of a Salesman (Miller) 13, 14, 18
The Deer Hunter (Cimino film) 148
Delaware 10, 28, 43, 45–47; auto companies 25; chemical companies 11, 46; Chesapeake and Delaware Canal 45; credit card companies 11; dream 11; first state 46; nightmare 46; working class 12; *see also* Baltimore; Collins Park; Delaware River; DuPont; New Castle; Philadelphia; Smyrna; Wilmington
Delaware River 12, 65
Delta Med 3, 6, 122; Charon 6; Graves Registration 6–9; NCOIC Raymond Massey resemblance 7
demilitarized zone (DMZ) 185; *see also* DMZ Tours

201

Index

De Palma, Brian: *Casualties of War* (film) 112
Dickens, Charles: *Great Expectations* 18, 28, 86
Dien Bien Phu 180
Dispatches (Herr) 111, 141, 178
DMZ Tours 188
doctor of philosophy (PhD) 175
Dong Ha 3, 5, 53, 59, 67, 91, 112, 122, 134, 145, 185, 187, 188, 189, 194, 197
Dragnet (TV series) 63
drowned Marine 77, 197
DuPont Company 11, 16, 46

Easter Offensive (1972) 112
Ehrhart, W.D. viii
Eliot, T.S.: "The Waste Land" 163
Elkton, Maryland 168
Ellis Drive-in 64
Ellsberg, Daniel: *Pentagon Papers* 181
Emerson, Ralph Waldo: "Self-Reliance" 73
English Renaissance 172
Evening Journal (Wilmington, Delaware) 169–170
Existential ethic 112

Fink, Mike vii, 2, 27, 74, 129, 130, 131, 132
First Indochina War 50–51; *see also* France; Viet Minh
Fitzgerald, F. Scott: *The Great Gatsby* 13
Fitzwilly (Mann film) 146
Flynn, Thomas ii, 2; *A Voice of Hope* 80–81
France 51, 115, 180; *see also* Dien Bien Phu; First Indochina War
Frantz, Roger 30–32, 34, 36, 41
Fromme, Lynette 28
Frye, Roland 172
Full Metal Jacket (Kubric film) 34
Fussell, Paul: *The Great War and Modern Memory* 1

Garrett, McClain ("Mack") vii, 27, 76, 105–106, 126, 127, 128, 185
Geneva Accords 180
Gentry, Bobbie: "Ode to Billie Joe" 97–98
Gibran, Kahlil: *The Prophet* 158
Going After Cacciato (O'Brien) 180–182
Good Morning, Vietnam (Levinson film) 99
Great Depression 13, 16
Great Expectations (Dickens) 18, 28, 86
The Great Gatsby (Fitzgerald) 13
The Great War and Modern Memory (Fussell) 1
Greene, Graham: *The Quiet American* 183, 186, 200
Greenwood, Col. John vii
Gulliver's Travels (Swift) 120

Haditha 139
Hamlet (Shakespeare) 2, 4, 8, 88, 134, 173, 200
harassment and interdiction fire (H&I) 60–61
Harry Potter (Rowling) 23
Heart of Darkness (Conrad) 198–199

Hein, Al ("Heinie") 40, 72, 73, 76, 79, 82, 94, 97, 99–100, 108, 127, 137
Heinemann, Larry: *Close Quarters* 112
Heinl, Col. Robert D., Jr., Award 185
Hemingway, Al: *Our War Was Different* vii
Hemingway, Ernest: "Away You'll Never Be" 139
Henley, William Ernest: "Invictus" 110–111
Herr, Michael: *Dispatches* 111, 141, 178
Highway Nine 3, 9, 68, 143, 145, 185, 189
Highway One 187
Hilton, James: *Lost Horizon* 53
Ho Chi Minh 179–180
Honda Dream (motorbike) 184, 200
Hue 53, 187
Huey gunships 128–129, 200

identification 3–9
Internet 2, 27, 184, 200
"Invictus" (Henley) 110–111
Iraq War 139–140, 200

Johnson, Lyndon 161–162
"Josh" (friend, pseudonym) 152, 155

K.I. Sawyer Air Force Base, Marquette, Michigan 93, 150
Klay, Phil: *Redeployment* 181–182
Kodachrome (color film) 134, 191
Korean War 180
Krulak, LtGen. Victor H. 49
Kubrick, Stanley: *Full Metal Jacket* (film) 34

Lamb, David: *Vietnam, Now* 198
Lang, Daniel: "Casualties of War" (article) 113; *see also Casualties of War* (film)
Lang Vei Special Forces Camp 192
Lembcke, Jerry: *The Spitting Image* 147, 183
Leonard, SSgt. Kenneth (pseudonym; OCS sergeant instructor) 173–174
Levinson, Barry: *Good Morning, Vietnam* (film) 99; *see also* Cronauer, Adrian
Lincoln, Abraham 200
Lockbourne Air Force Base, Columbus, Ohio 164–165
"Locksley Hall" (Tennyson) 30
Lost Horizon (Hilton) 53

M16 rifle 57, 131, 132, 136–137, 148, 200
Macbeth (Shakespeare) 61
Mann, Delbert: *Fitzwilly* (film) 146
Marine Corps Air Station, Cherry Point, North Carolina 175
Marine Corps Air Station, Iwakuni, Japan 175
Marine Corps Gazette 1, 80, 185, 197
Marine Corps Historical Center 1
Marine Corps, U.S. vii, 10, 24, 46–47, 173, 175; *see also* Camp Lejeune; Combined Action Program; Officer Candidate School; recruit training

Marine Enlisted Commissioning Education Program (MECEP) 174
Marine Officer Instructor, U.C. Berkeley 176
Marine Officer Selection Officer 173; *see also* Philadelphia Navy Yard
Marshall, Garry: *Pretty Woman* (film) 120
Marvin, Lee 152; *see also* Point Blank
Masarik, Albert 11, 15, 20; Vietnam verdict 149
Masarik, Joseph S. 14
Masarik, Joseph S., Jr. 15
Masarik, Julius 15, 150
Masarik, Katherine Omelka 14, 21; change-of-life pregnancy 15; family photograph 14–15; tuition assistance 150
Massey, Raymond 7; *see also Arsenic and Old Lace*
Mell, Donald C., Jr. 169
Miller, Arthur: *Death of a Salesman* 13, 14, 18
Miller, George 169, 172
Milton, John 29, 66, 160, 169, 175
monsoon 5, 53
MTV-Asia 200
My Lai 96, 112, 115, 141, 180; *see also* Calley, William

nation building 51
naturalism 125
nature moralized 5
Naval Academy, U.S. 176
Navy corpsmen 76, 80, 117; *see also* Papa One; Papa Three
neo-imperialism 181
New Castle Air Force Base 16
New Castle, Delaware 11, 65, 148, 154; *see also* Battery Park; Ellis Drive-in; New Castle Air Force Base
New corporal, Papa Three 108–109, 126–128, 133
New Jersey 12, 153
Newman, Franklin 169
Ngo Dinh Diem 180
Nguyen (pseudonym; Papa Three PF leader) 68, 93, 97, 98, 108
Nguyen Chanh Trieu 186–187, 193, 194, 196, 198, 199
Nguyen Thanh Duy 189, 193–196, 198
Nguyen (pseudonym), Trung-si 68, 93, 97, 98
Nordberg (pseudonym) 76, 88, 105, 106, 107
North, Oliver 199
North Vietnamese Army (NVA) 104, 143, 144, 197
Norton, Prof. (pseudonym) 171–172

objective correlative 165; *see also* Yashica camera
O'Brien, Tim: *Going After Cacciato* 180–182; *The Things They Carried* 1, 97, 119, 139
odd encounters 110–111
"Ode to Billie Joe" (Gentry) 97–98
Officer Candidate School 173–174

Old Customs House 30
Our War Was Different (Hemingway, Al) vii
"Ozymandias" (Shelley) 187

Palm, Andrea Muelenaer viii, 166–168, 199–200
Palm, Betty 83, 85–86, 164–165
Palm, Brian 165
Palm, Edward F. vii–viii, 1–2, 3–9,10–12, 29; *American Heart of Darkness* (PhD dissertation, 1983) 175; Combat Action Ribbon 102–103; early release 158–159; enlistment 30–33; family 19–25; girlfriends 63–66, 85–86, 152–160, 164, 166–168; great expectations 18; infantry MOS 158, 159; leadership 6, 101–102; 135, 136; military police 158, 159, 163; photography avocation 25–26, 61, 114, 133–134, 165, 169: regular commission 175; summer and after-school jobs 23, 156; supply MOS 43, 52, 55; *see also* Camp Lejeune; Caribbean cruise; Columbus, Ohio; Delaware; Frantz, Roger; girlfriends; Marine Enlisted Commissioning Education Program; Masarik, Katherine Omelka; Mell, Donald C., Jr.; Miller, George; Officer Candidate School; Palm, Andrea; Palm, Betty; Palm, Edward G.; Rice, Doris West; Salesianum; Sickinger, Josephine; University of Delaware, University of Pennsylvania; Whitlock, Margaret Elaine
Palm, Edward G. 14, 16, 19, 20, 21–22, 32, 83–87; active duty request 32; Army Air Corps 16; child support 19; divorce 83–84; early ambition 20; Edixa camera gift 25, 133; Japan 19; KC135 flight 84–85; Korean War 20; visits 19; World War II 16, 19, 20; *see also* K.I. Sawyer Air Force Base; Lockbourne Air Force Base; New Castle Air Force Base; Palm, Betty; Whitlock, Margaret Elaine
Papa One 59–62, 122; 134; claymore detonation 61; draftee 60; injury 61; sniper round 60; SSgt. Garcia 62; Tony, cook 60; transfer to Papa Three 62; village hospitality 59–60; *see also* harassment and interdiction fire; Yashica camera
Papa Three vii, 2, 9, 67–71, 96–103, 185–186; AC47 attack 104–107; ambush 125–132; assassination of village official 72; drug incident 96–97; first attack 80–81; flood 88–89, 90–92; harassing fire, pre–Tet 143–144; history of 80–82; leaving 145; Marine-PF schism 108–109, 141–142; old man and ambush 102; Papa Three Marines 72–79; patrol fired upon 102–103; PF patrol refusal 39–40; prisoners 131, 135–138; schoolbooks, delivery of 115–117; second attack 62, 73; tactical area of responsibility 70; "Tiger Papa Three" (radio call sign) 67; truck hits mine 72; unrecognized VC 101; *see also*

Index

Cam Hieu; Popular Forces; prostitution; Song Cam Lo; Viet Cong; village teacher; Walt, LtGen Lewis W.
Parks, Ronald vii, 2, 27, 74–75, 97, 126, 129, 130, 131, 132
pastoral 194, 169, 200
pathetic fallacy 5, 125, 132; *see also* nature moralized
Pentagon Papers (Ellsberg) 181
Philadelphia 45
Philadelphia Navy Yard 173
Philippines 123, 124
Phu Bai 3, 52, 53, 57, 145, 146
Playboy 119
Plebiscite, Geneva Accords (1956) 50–51
Point Blank (John Boorman film) 152; *see also* Marvin, Lee
Popular Forces (PFs) 6, 39–40, 48, 49, 50, 68–71, 80, 90, 93, 100–101, 104, 106, 107, 108, 116–118, 125, 126, 136, 141–142, 144, 193–194, 195, 197, 198; *see also* Papa Three; Viet Cong
post-traumatic distress disorder (PTSD) vii, 139, 165, 168, 179
Pregent, Dennis viii
Pretty Woman (Marshall film) 120
The Prophet (Gibran) 158
prostitution 119–122; *see also* boom-boom girls; *Pretty Woman*; *Two and a Half Men*; venereal disease
"Puff the Magic Dragon" (AC47) 104–107, 197
Purple Hearts 107; *see also* Nordberg; "Puff the Magic Dragon"; Scotty
Pyle, Gomer 76

Quang Tri Province 5, 67, 185, 196
The Quiet American (Greene) 183, 186, 200

Reagan, Ronald 179
Reaves, James vii, 3–5, 8, 58, 62, 72, 74, 76–77, 78, 82, 98, 102, 105, 117; death 127, 128, 137; girlfriend 8, 77; last patrol 126–129; Marine Corps ring 137; *see also* ambush
recruit training, USMC 34–38
Redeployment (Klay) 181–182
rest and relaxation (R&R) 123–124; *see also* Bangkok; Philippines
return to Vietnam (2002) 183–200
Rice, Doris West 25, 150
"Rime of the Ancient Mariner" (Coleridge) 88
Robb, Chuck 199
Rodney (pseudonym; Papa Three cook) 73–74, 91, 96, 97, 98, 145, 197
Roth, Philip 14
Rowling, J.K.: *Harry Potter* 23
A Rumor of War (Philip Caputo) 10, 115, 181

Saigon (Ho Chi Minh City) 177, 186, 187
Salesianum School for Boys 21–22, 30–31, 150
Samet, Elizabeth 147
"Scotty" 5, 58, 62, 72, 77, 78–79, 82, 106, 107

Scroggs, Larry vii, 2, 27, 77, 94
"Self-Reliance" (Emerson) 73
sexual double standard 64
sexual revolution 64–65, 153
Shakespeare, William: *Hamlet* 2, 4, 8, 88, 134, 173, 200; *Macbeth* 61; 29, 169, 172, 175, 200
Shelley, Percy Bysshe: "Ozymandias" 187
Sickinger, Josephine Masarik (aunt) 14,15, 21, 26; tuition assistance 150
Slovakia 14
Smyrna, Delaware 167
Song Cam Lo (Cam Lo River) 6, 39–40, 70–71, 76, 78, 80, 88, 129, 189, 194–195, 197
The Spitting Image (Lembcke) 147, 183
Springer, Jerry 35
Stallone, Sylvester (characters): "Rambo" 100; "Rocky" 32, 45
"Stanzas from the Grande Chartreuse" (Arnold) 194
Swift, Jonathan: *Gulliver's Travels* 120

Tennyson, Alfred Lord: "Locksley Hall" 30
Tet Offensive (1968) 143, 161
The Things They Carried (O'Brien) 1, 97, 119, 139
Third Engineer Battalion 52–55
Thompson, Hugh 112, 113; *see also* My Lai
Thon Vinh Dai 68, 185, 190, 192, 196, 197, 198; *see also* Cam Hieu
Thoreau, Henry David: *Walden* 46
"Tony" (cook Papa One) 60
Travis Air Force Base 147, 151
Twain, Mark (attributed remark) 32
Two and a Half Men (sitcom) 120–121
"The Tyger" (Blake) 67

University of Delaware 159, 166–167, 169–170
University of Illinois 170
University of Pennsylvania 169–175
Upper Peninsula, Michigan 83–87, 150; *see also* K.I. Sawyer Air Force Base
Uris, Leon: *Battle Cry* 34, 76–77

Valli, Frankie: "Can't Take My Eyes Off of You" 152
venereal disease 121–122
Viet Cong (VC) 6, 48, 51, 80, 81; main force 101, 131
Viet Minh 51
Vietnam 1–2, 32; China and 51; culture 51, 100–101; France and 51; Hai Van Pass 187; nationalism 180; Orderly Departure Program 186, tourism 192; *see also* Da Nang; Dong Ha; First Indochina War; Phu Bai; Quang Tri Province
Vietnam, Now (Lamb) 198
Vietnam War 32, 47; I Corps 49, 185; *see also* collateral damage; North Vietnamese Army; Saigon; Tet Offensive 1968; Viet Cong
Vietnamese exchange officers 177–178

village teacher 115–117; *see also* Papa Three
A Voice of Hope (Flynn) 80–81

Walt, LtGen. Lewis W. 49, 93–95, 96
"The Waste Land" (Eliot) 163
"A Way You'll Never Be" (Hemingway, Ernest) 139
West, Rose Masarik 14–15, 26, 150
West, William 26, 150
Westmoreland, Gen. William C. 49
Whitlock, Margaret Elaine Masarik Palm (mother) 11, 12, 13, 14–16, 15–16, 17, 18, 21, 23–24, 84–85, 148, 150–151, 164; birth 14–16; death 17, 84; divorces 16–17; family dependence 21; first marriage (Gordon Galloway) 16; fortune tellers 18; Great Depression 13, 16; high school 16; Kent Manor Inn 17; Japan 84–85; live-in boyfriend 17–18; materialism 13–14; name 15–16; Philadelphia College of Embalming 11; roomers 23–24; second marriage (Edward G. Palm) 16–17; Slovak heritage 14; third marriage (Reese Whitlock) 17; *see also* Collins Park; Delaware; DuPont; Masarik, Katherine Omelka; New Jersey; Palm, Edward G.; Sickinger, Josephine; West, Rose Masarik; Whitlock, Reese
Whitlock, Reese (stepfather) 12, 13, 14, 19, 26
Wilmington, Delaware 11, 65; *see also* Old Customs House; Wilmington Dry Goods
Wilmington Dry Goods 63, 66
winning hearts and minds 3, 114–118
Wolfe, Thomas: *You Can't Go Home Again* 197
Wordsworth, William: "The World Is Too Much with Us" 13
"The World Is Too Much with Us" (Wordsworth) 13
World War II 32, 149, 180, 181

Yap, Warren 25–26
Yashica camera 61, 165
Yost, Robert vii, 2, 28, 74–75, 91, 126, 127, 128, 131, 136
You Can't Go Home Again (Wolfe) 197